SOPHOCLES

SOPHOCLES

A STUDY OF HEROIC HUMANISM

CEDRIC H. WHITMAN

HARVARD UNIVERSITY PRESS

CAMBRIDGE · MASSACHUSETTS

Third Printing, 1971

Distributed in Great Britain by Oxford University, Press, London

Library of Congress Catalog Card Number: 51–10794

SBN 674–82140–8

Printed in the United States of America

TO JOHN H. FINLEY, JR.

PREFACE

THE best excuse for a new book about Sophocles is the number and diversity of those already existing. Great poets need frequent interpreters, but in the case of Sophocles more is involved than the shift of critical emphasis from generation to generation. Sophocles was an artist who hid his meanings under a glossy and almost impenetrable surface of simplicity. Like Dante and Goethe, he could wear the mask of orthodoxy; like Mozart, he could veil his human intensity in formal grace and refined brilliance. Beside his contemporary, Euripides, he has often seemed stiff and remote. Yet the most discriminating readers have always felt his inner fire, and since the fifth century B.C., scholars and men of letters have used all their philology and intuition to pierce his baffling exterior.

The attempt requires rashness, and this book may appear rash. In defence of it, I may say that I have tried diligently to relate my interpretation to what little historical evidence there is and to allow Sophocles to speak for himself as far as possible. Nevertheless, I am aware that at times my statements will seem dogmatic, and even polemical, especially when dealing with earlier scholars. It is not my wish to appear so, but I have felt the necessity of answering, and answering as firmly as I might, an array of time-honored assumptions about Sophocles which seem to me mistaken. I hope that my arguments will be received in the spirit of constructive zeal in which they were written, and not be mistaken for philological *Schadenfreude*. In the case of an ancient author, many points of view are possible, and nearly all are valuable. For this reason, as well as for the classical student's particular use, I have included a brief history of recent Sophoclean criticism, and have summarized in Chapter III many arguments relating to the chronology of the extant plays.

Throughout, the text used is the text of Jebb, with only one or two inconsiderable variants. The translations quoted are chiefly my own, though on a few occasions, out of personal regard, I have adapted the translation of the eighteenth-century clergyman, Thomas Francklin, and once, for its exactness, I quote the prose version of Jebb. For the benefit of those who do not read Greek, I have simply transliterated certain words which cannot be adequately translated, and yet are so basic to the argument as to be almost technical terms. The endnotes, on the other hand, are almost wholly for the classicist, and the selected bibliography primarily for the graduate student.

Little or nothing will be found herein about the lost plays — an omission which may be justly censured. In spite of Pearson's excellent edition, the fragments of Sophocles afford us only a hazy view of the lost works, and it is with great trepidation that I have once or twice made use of them in trying to sketch the poet's development. Should fuller knowledge of these plays ever come to us, it may well necessitate a revision — I hope, not a total rejection — of the picture I have drawn. Yet, since I was primarily interested in examining Sophocles' treatment of entire dramatic actions, I felt that the safest course was to leave the fragments to reveal what they may in the future.

Doubtless other omissions will appear. No one knew better than Sophocles that the defects of any effort, try as one will to forestall them, tend to reveal themselves too late. Meanwhile, I wish to express my sincerest thanks to all those who have criticized the manuscript and have exercised their patience in discussing it with me. Among these I should especially mention the late Professor F. O. Matthiessen, as well as my colleagues, Professor W. C. Greene, who gave me many helpful comments, both general and specific, and Professor Werner Jaeger, to whom I am indebted for seeing the unpublished manuscript of his *Theology of the Early Greek Philosophers*, a book which greatly influenced my view of the fifth century. I wish also to thank Mr. T. J. Wilson, Director of the Harvard University Press, whose painstaking critical reading amounted to far more than a publisher's duty. Finally, since this book had its origin in conversations with Professor John H. Finley, and owes so much to his insight and profound understanding of Sophocles, I have no choice but to acknowledge my debt to him on a separate page.

C. H. W.

Cambridge, Mass.
October 12, 1950

CONTENTS

PART ONE

THE ENIGMA
OF SOPHOCLES

*Boys will regard Sophocles
as a kind of enlightened bishop,
and something tells me that they
are wrong.*
                    — E. M. Forster

I

THE CLASSIC VIEW

ANCIENT Greek poetry has only recently begun to disclose its vivid meaning to the modern world. When the men of the Renaissance rediscovered Hellenic culture, it was not long before the motifs of antiquity had passed through the hot creative fires of the fourteenth and fifteenth centuries and emerged in new and highly changed forms. The focus of those generations was centered so keenly on the new product that much which was purely Greek was lost, or, to put it more fairly, lay still buried. Unquestionably the work of the Renaissance artists and poets was in every way a legitimate extension of that very process of combining the traditional with the new, the universal with the individual, which the Greeks applied first to themselves and later to the Romans. By this road they themselves became Hellenes, and European culture Hellenic.

But the task of the literary historian remains to understand the Greeks themselves, apart from their effect on succeeding ages. The obstacles on this path, however, do not date from the Renaissance — for one spark of whose fire we would happily exchange whole libraries full of scholarship — but from a later time. If the eighteenth century produced such brilliant scholars as Bentley and Wolf, it also evolved a special variety of neoclassicism, which made it one of the few periods in European history when an ancient Athenian, with all his versatility, would have been utterly unable to adjust himself or comprehend a thing he saw. From this period come our general formulations about "classicism" and the "Greek spirit," terms for which we are doubtless grateful, since we all use them, but which defy definition, and like most common property offer as much opportunity for mutual understanding as for bitter dispute.

More than any other author, Sophocles has suffered from these terms, for instead of being interpreted by his works, he has been somehow identified with all that is "classical," and praised as both the prophet and the example of those qualities of harmony, piety, and self-restraint which we have come to look upon as so essentially Greek. Hardly a scholar who has written at all extensively on Sophocles has failed to dwell upon even those physical gifts which marked him out, as it were, to be the true type of Greek culture, from the day of Salamis on, when, naked and with lyre in hand, he led the boys' triumphal dance. His beauty, his charm of manner, his musical accomplishments, no less than the supreme ability he showed in refining Attic speech and drama into a matchless artistic vehicle, all shared in creating an impression which doubtless had its beginnings even before his death, and in any case is not wholly the creation of modern times.[1] Above all, his well-known piety, which appeared to be so eloquently reinforced in public by the tenor of his plays, recommended him as the last great guardian of the myths — the special symbols of Greece — and won him a title almost the equivalent of Defender of the Faith.

Perhaps also, there was another more subjective factor involved in electing Sophocles the "classic" poet. Sophocles stood for nothing else. Of his contemporaries, Aeschylus was a direct theologian in his art, almost a dogmatist at times, while Euripides was inwardly divided by the conflicting attitudes of the Sophistic Enlightenment. Other poets had their individual grooves and labels by which they might be known, except possibly Homer. But Sophocles defied all pigeonholes and programs. His simplicity was veiled in a kind of mystery, an indefinable but familiar aloofness and perfection which recalled nothing so much as the Greek spirit itself. Hence there arose a natural instinct to let these two unknowns equal each other. Sophocles illustrated the Greek spirit, while the Greek spirit explained Sophocles.

The classic view had its origin as well as its culmination in the contrast of Sophocles with Euripides. The latter made himself the spokesman of the younger generation with its ever-increasing emphasis on naturalism, its veering allegiances, its war-enthusiasm, or its war-weariness. But Sophocles maintained a level. The contemporary scene made little difference in his art, or so at least it seemed, if one compared the program pieces of his rival. Furthermore, Euripides had written plays which were little more than studies in eroticism, for which Aristophanes, speaking through the ghost of Aeschylus, roundly berated him.[2] Sophocles, on the other hand, seems to have been less interested in this aspect of human nature, and therefore, of course, more respectable in the eyes of the proper. Worst of all, Euripides not only derided openly the official gods, but even occasionally introduced "new gods" — that is, he treated almost as cult divinities those natural forces such as Air and Vortex [3] which the natural philosophers of the sixth and fifth centuries looked upon as causal and creative. Sophocles offered no new gods, and gave at least a strong impression of being very reverent toward the old ones. In his plays, oracles came true, and the gods seemed to assert themselves. Hence, for the most part he escaped the comic poets. They had a much better butt in the radical Euripides, whose new musical styles were easy to parody, and whose characters and ideas were obvious matter for conservative ridicule. To Sophocles therefore went the prizes and the respect. Euripides might be fascinating; he was unquestionably more fully understood, but he was not quite decent. He said in public what everybody thought was true, but it should not have been said in public. If Sophocles sometimes said things which were almost as bad, he said them much more subtly, and they went by unnoticed in his disarmingly smooth and pious-sounding plays, where the choruses regularly declare the majesty of the gods. Sophocles' heart was anywhere but on his sleeve, and his countrymen naturally and sympathetically assumed it was in the right place. Finally, half a century after his death, Aristotle's preference for Sophocles, and his derivation of the so-called rules of tragedy from his plays, were all that were needed to put the final touch on the picture of the perfect poet who taught piety and prudence to his fellow citizens through the medium of a supreme technique.[4]

For centuries this view was the accepted one, but its apparent clarity and simplicity led in the long run to depressingly sterile results. The masters of the *Klassik* revered Sophocles and imitated Euripides. Goethe himself, in search of the classic spirit, settled on Iphigenia, whose tradition went back to the earliest roots of Western romanticism, and even his *Helena* had for its model the *Helen* of Euripides. Hegel's theory of the *Antigone* achieved wide acclaim for a time, but has slowly crumbled, and eventually Sophoclean scholarship flagged altogether in the nineteenth century, except for the great commentary of Sir Richard Jebb and the permanently valuable textual work of Elmsley, who discovered the importance of the Laurentian manuscript. But as poet, Euripides had won the day. To the Brownings he was "our Euripides the human, with his droppings of warm tears," while Sophocles was only a "great name." Landor could see Sophocles as the heir of Aeschylus, quiet-voiced and modest, but no more. Matthew Arnold brought Sophocles into "Dover Beach," but in a Victorian incognito. In Germany, the great Wilamowitz orientated his whole approach to Greek drama through Euripides, and died after having dealt with almost every author and branch of Greek studies except Sophocles.[5] As a poet, artist, and thinker, Sophocles had all but died of his own magnificent fame.

The reaction has already begun. With the growth of a more historical mode of literary interpretation, some attempt has been made by recent scholars to see Sophocles in the context of his time, and more specifically, to outline and explain the moral and religious content of the seven extant plays. But so far, the classic view continues with scarcely abated force as an assumption always in the background, a cliché to which it is always possible to retreat with safety. Its principal symptoms may be identified for purposes of clarity with certain words which are traditionally associated with Sophocles and with the Greek spirit in general: serenity, self-restraint, piety. Now it is not to be denied that these words do apply in some sense to Sophocles, but in exactly what sense is a large and difficult question. When Aristophanes calls him "serene-natured," [6] it is agreed that he is speaking of his disposition. But this serenity has been universally detected in his art as well, which is surprising in view of the agonizing intensity of some of his scenes and the disturbing impact of his plays as wholes. Doubtless some part of this notion arose from the style, especially the verse technique, of his tragedies, even as the style of Mozart has earned for him such dreary and thankless popular titles as "cheerful," "sunny," and "sprightly." But also, from the beginning, the classic idea has been that the "serenity" of Sophoclean art denoted in the poet a special quality of spiritual peace, which arose from a settled, unquestioning faith, whose reward was mental harmony and whose rule was that well-known kind of self-restraint which the Greeks called *sophrosyne*.

Thus all three words are linked together and defined in terms of each other. Yet if it be asked what Sophocles was pious about, one can only say, "the gods," an equally equivocal word in this case, for the plays offer no very clear picture of the gods, no comprehensible theological idea such as the Athenians admired so justly in Aeschylus. Indeed, if the plays be read with only this assumption, one is left with the feeling that Sophocles was either more unquestioning than pious, or else more pious than intelligent. It has long been known that Greek religion had no creed, no developed body of dogma upon which such piety could be built. But the tacit assumption has been that Sophocles had some such creed, and that his religious and moral attitude was the very apotheosis of those saws and sayings of popular tradition, those clichés, chiefly of early Delphic origin, with which any average Greek could meet the various circumstances of life, without worrying any more about their mutual reconciliation than the New England farmer does about the Golden Rule and his more hardheaded penny-wisdom. Among scholars the belief still widely prevails that, while Euripides peddled the latest intellectual wares, Sophocles proved in play after play that excess is an evil, that man must not try to be a god, that not to be born is best, and all things are insecure; and that he had more or less schematized these commonplaces into a serene and pious system of life, whose watchword was *sophrosyne*.

The term *sophrosyne*, like most of the moral terminology of the Greeks, evolved from a specific root-meaning and underwent various changes before it became crystallized as "temperance" in the systematic world of Plato and Aristotle. But the idea of sophrosyne came first from Delphi. The motto of the Delphic Oracle, "Know Thyself," meant simply, "Remember that you are mortal, not a god." This had been from earliest times the first commandment of sophrosyne; hence the word originally had indicated an ability to keep the mind free from presumption and based firmly on the irrevocable facts of birth and mortality, within whose limits all human hopes and deliberations must find their fullness. To Socrates, however, Apollo's warning was a signpost to the new inner world he was discovering: "know thyself" meant "search thyself" for the real significance of life, the essence of good which existed only in a state of soul and in the activation of that knowledge which is virtue. Finally in the *Republic*,[7] Plato defined sophrosyne as a kind of contentment, especially appropriate to the artisan classes, a satisfaction with the existing ideal order of government based on a knowledge of its justice and an understanding of the place they fill in it.

We need not trace the concept of sophrosyne further in order to see that, while its exact implications for behavior varied, there remained a central idea that did not vary: the idea of self-knowledge. To the Greeks of Homer's time, the self may have seemed hardly more than skin-deep; the wrath of Achilles hurled the souls of the Achaeans into Hades, but left "the men themselves" as carrion prey to dogs and vultures.[8] Socrates and others found deeper recesses in the self. But the knowledge of the self lay always in the discovery of a limit, and if that limit became in the fourth century more consciously moral in our sense of the word, nevertheless it had always been moral in import. Sophrosyne always had moral intentions, but its effects depended entirely on what one discovered in the self. In the *Iliad*, Achilles felt, and doubtless he was, in some sense, justified in his first refusal to bow tamely to Agamemnon's outrageous insult. If Socrates had been there to tell him that because of the structure of the soul it was better to suffer injustice than to commit it, Achilles might well have been deafer and more violent than Callicles, or any of the others to whom Socrates tried to prove his point. But there is a grave difference between the position of Achilles and that of Callicles as Plato represents him in the *Gorgias*. Achilles was morally obliged to take umbrage at an affront because of the laws of heroic behavior by which he felt himself limited. In his way, he preserved sophrosyne. Callicles, however, stood deliberately and proudly on no moral ground, denounced sophrosyne as folly, and argued that there was no limit beyond which man ought not to go.

A contemporary of Socrates, Sophocles too studied the problem of self-knowledge, but his approach and his conclusions more nearly resemble Homeric than Socratic ethics. Those who say that his plays teach sophrosyne have generally failed to recognize how refined and true may be the understanding which the Sophoclean hero has of himself, and how the man who is, in the eyes of all the world, a law unto himself may yet be acting in obedience to a true law which is beyond the vision of those who observe him. Sophocles' dramas may well teach sophrosyne, but it is in the character of the hero that this sophroysne is to be found, and not in the commonplaces and clichés of the chorus and lesser characters. It is the hero himself who has the real self-knowledge; the others have only rules of behavior. And yet, because in the mid-fifth century these rules of behavior had already become identified with sophrosyne in common intercourse, it forever appears that the protagonist moves blindly and arbitrarily along his fated road, while the static chorus and all the secondary figures stand firmly on the bed-rock of a settled and utterly correct ethic, approved and protected by the sanction of the gods themselves. Not even the hero himself can say that he acts from sophroysne, for the word has already been pinned down to a code of behavior closely resembling philistinism. Rather the hero proudly transgresses this code, and, if he is articulate on the subject at all — as Electra is — rejects sophrosyne as a course applicable only to those who desire safety more than moral action. And there it must be left. For Sophocles, the word belongs to the little people who wish to be safe. It remained for Socrates and Plato to rejuvenate the word and transform it again into a positive moral force. Sophocles focused on the morality which conflicted with it.

The interpretation of Sophocles from earliest times must have suffered from such a conflict, where the everyday values of sophrosyne met those of the larger sphere of heroic moral perception. It is incredible that the citizens who admired the works of their great poet did so because they were always in complete alliance with a hero whose ethic so violently contravened their own. Surely the audiences of antiquity felt some degree of our puzzlement. Many of them must have assumed, as have so many modern scholars, the simple formula that the almighty gods were just, and that he who crosses certain limits of behavior — be he as puissant as Ajax or sagacious as Oedipus — is guilty of *hybris* (the opposite of sophrosyne) and is in some sense justly doomed. In any case, this formula emerges in many a treatment of Sophocles. It is one of the most fundamental, if not the most fundamental, assumption in our classic conception of the poet's import, and if it is not wholly untrue, it is almost wholly untragic.

Closely allied to this belief, and in fact necessarily derived from it, is the search for the exact guilt of the protagonist. This has not always been easy to determine, and all too often critics have contented themselves with the conclusion that the protagonist is guilty of differing with the gods because he differs with the chorus. The divine forces in Sophocles are subtle, to say the least, and the danger of over-simplifying them is always at hand. Since the chorus asserts so often that the gods are almighty, all-wise, and infallibly just, it is natural to seek in the tragic circumstances of the hero the results of some deep moral offence against the world order, rather than to accept the more bitter implication that these circumstances themselves, this very dichotomy between what is believed of the gods and what shows itself in their active dealings with men, may indeed be the world order — in short, that the world may be not subject to simple moral rules, but may really be tragic. In any case, the search for crime as the cause of tragedy has gone on uninterrupted for centuries, embarrassed only by the variety of possibilities in the case of each hero and the peculiar monotony of the results. And this aspect, too, of our classic point of view has its roots in antiquity, in Aristotle's famous theory of the *hamartia*, or tragic flaw, of the hero. Aristotle was the first to schematize tragedy into a moral system involving sin and punishment and his reason for doing so is obvious. Only by some such formula could the statements of the chorus about the justice and omnipotence of the gods appear valid.

The answer to these two main tenets of common belief regarding Sophocles demands a detailed inspection of Sophoclean scholarship and of the whole theory which underlies the sin and punishment formulas. But there are other tenets as well, or rather bland concomitant assumptions which still affect our outlook on the poet. We still, for instance, interpret the known events of Sophocles' life and sundry anecdotes about him in the light of our classic prejudice, whereas a deeper scrutiny of the historical background of these anecdotes might well force a considerable change of ideas.

The problem of giving Sophocles his proper historical setting must remain a difficult one, of course; his maturity coincided with those fifty years of Athenian expansion for which, to our eternal regret, we possess no full-sized contemporary document. The great poet of the Periclean Age stands divorced from his time as much by our lack of knowledge as by his own timelessness. Our scanty information about his life comes from a variety of sources of varying trustworthiness,[9] the chief of which is the anonymous *Vita*. Yet it is not so much the acquisition of new material that is needed as a reinterpretation of the old. Sophocles' art has been generally interpreted in the light of certain acts of piety and marvelous legends which are associated with his name.[10] When he led the boys' dance after the battle of Salamis, that episode became for all time a kind of melodious prologue to the whole tradition about him. In later life he seems to have dedicated a chapel to Heracles,[11] an act which is generally taken as illustrative of some special reverence toward that hero, or at least of some remarkable religiosity. Yet it is a well-known fact that piety of this sort among the Greeks was a public matter, a function of citizenship and the social obligation of the financially able. It did not signify anything about a man's real spiritual beliefs.

There is another story which has been even more influential.[12] In the year 420 when the Athenians sent to Epidaurus for the god Asclepius to come and purify the city after the plague, it became necessary for some eminent citizen to house the illustrious guest until a fitting temple should be prepared. Sophocles either offered or was chosen for this honor. In either case his reputation for uprightness and religious scrupulosity was involved, as well as his connection, perhaps hereditary, with the cult of the god of healing. Precisely what he received into his house is a matter for question. Possibly it was a statue,[13] but it seems most likely that Asclepius elected to come as a serpent, the form in which he was generally exported by the Epidaurians. One scholar who relates the story remarks ironically on the dignified and aging poet solemnly offering eggs to a sacred snake.[14] The picture is an amusing one, and doubtless Sophocles was amused by it. Theriolatry of any kind could only have been a formal survival in the fifth century, and such functional state gods as this, whether bleating or hissing, could hardly have swayed very far the subtle mind of Sophocles. At least, it is hard to see in them the germs of the *Electra* and the *Oedipus at Colonus*.

When Sophocles died in 406, the god of the theatre, Dionysus himself, was supposed to have guarded his funeral train along the road to Decelea, then held by the Spartans.[15] Significantly, the gods play a considerably greater part in the life of Sophocles than in the lives of Euripides or Aeschylus, and it is a known fact that after his death the poet received heroic honors, at least from some private religious body, under the divine name of Dexion, the "Receiver." [16] His worship, if such it can be called, was associated with that of Asclepius and another local hero. The site of the chapel, known to archaeologists, holds its place today in our imagination as a symbol of the piety of Sophocles, rather than of the piety of those who built it, Iophon or whoever. The poet's shade may have been touched by these attentions, but it is the admiration of his audiences, more than their understanding of him or his own intention, which linked him with the gods. He himself, a tragic poet, linked his life with humanity.

There is a famous passage in the first book of the *Republic*, where Plato makes old Cephalus say: "How well I remember the aged poet Sophocles, when in answer to the question, How does love suit with age, Sophocles, — are you still the man you were? Peace, he replied, most gladly have I escaped the thing of which you speak; I feel as if I had escaped from a mad and furious master." [17] Plato used this anecdote to his purpose, to accentuate the character of the tranquil Cephalus, but its significance for the critic of tragedy should be not so much that Sophocles enjoyed a peaceful old age, free from passions, as that he had passed through a youth full of strong ones. We need only compare Cicero's story [18] of how Pericles once rebuked the poet for admiring a handsome boy instead of attending to his business as a general, or the epigram which, on a somewhat unseemly occasion, he addressed to Euripides,[19] in order to realize that Sophocles had his human and even embarrassing moments. Again, the episodes recalled by that eminent traveler and man of *belles lettres*, Ion of Chios, who met Sophocles at a symposium during the time of the Samian War, reveal his nature as charmingly deft and sophisticated, but decidedly sensuous and passionate.[20] Ion was enchanted as much by his skill in getting a kiss from a pretty cup-bearer as by his witty discomfiture of a carping grammarian. Another remark of Ion's, that Sophocles in general behaved like a regular Athenian nobleman, has tended to put him in the serene bright light of *kalokagathia* — that ideal of Greek gentlemanliness which embraced everything fair and upright in both body and soul. Yet, before we content ourselves with that attractive picture, it is well to remember that Sophocles was not a nobleman by birth,[21] and that this particular comment was not meant entirely as a compliment, but at least in part as a reflection upon the competence of many an Athenian aristocrat. What Ion meant was that, as a general, Sophocles was no better than the rest.

Such little notes are in truth the most lifelike details we possess about Sophocles, and should serve to give our picture of him dimension and movement. Yet even in antiquity they seem to have been smoothed over to fit the classic mask, so that a comic poet, shortly after his death, envisioning him as a kind of Herodotean Tellus, could exclaim: "O fortunate Sophocles, who, having written many beautiful tragedies, a happy and skillful man, died without suffering any evil!" [22]

In modern times there have been two scholarly attempts to reconstruct the life of Sophocles. Gotthold Ephraim Lessing wrote a scrupulously detailed and learned commentary on the extant material, in the attempt to establish factual truth and exact chronology. More recently, Perrotta has prefaced to his *Sofocle* a "Life" designed more or less in the manner of Wilamowitz' famous historical reconstruction of Euripides.[23] Perrotta's effort was worthwhile, for it unearthed among other things a new possibility about Sophocles' birthplace.[24] Furthermore, Perrotta has tried to build upon the intellectual associations of Sophocles and his relations with such figures as Archelaus of Miletus, though his conclusions on this matter are open to doubt.[25] Yet even Perrotta, though the avowed enemy of classicism in its smaller details, has seen little if any beyond the traditional and classic interpretation of the larger questions. Sophocles emerges as remote, serene, and apart from his age as ever.

One of the most provocative aspects of Sophocles' life is certainly his connection with Pericles. But this in itself does not imply conservatism[26] or traditional piety, but, especially in Pericles' earlier years, rather the opposite. The situation is further complicated by the fact that Sophocles was apparently friends with Cimon who was a conservative and the political enemy of Pericles. If we knew more of the chronology of the matter, we should know whether Sophocles simply shifted his allegiance after Cimon's death, or was tactful enough to be intimate with both sides when their opposition was hottest. Whichever it may have been, this whole aspect of the poet's life deserves greater consideration than it has had, especially when we realize that in Cimon's circle Sophocles surely met the philosopher Archelaus,[27] while on the other hand it is scarcely possible that he failed to meet Anaxagoras, the preceptor of Pericles. The exact purport of these hints and scraps cannot of course be established. But they do help to place Sophocles in the milieu of the leading thinkers of the day and vitiate the general impression of his intellectual and political detachment from his age.

The one contemporary with whom Sophocles has been allowed a spiritual affinity is Herodotus. This relationship, which obviously appears on occasion in Sophocles,[28] has been carefully studied.[29] It has been shown that Sophocles did use Herodotus as a source, but many scholars have therefore tended to stretch the moral and religious formulae of Herodotus to fit Sophocles as well, on the basis of his borrowing of more peripheral ideas. Only the traditional, classic prejudice could take such a means for stressing the "naïveté" of the poet who is supposed to believe in oracles and to adhere to the old divinities and the old sentiments about the envy of the gods. The envy of the gods plays no great part in Sophocles, and the oracles, as Sophocles uses them, give evidence not of religious naïveté but of sophistication. Herodotus can provide no very great index to the meaning of Sophocles. It is rather Thucydides, whose pages are filled with the insights of the dramatic psychologist, who offers a real source for a historical understanding. And once he is given even a slight historical foothold, Sophocles himself should provide the best possible key to the intellectual history of the middle fifth century, even as Aeschylus and Euripides illuminate the generations before and after, and as Hesiod provides the only literary source for the Greek Dark Ages.

After the glibness of the classic assumption, with its easy ethic and its clichés about piety, serenity, and sophrosyne, a return to the mystery of the virile and passionate lines of Sophocles himself is a disquieting and bracing experience. What kind of serene simplicity can embrace the world of Oedipus, or conceive the terrible lines which close the *Trachiniae*? What lessons of prudent restraint can we draw from the fierce and openly justified extremes of Antigone and Electra? Once more, like Mozart, Sophocles veiled his passions in elegance, but they are only the more fearful for being veiled. It is an error to take elegance for meaning, to mistake the artistry for the art and leave the veil drawn. Yet the answer is not to tear the veil and separate the two; elegance is part of meaning, and artistry is necessary to art. If the tragic spirit is to penetrate to the central mysteries of life, it must, in order to remain intelligible, do so within a formal scheme. And the stricter the scheme the better, for thus the mystery grows incandescent by contrast with the innocence of the form. Of this essence also are Shakespeare's fools or the deft grace of the violins as Don Giovanni invites the statue to supper. Such motifs buoy the action suddenly into a sphere of ambiguity where the listener must either formulate the mystery for himself, or lose the thread entirely. *Don Giovanni* is what it is because, though tragic in implication, it is written in *buffa* form; and Sophoclean tragedy perhaps owes its peculiar power to the dichotomy between the formal security of the framework, which is the world of tragedy, and the heroic fate which evolves within that world. No one moral formula can adequately describe that dichotomy, for the heroic fate may include too great a variety of actions and values, as the sum of Sophocles' extant work shows. Our formulae have all been based upon the framework, none upon the action, and none can be, for there is no single moral scheme which can include the actions of both the *Ajax* and the *Oedipus at Colonus*.

For centuries the moral and religious force of Sophocles' plays has been lost in a waste of flat formulations, not one of which has ever fitted all the plays; and the most popular formula of all, that of *hamartia*, or sin-and-punishment, seems scarcely to fit any. Those who recognized this fact have offered the counter-formula that Sophocles proclaimed not the justice but the power of the gods, and consequently the nothingness of man. But this formula too seems to fail in the light of specific values set upon man in all the plays, and deliberately brought to triumph in the last three. There is also the difficulty that such a nihilistic scheme is hardly consistent with serenity or the necessity for self-restraint, and least of all with the famous humanism of Sophocles. This humanism also wants definition; presumably it arose from the fact that Sophocles' characters are usually men, not gods, in contrast to those of Aeschylus. But the real reason for this change, the driving power behind Sophocles' humanism, has been ignored. We have tended to find in the perfection of Attic drama both the motive and the result of Sophocles' efforts with the single play as against the trilogy, as if the artist felt no necessities beyond those of his art. And thus another inconsistency in the classic assumption arises: Sophocles the pure artist cannot be identified with Sophocles the pious teacher of sophrosyne and heir of Aeschylus' post as educator of people. Once these contradictions and circular arguments have been removed, it may become apparent wherein Sophocles was really serene, and wherein we must admit that he was not. The most intense of tragic poets could scarcely have lived entirely above the tragic emotions.[30]

In the light of the dramas themselves, it seems impossible that Sophocles' innermost allegiance could have been to the official gods of Olympus, or that the heroic figures of his tragedies were created out of the straw of hybris in order to be knocked down as an object lesson in sophrosyne. Sophocles is one poet for whom oversimplification is not only misleading but fatal. Mystery must be taken as part of the meaning, if we are ever to know what the stories and myths really signified. That the meaning was moral and religious is axiomatic; but the search for it must center around the "higher personal, as distinct from the purely social, religion of the Hellenes." [31] Whether or not it is "higher," it is this personal religion of Sophocles which alone can reveal the meaning of divinity and the moral canons of the heroic Sophoclean world.

These canons form the dynamics of the poet's spiritual experience and artistic impetus, and they have been confused or passed over by the formulae relating to the framework, not the heroic action, of tragedy. The only possibility of an advance, therefore, lies in a totally new point of view. Attention must be focused not on the chorus, which embodies the framework, but on the hero himself. The real moral nature of his position must be judged only by his own standard as he reveals it in the play, and by the moral choices open to him in the action. It is the essence of the time-honored prejudice to take sides with the forces which oppose the hero, in the belief that they, and they alone, are divine. Usually they are divine, but whether they are also morally right can be decided only after each play has been analyzed in the light of its real issues and their place in Athenian thought.

One difficulty arises at the start. Total actions of plays can seldom be adequately illustrated by specific, individual passages. In the case of Sophocles, perversely enough, the most explicit moral statements are made by the chorus, as a rule, and therefore tend rather to bear out those formulae which must be particularly rejected as unfitting to the whole. But this fact only illustrates the function and necessity of the tragic framework, with its simple elegance and apparent clarity, within which the poet must let his real intention half reveal itself by subtle contrast and innuendo. The veil which Dante spreads is only occasionally lifted a little at one corner to reassure us and provoke us to deeper reading. And so it is with Sophocles. What is most explicitly declared is often most subtly and implicitly denied; somewhere in the inconsistency between what the hero does and what the chorus says may lie the secret of Sophocles' own moral judgment.

Another kind of evidence will be found in certain themes which recur: the theme of "knowledge too late," or "wisdom and time," or "shadow and reality." These are, of course, no more than hints, momentary liftings of a corner of the veil, but they cast some light. Another perhaps more valuable method will be the observation of characters and modes of speech which correspond to certain political and social ideas by which we may set definite historical values against the background of the fifth century. Finally, in the wake of Professor Werner Jaeger, whose *Paideia* has demonstrated the centrality of the idea of *arete* in all stages of Greek culture, we must seek for commentaries on this and related ideas as inevitable elements in any treatment of Greek morality.

It is impossible to give here anything like a full account of the significance of the word *arete*. For that, Professor Jaeger's work must be consulted. In the course of its long development over the centuries of Greek culture, arete came to embrace at one time or another practically every kind of ideal or aspiration which the Greeks conceived. Like sophrosyne, it achieved a certain schematic poise as "virtue" in the world of Plato and Aristotle; but earlier it had indicated a wider kind of excellence, whether physical, intellectual, or spiritual, and it could even be applied to things as well as to human beings. But in the human realm, it indicated that quality which was most perfect in an individual or race. Not necessarily moral, arete nevertheless could be moral, and throughout the fifth century gradually became more so. Yet even Aristotle's definition of it is not so narrow but that he can distinguish both a moral and an intellectual kind of arete. But Sophocles is the last who uses the word, and even more the idea, with all its old heroic and resplendent connotations, which lie close to the roots of that belief in human glory and strength upon which the Greeks built their civilization. Socrates was the first to try to define it exactly. Before his time, anyone who used it expressed not only his own immediate meaning but also the whole long history of meanings which the word had gathered, and thereby referred his hearers to the core of his cultural heritage, that self-conscious standard of being which drew the line between Hellenes and barbarians. After Socrates, it can usually be translated, but before his time it had no synonyms, even in Greek, and so must remain "arete." The meanings which one after another reveal themselves in Sophocles' treatment of this idea provide an excellent clue to Sophocles' own development as poet and moralist, and cast great light on the puzzling variety of his works, as well as on the main thread of his inner life.

From this vantage point, it is possible to see the nature of Sophocles' tragic heroes. Moreover, much will be revealed about the gods, as he conceived them, and about tragedy itself. For the nature of the gods determines the nature of tragedy; and to some degree tragedy is an attempt to ascertain or declare the nature of the gods. Now the Greeks, especially the Athenians, were never perfectly sure of the moral virtue of the gods. Pindar often took pains to whitewash mythology, but the tragedians of Athens looked at the gods as the myths presented them — that is, as they really were for them — and thus fell under the necessity of explaining them. Certainly the gods were not always commendable. They lied and stole and committed adultery,[32] but that was perhaps their business. What concerned the tragedians was their treatment of man. For while the Greeks did not generally believe that "every good gift and every perfect gift cometh from above," there was never any doubt where evil came from, especially that irrational evil which seemed to have no cause or moral meaning. Somehow it was necessary to explain this evil, to face this question which in all Western culture is identified with the problem of life's own meaning.

It was precisely this doubt about the moral trustworthiness of their gods, together with the peculiar willingness of the Athenians to face and argue that doubt, which stimulated a hundred years of tragic poetry. The austerity of the form, as contrasted with the earlier poetry at the courts of Peisistratus or other tyrants, finds its parallel perhaps in the austerity of fifth-century sculpture as compared to the earlier Maidens of the Acropolis, or in the change from the luxurious Ionian to the more severe Dorian mode of dress which Thucydides notes.[33] Unquestionably, the seriousness with which Athenian genius took up this weighty matter arose from the sudden burden of responsibility and alertness to major moral issues which the newly founded democracy put upon the individual.[34] Professor Jaeger observes: "But as man becomes increasingly conscious of his self-hood, he tends to consider his own will and reason independent of higher powers; and thereby he becomes more responsible for his own fate." [35] Man as responsible, as morally capable and not as the imbecilic toy of outer forces, was the vision which gave the first impulse to the theodicy of Aeschylus and led him to see behind tragic suffering the unexpected but inevitable judgment of God upon some long-hidden crime.

And yet, tragedy also embraces man as morally imbecile — especially the later work of Euripides; the youngest of the three great poets ended his life with a paean of the world's irrational evil, the god Dionysus, patron of tragedy. And this is equally significant — significant of Euripides' confessed failure to make life morally intelligible; it was perhaps his very honesty, the fullness of his vision of evil, which brought him in the *Bacchae* to his most magnificent heights. Somehow it impresses us as the play Euripides always meant to write, for with all its negativity and despair, it is a kind of yea-statement, a realistic grasping of the tragic essence in terms of myth, unmarred by rationalistic doctrine or sardonic disapproval. Emphasis has been laid on the relation between the cult of Dionysus and the nature of tragedy itself; [36] tragedy seeks the inner springs of life, whatever they be, and Dionysus well symbolizes them, in their evil as well as in their good. But be it observed that Dionysus was never a god bound by moral responsibility, as Apollo was; and the question of moral responsibility was as fundamental to tragedy as was the cult of Dionysus. We may therefore observe in tragedy something analogous to the Nietzschean antinomy between the Apollonian and Dionysiac spirits, a tension between what is morally and intellectually intelligible and what is forever darkly fascinating, but destructive and full of peril. Aeschylus was completely committed to the former, and Euripides seems slowly to have embraced the latter. The question remains, where does Sophocles belong?

To say that he neglected the problem and concentrated on man alone is to deprive him of his birthright as a tragedian. The humanism of Sophocles was not so limited. True, he did not proceed like a dogmatic theologian, but he proceeded, and in his successive stages he seems to have faced the problem of evil in its most acute and disquieting forms. In him the conflict between the intelligible and the perilously daemonic is as intense as possible. Nor could he well have retained the old answers of Aeschylus — the inherited curse, the divine Justice of Zeus — in the rapidly changing years after the fall of the Areopagus. With the world developing around him, and new religious ideas constantly springing to life, Sophocles could not help meeting the challenge of the times and raising the old tragic questions anew,[37] to answer them as he could in his own terms: what justice is there for man? where is the moral balance of life to be found? to whom is man responsible? We have been too prone to think that Sophocles resisted all the novel forces of his day, and to put him in the conservative camp, as if he foresaw in the Sophists the breakdown of Athenian morale, or in the growing power of Athens the as yet untraceable seeds of her decay. How are we so sure that this fortunate and deeply gifted poet, whose genius is so closely allied with the genius of the expansive and forward-looking Periclean Age, was in truth a wary reactionary, suspicious of all new doctrines and shaking his head over the very release of the individual which made his city the mistress of the Greek world.[38]

It cannot be so. Tragedy lies deeper than religious or political conservatism. And in Greece, where until the age of Plato the poets were the creators of religion, it would have been highly singular and inappropriate for Sophocles to assume the backward gaze and ally himself with all that was religiously archaic and outmoded. The gods

of Olympus were slowly becoming mere public figureheads, and so
we may assume they were for Sophocles as well. Divinity was elsewhere — a conclusion which logically followed from the realization
of man's moral responsibility. The more we look closely for a satisfying justice in the world, the more inevitably we are driven to disillusion and to the admission that justice is with man, not the gods;
that man is more responsible than he dreamed, though in a different
way; and that perhaps this very quality in man is a kind of divinity.
Some such change seems to have taken place in the fifth century,
and it is well described by one German scholar in a monograph on
Sophocles: "The earlier divine individualities step out of their stiff
shape, the religious element becomes fluid; it shifts from the remote-
ness of the world of the gods into the human breast, until finally the
divine idea is completely evaporated and emptied in the shadow-life
of allegorical images." [39] The final stage of that change does not occur
in Sophocles. He never becomes allegorical. But there is surely much
that is fluid in his view of divinity, and much that is only to be found
in humanity itself. The task of the interpreter of his plays is not to
crystallize that view, but to try to show it, or distill it from its context.
Some crystallization, some loss of subtlety, must inevitably occur, for
Sophocles is not to be translated or explained in prose. But the poetry
of man as a fully responsible moral agent, yet confronted with the
irrational, inexplicable evil of the world, led to certain inevitable
conclusions which Sophocles traced out with characteristic Greek
thoroughness and intensity, and laid down as the basis of his tragic
art.

II

SCHOLARSHIP AND HAMARTIA

THE traditional conception of Sophocles, with its virtues as well as its insufficiencies, found its most monumental expression around the turn of the century in the edition of Sir Richard Jebb. Jebb was a great scholar, but his affinity for Sophocles, one suspects, was founded on Victorian sensibilities which sought and discovered in certain of the ancients a satisfying if misleading similarity to modern values. The Victorians did not invent this moral provincialism. It was the natural outcome of the formal and rational humanism of the eighteenth century which, after the vast revelations and researches of the Renaissance, endeavored to schematize values and define man. The Victorians merely trailed behind, striving with failing hearts to retain that faith.

Jebb's work fixed the point at which all coming editions of Sophocles must begin, and it may be some time before any scholar feels the confidence to measure himself against those formidable commentaries. And yet in Jebb's edition there is a notable absence of any full exposition of Sophocles' moral intentions as an artist. Perhaps for him an artist did not have to have moral intentions. Still, Sophocles taught piety, and if such perfect works of art needed any motivation besides their own beauty, piety was the answer. Be it said in tribute to Jebb's honesty, that he more than once admitted to his students that the *Electra* puzzled him greatly, and that he had never found a way to fit that matricidal paean into his general view of the poet. Perhaps if Jebb had tried to formulate at length the substance of Sophoclean piety, he would have found more and even greater difficulties. But he usually contented himself with the classic assumption. Once in a little essay he explained that Sophocles was an adherent of the ancient religion in a more spiritual form.[1] But the "spiritual" is left to mean what it may, as is the "ancient religion." If Sophocles seemed vague, his expounders could be even more so. Such scholarship had a serious, complacent expansiveness which was typical of its time and which may never again be rivaled.

In 1917 came the beginning of a great change and a reawakening of Sophoclean criticism, with the posthumous publication of Tycho von Wilamowitz' *Die Dramatische Technik des Sophokles*. The young author died in the war, and the last chapter was written by his illustrious father, Ulrich von Wilamowitz. After the shallows and sand-bars in which Sophocles had been becalmed so long, this rigorous and cold-blooded examination of the poet's method was, to say the least, a stimulating blast. With utter disregard for prettier notions, Wilamowitz approached Sophocles as a craftsman and proposed the theory, on the basis of certain inconsistencies in action and characterization, that Sophocles worked primarily for the optimum effect of particular scenes, and for this end was even willing to sacrifice, if need be, the unity and harmony of the piece as a whole.[2] He was peculiarly averse to psychological explanations of motive, and asserted that "complicated psychological motivation lies entirely beyond the possibility of ancient tragedy, and especially of Sophocles,"[3] and that therefore Sophoclean characters are no further characterized psychologically than is made necessary by what they have to do and say.[4] Action and character were determined primarily by the myth, and then further qualified by the limitations, technical necessities, and dramatic possibilities of the stage production. The purpose of the play was ultimately the effectiveness of its principal scenes.

In such doctrine the effects of a highly developed taste for Euripides are obvious. It is hard to believe that Sophocles had so episodic an ideal of tragedy. Nevertheless, Wilamowitz' theory was applied brilliantly, though narrowly, and at least in the case of the *Electra* it pointed the way to wider and more generally illuminating conclusions. On the other hand, it confessedly ignored all the moral problems of the plays in making their purpose a mere display of art for art's sake. Furthermore, it labored the small inconsistencies into a whole theory of scene-by-scene composition which is foreign to Sophocles, and somewhat self-contradictory. For small, intentional inconsistencies, whether in character or situation, are generally admitted by an artist with the purpose of increasing the harmony and unity of the piece as a whole rather than as a means toward heightening the effect of individual moments: that is, presuming they are purposely committed, they are committed in the interest of the plan of the whole. A good many of the little contradictions in Sophocles, however, are not so significant as Wilamowitz thought them, and it would require no very complicated psychological reading of character to explain them quite simply and naturally. The whole interpretation went to the utmost limit of concreteness; but in revealing and extolling the technical merits of Sophocles, Wilamowitz at times made art seem the master of the poet, not the poet master of his art. The necessities of the Greek stage — the limitations of the number of actors, the length of time the *eccyclema* and other stage mechanisms required, and so on — carried the day, while a more important consideration was ignored: namely that supreme dramatic art means, among other things, the ability to fit together the technical necessities and the poetic intention.

In direct answer to Wilamowitz, Wolfgang Schadewaldt [5] approached Sophocles as a psychologist, and found him perfectly mature and sound. Attacking some of the same inconsistencies of character which Wilamowitz had explained on technical grounds, Schadewaldt urged, for instance, that the characters of Ajax and Antigone suffer actual change. The implications of such an idea were immense, apart from the fact that it contravened the more usual notion that character in Greek tragedy is static. Value-change is implied in character-change, and hence the whole inner world, which Wilamowitz had avoided, came into play. Schadewaldt did not avoid the issue, or content himself with mere secular psychologizing. He offered a general theory of Sophoclean tragedy in this form: "Man, overthrown by a fate which he has unwittingly brought upon himself, comes to his right mind and conquers himself, and thereby his fate, in his own destruction." [6] But there, in those words "unwittingly" and "comes to his right mind," we find ourselves back where we started. The sin-and-punishment formula is at work again in the service of simple piety. Schadewaldt could see the antinomy between the hero and the world, but in interpreting it, he fell back upon a tragic flaw, and called the difference hybris, or pride. Aristotle had come in by the back door and completed the formula.

Schadewaldt assuredly read Sophocles with the eye of an artist, but his conclusions were disappointing. Thus he observed, in describing the hero's difference and isolation from his fellows, that the hero's values emerged in what he called the "aristocratic" words, that is, words which connote the training and standards of the old aristocracy, such as "glory," "nobility," "honor." On the other hand, the values of the city-state — with which Sophocles supposedly identified himself — appeared in the so-called "democratic" words of intellectualistic import: "sense," "prudence," "good-counsel," and above all, "sophrosyne." [7] The verbal antinomy certainly exists, and cannot be denied. But the assumption that Sophocles himself stood for the democratic words, with their emphasis on sophrosyne, would have seemed more arbitrary had it been less traditional. Equally arbitrary, however, was the further assumption that to the mind of Sophocles the structure of the city-state, or political cosmos, corresponded to a divine cosmos — a world, presumably, in which the "democratic words" were codified in eternity. So Sophocles would stand forth as the true poet of the democratic Athenian city-state,[8] from whose divinely authorized design the hero is a tragic deviation. And yet, these "democratic words" do not always represent sound morality, and what is more, the evidence for such a divine cosmos corresponding to the political one is totally lacking. At least, it cannot be shown that Sophocles believed in it for any longer time than it took him to write a chorus. The whole view harks back to Aeschylus, for whom the city was indeed the repository of sacred and eternal values. Sophocles was never so schematized.

The vision of Sophocles, however, as poet of the city-state, or *polis*, marked a great advance in the historical understanding of his work. It brought him one step out of the vacuum, and allowed him a moral function, a responsible position in the roster of Greek poets as well as in his own time. It now became important to find out exactly how he performed that function, and what his moral position was. Max Pohlenz, in his general treatise, *Die griechische Tragödie*, tried to show that Sophocles stepped into Aeschylus' shoes as teacher of the people and proved himself a strong religious conservative, even reactionary, who reflected the released individualism of the times in the artistic viewpoint of his plays, and yet defended the old groundwork of Aeschylean religion.[9] Strangely enough, in this difference between his religious beliefs and his artistic point of view, Pohlenz found the secret of Sophocles' harmony. He made the poet an apologist for the old optimistic beliefs, who imparted to his works a "spiritual peace, a harmonious balance which does not lose its effect even on him who does not share these beliefs." [10] Hereby the Sophocles of the classic pattern also embraces a kind of primitivism, if by the old religious beliefs be meant the mythic tales in themselves, the *fabulae sacrae*, as it is now popular to call them. If, however, the old religion is the religion of Aeschylus, it remains to be shown where Sophocles really expounds or defends it. Certain traces may be detectable in the *Ajax*, but where in the bitterness of the *Trachiniae* is the solid faith of Aeschylus to be found? Pohlenz throughout treats the question of individualism as a very central one, and indeed it is. But also he asserts, not very convincingly, that the characters of Creon and Menelaus issue the poet's warning against too great freedom in the individual personality. [11] Sophocles cannot thus be forced into a conservative pattern; he set no arbitrary or fixed limit to the potential of the heroic individual.

Two very brilliant German works, by Karl Reinhardt and Heinrich Weinstock, have done much to refine and sharpen sensitivity in the attitude of the present day toward Sophocles. Reinhardt especially has read him with the closest care and has revealed subtle contrasts and ambiguities in the text which must undeniably affect any general interpretation. The chief virtue of Reinhardt's book, however, which is detail, has militated somewhat against the formation of a complete understanding. It offers no Procrustean formula, but on the other hand, it leaves much to be asked. One general theory does emerge, that of the isolation of the Sophoclean protagonist, which sometimes tends to dominate the interpretation. [12] But for the most part, Reinhardt attends to the moral and religious questions in individual situations, and stresses no dogma.

More than any other critic, Weinstock has escaped the smooth superficies of classicism. In his preface he openly condemns it as a weakening of the poet, whom he approaches as the interpreter of life as it is, a realist in the best sense of the word: "That long perceived depth of surface in Sophocles lies in nothing but in the poet's will to reality. The pattern of an idealistic and overblown classicism has changed into the inexorable poet of reality, of human reality with all its foundations, backgrounds, and abysses." [13] Weinstock's approach is fresh and courageous, and his insight into Sophoclean character and symbolism is immense. For him, Sophocles' message is one of "responsibility for the present," a rather general formulation which owes its particular character to the Existentialist philosophy to which Weinstock adheres, and which is also sometimes apparent in the pages of Reinhardt. But Existentialism is hardly an adequate summary either of Sophocles or of these critics' understanding of him. Weinstock's conclusions, which are the bolder of the two, indicate the liveliness of an interpretation which has freed itself from the conventional repressions about Sophocles and which has seen in his characters types of the heroic human spirit, instead of examples of various kinds of fault. On the other hand, Weinstock ignores all the historical questions, and so his book remains more an appreciation than an interpretation. As such, however, it could scarcely be surpassed, especially in its understanding of the function of divinity.

The works of these five scholars are perhaps the most important large contributions to a modern interpretation of Sophocles. They all have a certain consistency and clarity in their approach, which is more than can be found in the recent books by Gennaro Perrotta and C. M. Bowra. For instance, Perrotta's attitude differs scarcely at all from the traditional one he condemns, except insofar as he insists that Sophocles was a pessimist — a conclusion hardly compatible with his other view that the gods are just and good. Perrotta stands confused between the classic outlook which he cannot avoid and his reaction to Pohlenz. He makes the general observation that Sophocles taught piety and sophrosyne on the one hand [14] and, on the other, that he avoided all moral problems except in the *Ajax* and *Antigone*.[15] The latter fact, however, does not prevent him from explaining Sophocles' moral attitude in the other plays.

A comparable confusion exists in Bowra's *Sophoclean Tragedy*. It is never made entirely clear, for example, whether Oedipus is responsible or not for his destruction; indeed Bowra never really raises the question of whether the gods meant power or righteousness to Sophocles; he seems to assume the poet's complete piety on either basis, depending on the passage in question. Thus the gods exhibit their power arbitrarily in the case of Oedipus; but when Hyllus cries out against them in the end of the *Trachiniae* Bowra interprets the speech as impious and states rather surprisingly that "Sophocles allows no doubts, no criticism of the gods." [16] Bowra has left untouched the roots of the religious question and has re-created the traditional view of Sophocles, with all its bland inconsistencies, and with hardly an addition or subtraction. Everything is taken at face value, from the coming and going of the gods themselves, or the apparent yielding of Ajax, to the choral tags to which a rather arbitrary importance is attached.[17] The evidence is merely heaped, not sorted. Bowra is generally committed to a sin-and-punishment formula for tragedy and therefore, since he finds Antigone and Electra innocent, is constrained to draw the moral of these plays not from the tragedy of the protagonists, but from the punishment of the villains, Creon, Clytaemnestra, and her paramour — a result more fitting for melodrama.[18]

Bowra's book shows little advance over many another attempt to solve the moral questions in Sophocles within the classicist mold. The fundamental errors in this view arise, no doubt, from the feeling that the impossible gulf between man and God makes it necessary to leave the Divine inscrutable — a kind of self-restraint alien to the Greek, especially the Greek tragedian whose business it was to find out God. Although Bowra has made some allowance for the gods to function through character, especially in the case of Oedipus, he nevertheless believes that they inhabit a separate world and affect man from without, for their own purposes. Long ago Evelyn Abbott, in his *Theology and Ethics of Sophocles*, tried to work on these assumptions and was forced on the one hand to allow a kind of teleological design to justify tragic suffering,[19] and on the other to say that "Sophocles, as a rule, does not inquire into the motive of a legend which he finds serviceable for dramatic purposes." [20]

Thus between art for art's sake and various types of sin and punishment, the classic view of Sophocles wavers, growing more and more transparent, but refusing to give way entirely. It seems on the surface completely justified; Sophocles' religious attitude, as John Moore said, appears so "suspiciously like mere conventional pietism," [21] that any other interpretation risks seeming far-fetched. Yet Moore, as well as some of those whose work has just been described, have made at least a partial beginning. But the old assumptions remain, a fashionable array, with ancestors reaching back to the earliest of all the formulae for tragedy, the Aristotelian theory of *hamartia*.

It is not unfair to say that practically all, if not all, Sophoclean criticism has been affected to some degree by the hamartia theory. Not all scholars have embraced it wholeheartedly, and very few have been willing or even remotely able to interpret all seven tragedies according to its schematized moral plan. Most have preferred to keep it in reserve and to bring it forward when all other explanations seemed either impious or empty. Nor has there been any universal agreement as to what is meant by this word, usually translated "tragic flaw," which has come down to us, encircled with the aura of Aristotle's vast authority, as the true key to the tragedy of all ages. Not only the drama of the Greeks, but also the plays of Shakespeare and Marlowe, *Samson Agonistes*, and the tragedies of the Restoration have all been interpreted in deference to it, not to mention the drama of the Continent, and the hosts of frigid tragedies written to fit the rule. And so many and so various are the tragic flaws that have been discovered that, historically speaking, "hamartia" has now come to mean almost any characteristic or event which happens to occur in a tragedy, so long as it can be considered even remotely connected with the hero's fall, whether it be the blackest of crimes or the merest bad luck.

The word seldom appears in the critique of Aeschylus or Euripides. The criminal actions which set the former's monumental works in motion hardly qualify as convenient examples of hamartia, which, as Aristotle says, is definitely not a great evil or misdemeanor.[22] Neither has it been thought necessary to apply the rule to Euripides, for his moral is generally clear without it. Where his moral is not clear, however, hamartia is very useful; thus his Hippolytus may be looked upon as guilty of prudery, or his Pentheus of hybris.

Indeed, hybris, generally translated "pride" and interpreted according to St. Paul, has been very useful in this context. Originally it meant assault and battery, and it never quite lost the overtones of physical violence, even when it later was associated chiefly with the overweening arrogance of the rich and mighty. In any case, it is too serious a matter to qualify as hamartia, though the two are often equated in an effort to make the tragic hero deserve his fall, and save the moral order.[23]

Significantly enough, only Sophocles seems to be in need of this kind of moral assistance; indeed, the hamartia theory in all probability was invented to explain Sophocles, and it has remained ever since the governing feature of the several moral approaches which the critics have tried. The feeling has apparently been that the reverent and morally sound Sophocles would not have been guilty of showing the fall of the innocent, which was offensive; [24] yet obviously, his tragic characters were not abandoned villains. Ergo, he must have been following that middle road which was so consistent with piety and the Greek spirit, and motivating his catastrophes by means of that rather vague but morally defensible formula, the tragic flaw. If some of his people seemed utterly innocent, then it behooved the critic to stretch his historical sense and find the flaw. There was challenge in this for any scholar. What kind of fault would the Greeks have considered a just cause for the just gods to destroy an otherwise just man? Thereafter, it was merely a matter of procedure. Critics such as Jebb and his contemporaries assumed and believed in the impeccable justice of Sophocles' gods with surprising fervor. Piety was piety, whether it be in the nineteenth century or the fifth century B.C. Others, such as the elder Wilamowitz, realized that the gods might not be just, exactly, but they were powerful, and that was enough to keep Sophocles serene and respectful.[25]

But for those who sought for tragic flaws, the chorus was of immense assistance. For the Sophoclean chorus regularly did just what Horace, after reading Sophocles, said it should do:

> Favor the good and friendly counsels urge,
> Control and soothe the wrathful bosom's surge;
> Praise modest feasts, unspoiled by luxuries,
> Sound Justice, Law, and the open gates of Peace;
> Keep secrets, pray the gods, and supplicate
> Fortune to bless the weak, and mock the great.[26]

In short, it ought to preserve the amenities and the norms of everyday life, a common-sense attitude, and a certain level of decency in contrast to the extremes of action on the stage.

The chorus of Aeschylus does a great deal more than it should, according to Horace: it teaches the moral lesson. For Aeschylus it was still the prime vehicle for his ideas, and it is in the lyric portions that the central meaning of most Aeschylean drama lies. Because of this fact, presumably, it was assumed that the chorus of Sophocles equally expressed the poet's main thought, in spite of the fact that the obvious self-consistency of Aeschylean lyric is quite absent and no clear doctrine can be drawn from it. It does, however, provide judgments, always on the side of moderation, and seldom fails to calm the angry, keep secrets, and pray for justice; from this source most of the tragic flaws have been derived. Thus from choral criticism Antigone is convicted of harshness and stubbornness, Oedipus of rashness of temper, Philoctetes of obstinacy,[27] and so on. It is a surprising fact that all these faults, or most of them, really come down to the same thing — stubbornness, or more specifically, that special quality of self-willed independence, called *authadeia* by the Greeks, which keeps a man from yielding to his fate and makes him talk harshly and proudly. So too Ajax is urged to put away his noble but overweening attitude, and Electra is reproved for drawing more trouble on herself than is necessary by her constant mourning for Agamemnon.[28] The chorus in the *Trachiniae* is remarkably sympathetic to Deianeira, but can still rebuke her inability to bear her loneliness more hopefully.[29] It is all one: if we trust the chorus, Sophocles wrote about nothing but the evil effects of stubbornness.

The mind of the chorus, with its common sense, its amenities and polite norms, is not a sufficient moral guide to Sophocles, but rather a mirror of the normal, nontragic outlook, psychologically nondramatic, always trying to retard or stop the action, but only succeeding in accentuating its superb and fatal rush. The chorus must, of course, be taken into account in estimating the action of a play, but the lyrics of Sophocles are not gospel. The results, in fact, are quite surprising, if one analyzes from the standpoint of the protagonist the "faults" which have emerged as tragic causes from the chorus' judgments. What, for instance, is this stubbornness?

If stubbornness is a fault which the gods punish, why is it not consistently punished? Of the six protagonists, all supposedly with the same failing, why is Antigone punished, while Electra goes off in triumph? Why is Ajax allowed to die, while Philoctetes is divinely enlightened? Why is the essentially gentle resistance of Deianeira consigned to an ignominious fate, while the rash individualist Oedipus, though temporarily humbled, is eventually taken up into heaven not a jot more subdued, with all his rashness and violence on his head? Where in this confusing tangle of uncertain crimes and all too certain outcomes is any pious doctrine to be found? The extenuating circumstances prove little, for the protagonists with the most extenuating circumstances, such as Deianeira and Antigone, come to the worst fates of all. Ajax alone, it has been urged, really deserves his fate, because, by scorning her aid in battle, he committed an actual offence against the divinity of Athena.[30] This is in some sense true, but there is also a great deal more to be said about Ajax, in the light of which his hybris, as it is sometimes called, may appear merely superficial (see Chapter IV).

If stubbornness, or authadeia, is an example of hamartia, its results are various, to say the least. One is furthermore tempted to ask what the results would be if the obstinacy of Antigone or the "temper" of Oedipus were removed. Would Antigone really have been a better person for yielding to the tyrannical decree of her uncle? Or would Oedipus seem nobler for taking the blow with the ox-goad as patiently as a Christian martyr? [31] Few Greeks before Socrates would think the latter; and as for Antigone, even Socrates, when ordered once by the Thirty Tyrants to commit an act which he considered unjust, refused (obstinately) and went home. Or again, should Oedipus have believed Teiresias' word at once and gone into exile, or neglected the problem of the murder when he saw it was beginning to involve himself? To rebuke these protagonists for their faults implies that one knows what they should have done.

The question of the supposed guilt of Oedipus leads directly to the question of the real meaning of hamartia. Indeed, so closely are the two problems related that it seems possible that the whole hamartia theory had its genesis in the mystery of the *Oedipus Rex*. There are two fundamental ways of explaining the tragedy, corresponding in general to the two possibilities involved in hamartia. One is to attribute Oedipus' fall to the rash, self-willed temper already mentioned. But others maintain that no such moral failing is involved, but rather an intellectual slip, an error, entailing no moral guilt, but merely the well-known cataclysmic sequel. This error — "trifling," as Aristotle said — occurred when Oedipus slew his father and married his mother. He was innocent, in that he acted in ignorance, but he was wrong in that he did these things.

In these two views of the *Oedipus* we see the two interpretations of hamartia which have divided Aristotelian scholars. Butcher [32] defends in general the moral interpretation and translates the word as "frailty," [33] while Bywater and others maintain the purely intellectual significance and translate, "error of judgment." [34] The relative significance of these two views for tragedy itself is, of course, immense. But the important question for the present is, which did Aristotle mean? Did he intend us to find a morally culpable act or merely a mistake as the cause of tragic catastrophe?

There can be no real doubt that Aristotle meant by hamartia a moral fault or failing of some kind. It is due only to the influence of the romantic era that people sometimes imagine the Greeks as happy pagans with no sense of sin. Socrates may, indeed, have defined sin as a kind of ignorance; but the mission of his life was to prove that such ignorance, the ignorance of values, was itself sinful. In all Greek literature, wrongdoing goes hand in hand with folly; there is an intellectual element in all Greek ethics. But no literature is more directly moral than the Greek. Specifically, in the chapter on hamartia in the *Poetics*, Aristotle discusses the moral stance of the hero of tragedy: he should be neither perfect nor a villain. The whole context is that of good and evil, and the upsetting effect of seeing a perfectly just and upright man destroyed. He must be only a relatively good man, whose goodness is somehow obviated by a minor moral flaw.[35] It would hardly make a play morally gratifying to have its hero ruined through some trifling error of brain-work, which, however it involved him in some ritual pollution, implied nothing about his character. If the moral order is to be saved by making the hero deserve his fall, he ought at least to deserve it. Of all men, Aristotle was clear about the difference between inner and outer guilt.

A relevant passage in the *Nicomachean Ethics* proves the point.[36] Aristotle divides wrongdoing into three classes: *misadventure* (ἀτύχημα); *mistake* (ἁμάρτημα); and *unjust act* (ἀδίκημα), which is further subdivided into unjust acts arising from passion or lust, but without deliberation, and those arising from deliberate intention. Aristotle says specifically that these all involve moral guilt except the first, misadventure, which simply means *unforeseeable accident*; and he refers generally to all except the first by the term "hamartia." In defining the second class (*hamártema*), he notes that it differs from a misadventure in that the fault originates in the agent himself, though it may not imply rooted vice. In any case, it is clear beyond doubt that Aristotle did not use the word without moral implications. The moral interpretation of the tragic hamartia is the only one that is consistent with Aristotle's thinking and that preserves the universal validity of poetry which Aristotle himself said made it more philosophic than history — a view which the particular "error of judgment" theory would seriously violate.[37]

Such then is the meaning of the word in Aristotle. As used in tragedy itself, however, its meaning seems to differ. The world of values was not yet schematized, and the word "hamartia," which had originally meant simply "failure to hit the mark," was still used indifferently to refer to anything which went wrong, whether morally or circumstantially. Thus old Oedipus, defending his innocence in the later play, can say:

> For not in me, not in myself, could you
> Discover any stain of sin, whereby
> I sinned against myself and mine.[38]

Both words translated here as "sin" contain the root of "hamartia." Old Oedipus can use the same word for the deeds he did and for the moral guilt which he disclaims. When Sophocles wrote these lines, the implications of the word were still not entirely fixed, nor was the distinction between inner and outer guilt clarified — a process which the play unquestionably helped to advance. In tragedy, the word is used with the completest freedom, in contrast to its strict significance in Aristotle, to cover a multitude of errors, sins, crimes, petty mistakes, and transgressions of authority, whether for moral or immoral reasons. There is no English equivalent which can embrace all its internal and external aspects, its moral or merely technical constituents of guilt. With so many meanings, then, the word "hamartia," as used by the tragedians themselves, becomes relatively unimportant for our moral interpretation of tragedy. It remains to question Aristotle's use of it, and therewith the whole moral scheme which he imposed on the drama of the preceding era.

Fifth-century tragedy was in itself morally sufficient for its time. It had its own scheme. Aristotle's attempt to understand that scheme was based on the philosopher's ethical requirements more than on the values of the older poets. Hence it cannot help contradicting the facts, and scholars who have made use of the hamartia theory have had to suspend their historical judgment in order to do so. But where Aristotle falters, others may be forgiven. It is indeed surprising that Aristotle, as a rule so historically minded, should have been so bound by his own moral beliefs as to think that a play which presented the fall of a perfectly just man would be "disgusting."[39] Many a play showed the fall of a just man, and the men of the fifth century seem not to have been disgusted at all. Plato's original complaint against poetry was just this — that it was not moral enough, that the good man did not receive his deserts, and that therefore poetry was inferior to philosophy as education.[40] Plato's attitude was typical of his own philosophic position and of the tone which his thought gave to a later age; but it should be remembered that his complaint was a real one. Tragedy did show the world's injustice.

Aristotle, however, though not more sensitive than his master to poetry, was yet more indulgent of its claims as an educative force, and his *Poetics* is an attempt to reconcile Plato's original objections with the undeniable, though almost undefinable, moral value of tragedy. But Plato's view remained unassailable; for the ideal state, tragedy — and Plato's attacks on poetry are aimed chiefly at tragedy — is the wrong educational mold, for of all the arts it arises most directly from the experience of irrational evil and implies a careless godhead. Aristotle, of course, was not speaking for the ideal state; nevertheless, the failure of his attempt to fit poetry into the political scheme of even a good state lies not in the fault of his ethical system, but simply in the fact that poetry does not, and cannot, exist to fulfill a political function, such as the catharsis of pity and fear. Its function is personal and universal, though it may fill an apt social niche, as it did in the fifth century, when the circumstances and natural properties in the Athenian democracy were peculiarly felicitous to its development.

Poetry may proclaim the law, as it did in the early days of the fifth century, when Aeschylus saw his hopeful city overarched and sanctioned by the infinite justice of God; or it may deny the law, as it did when Euripides saw no justice in God or man. But poetry will not obey the law. And that seems to be the chief trouble with the *Poetics*. Aristotle tried, experimentally, to see tragedy within the moral law as systematized by the Academy and his own efforts; his recommendations for the best kind of tragedy are a curious mixture derived partly from what he found so effective in the works themselves, and partly from what he felt must be there in order to satisfy moral necessity. From the first source comes the suggestion that tragedy should show a change from good to evil fortune,[41] and from the second comes the theory of hamartia. And these suggestions, or statements of preference perhaps, innocent and tentative as they doubtless were in Aristotle's original lectures, have become rules of thumb, in spite of the fact that the steady search for hamartiae has all but taken the life out of Sophocles' vital works, and in spite of the difficulty that no hamartia has ever yet been found to fit the facts. It is a choice between Aristotle's theory or Sophocles' plays. Sophocles' plays all break the rules, and the last three, perhaps his finest products, even show a change from evil to good fortune, without the slightest violence done to the high art of tragedy.

The hamartia theory has survived through its sheer vagueness and unbounded adaptability. Anything which offends the ethics of the critic's own day is likely to emerge as an hamartia. Thus the famous Hegelian interpretation of the *Antigone* involves the strain exerted by the individual and the state on each other's rights, a question very much alive in the romantic era, but hardly conceptualized in those terms in 442 B.C.[42] Yet on the basis of it, Antigone and Creon are both given tragic flaws. Similarly, the gentlemanly standards of modern English society shine through some of Bowra's interpretations: in the *Ajax*, Odysseus is chosen as a pattern of true virtue, while the pride of Ajax, the great hero, which led him to forget himself, is deplored and blamed; the outbursts of Oedipus and the attempt of Deianeira to "dominate her husband" are duly condemned as prideful and improper. Bowra's book, in fact, illustrates most aptly the full range of confusion over the motivation of Greek tragedy. On the one hand, it is stated that Sophoclean characters fall by the same qualities which make them great, and not by flaws at all; on the other, it appears that the flaws in Sophocles are kinds of delusion which lead to harm and teach the essential moral lesson; at the same time Philoctetes is guilty of an "error of judgment." Thus moral, intellectual, and even teleological views of hamartia make their appearance. The term itself is avoided, as is often the case, though both moral and intellectual errors are spoken of as causes of catastrophe.[43]

The protean metamorphoses of the sin-and-punishment formula are numberless. Each time it is attacked, it turns into something else, outwardly, but inwardly it is always confusion. The *Antigone* turns on a "flaw of prudence" — certainly moral, according to Aristotle — while the "rashness" of Oedipus entails no moral guilt.[44] Or Sophocles is supposed to believe in gods who deliberately make the world hard, out of a kind of divine justice which must punish sin.[45] Or again, the poet's mind was identical with that of Herodotus, who taught that satiety of wealth (*koros*) bred hybris, and hybris madness and death (*Ate*). These are all interpretations of Aristotle, not of Sophocles. The hamartia theory may take many forms, but it always fits the critic better than it fits the play.

If the imposition enriched the poet, one might find in that fact some lame excuse for its perpetuation. As it is, Sophoclean scholars are unduly indulging the prerogative of criticism to be less inspired than poetry. Sophocles, presumably, marks the height of Greek dramaturgy; the subtlety of his hand is apparent in every line; he is a master of artistic control, of lights and shadows, and sometimes of an intensity that not even Aeschylus can equal. If we are to believe the sin-and-punishment formulae, this miracle of poetic inspiration and skill was exercised during a ninety-year lifetime in some hundred and twenty plays in order to prove to the sophisticated men of Athens a Sunday-school lesson: Be humble, be careful, and you will be happy. If that is all, it is worse than disappointing; it is vulgar. Greek mothers long before Sophocles taught their children lessons of piety and sophrosyne. However he may have admired these virtues, Sophocles did not write tragedy in order to teach them.[46] In fact, though the Greeks praised these traits, and asserted them, it is far from certain how much Sophocles or any of his countrymen really admired them.

Sophrosyne is in an especially doubtful case: Plato, himself, probably the greatest moralist of antiquity, made it the least of the cardinal virtues, and most suitable to the lowest mentalities in his polity.

No tragedian, faced with the paradox of human evil and human dignity, could approach it, were he honest, with any such glib formulations in mind. The problem of evil for the Greeks was made difficult from the first by their mercilessly truthful concept of the goddess Ate, whom Professor Jaeger has defined as the "madness of doom." [47] The phrase is particularly felicitous in that it includes both the subjective, psychological aspect of Ate and the objective and external aspect. It would be wrong to consider the first as cause and the second as effect, for the conception of her in the *Iliad*, where she first appears, is not so clear-cut; only in the *Odyssey*, which represents the first rudimentary rationalism at work upon the primitive goddess of evil, does the schematic question of cause, guilt, and responsibility arise. The history of Greek moral thought is chiefly the history of this rationalistic effort to see in the world a divine justice, in whose light man becomes a responsible agent. But the dual nature of evil, its inner psychological manifestations and its outer form of destruction, never faded from view. After Homer, Hesiod and Solon took up the problem, and tried to explain, if possible, the external at least in part by means of the internal, and to prove that man's own fault lay behind the wasteful and destructive behavior of the gods. On the tension of this effort rose the cosmos of Aeschylus, prophet of human responsibility and divine disposal. His trilogies assuredly contain the fullest doctrine of theodicy before Plato, and they utterly refute, incidentally, the popular notion that the Greeks had no conception of sin. Aeschylus covers his pages with words comprising the idea of offence against divinity.[48] The moral and theological substratum of Aeschylus' works remains profound and convincing, for it admitted many elements of mysterious import — the subtle ministration of time to the world's progress, the adjustment of God himself to the *Ananke*, or fatal Necessity, created between His nature and man's, and finally the problematical doctrine of wisdom won through suffering.

Why then are we not free to interpret Sophocles, his successor, according to these same views? He certainly refers to them, as in the passage in the *Oedipus* where the chorus cries that "time has found out" the king,[49] or where old Oedipus says the gods "look well, but late" upon man's crimes.[50] But the action of the plays does not bear out an interpretation of these observations at face value. For these are single plays, not trilogies, and the scope is too limited to include the vast evolutions of Aeschylus. That which happens in the generations of the *Oresteia* or the myriad centuries of the *Prometheia* cannot be compressed into a day and retain any conviction.[51] The trilogy was the perfect vehicle for divine justice. Why then did Sophocles abandon it? It is customary to say that he was more interested in individual fates; but it is clearer to observe that he was not concerned with divine justice, but with divine injustice.

The single play offered Sophocles that form of moral problem which for him was most pertinent: the morality of individual man in the face of irrational evil. Aeschylus had shown how evil in the long course of things fell within the just and progressive cosmos of Zeus, bringing wisdom with time in the wake of suffering. But the fate of the individual who did not live for centuries presented a spectacle of suffering within whose sphere evil could be and still was irrational. It is impossible that Sophocles could really have believed in the theodicy of Aeschylus and yet have concentrated upon the fate of the individual exclusively, or written single plays; for if the Aeschylean scheme had been true for him, it would have compelled some mention, or proof — in short, a trilogy. The emergence of the single play as the typical form for Sophocles is one primary indication that Aeschylean theology no longer satisfied the poet of the middle fifth century.

The time was no longer right for such theories. Many of the Sophists were already casting doubt on the very existence of the gods, and Sophocles, far from being a reactionary, felt the pull of this new thought, and sought in his art the right form for the problem of Ate in its new shape. The emphasis consequently shifts, not merely from god to man, but from the structure of cosmic justice to the structure of human morality. Human responsibility now fills both foreground and background — a development consistent with that of the Athenian democratic temper as the Fifty Years went forward — and the position of the gods becomes more and more vague. Their will, which had been so clearly pronounced and illustrated by Aeschylus, is no longer clear. It is almost idle to speak of them in Sophocles as separate entities, for their operation is so dimly outlined, where it is outlined at all, that if we explain anything by them we speak in a circle. The simple fact is that for Sophocles, the gods, whoever they are, no longer stand within the moral picture. Morality is man's possession, and the cosmos — or chaos — may be what it will. The Aeschylean scheme is not openly denied, but rather ignored with a kind of agnostic aloofness analogous to Protagoras' attitude toward the existence of the gods.[52] Behind this agnostic attitude lies an indifference which is more challenging to the interpreter than the painful doubts of Euripides. And the reasons which Sophocles had for not caring any longer to justify the gods and rationalize evil seem to be two: first, he felt that Aeschylus had already done so in the only way it could be done; and second, he recognized that even so, evil could not be fully rationalized and perhaps should not be. Nevertheless, he did not, like Euripides, abandon man's responsibility, but rather gave it a different point of reference: man for Sophocles is no longer responsible to the gods and cannot be, for the evidence of their justice is too thin; man is responsible to himself as the repository of the ideas of justice and morality.

This is not to say, however, that Sophocles disbelieved in the gods, or in divinity in general. There is nothing irreligious in the belief that God does not punish sin or that man is morally responsible for his acts only to himself. Indeed, the Book of Job points to God's freedom from man-made rational schemes of morality. Sophocles was religious rather than pious; and the Sophoclean hero, all critics to the contrary, seems to be less under the obligation to worship the gods than to fulfill his duty to himself. If that duty sometimes appears in the light of a present deity, such a concept, though it may lie at a far remove from orthodoxy and Aeschylus, is nevertheless deeply religious.

Moderns have been misled by their own conceptions of piety and divinity; they have been drawn by the rational scheme of Aeschylus, which is very sympathetic in its optimism, into the assumption that all piety implies belief in a moral deity. It follows naturally, therefore, that Sophocles' public reputation for piety should have turned critics, from Aristotle on, toward the hamartia theory, with its various forms, as the most available key to that piety. Thus the poet has been squeezed into the framework of his great predecessor, and it only remains to admit that, if all this be true of him, then Sophocles' works are the most banal examples of poetic justice anywhere in literature.

But it is not true. The two poets lived in different worlds. Evil in Sophocles is nonrational. For him the importance, even the very existence, of man's moral life depends in great part on the absence of any teleological scheme of cosmic justice. Sophocles perceived clearly that man may come to grief by means of action, but without crime; in short, that all action, and not merely sinful action, may entail suffering. He turned deliberately away from the suffering which was caused by sin, which is first schematized in the *Odyssey* [53] and which forms the backbone of Aeschylean tragedy — to the suffering which comes of moral action or simply of itself — the unmitigated fact of Homer's old goddess, Ate.

Thus an understanding of Sophocles' religion will depend first upon an abandonment of Christian, Aristotelian, and Aeschylean values, which can only prejudice the mind's approach to a difficult and subtle text. Sophocles alone can tell us what he regarded as divinity, and what he meant by his so-called humanistic treatment of the problem of evil. Our task is to accept only what is historically possible and poetically true.

III

CHRONOLOGY

THE *Philoctetes* and the *Oedipus at Colonus*, for which ancient evidence gives the dates 409 and 401 respectively, are the only two of Sophocles' plays which can be definitely dated.[1] About all the rest there is the widest range of uncertainty and disagreement among scholars.[2] There exist, however, certain basic likelihoods that enable us fairly well to establish the order in which the preserved works were composed. These likelihoods can be further bolstered by reference to certain phases of Athenian history, notably the Sophistic Enlightenment. A restatement of the evidence will show that Sophocles can be related a little more closely to his age than has sometimes been thought, and it will point the way toward a discovery of his inner development and the three chief periods into which his work falls.

AJAX AND ANTIGONE

Plutarch says that Sophocles himself thought of his work as falling into three chief styles: the first, in which he imitated the "majesty" (ὄγκος) of Aeschylus; the second, which he characterized by the somewhat puzzling description, "pungent and contrived," or "artificial" (πικρὸν καὶ κατάτεχνον); and the third, his own style, "most full of character and the best" (ἠθικώτατον καὶ βέλτιστον).[3] The grouping of the plays here adopted is based on the development of religious beliefs rather than on style; but Sophocles' remark will be a helpful point from which to start. Professor Finley is doubtless right in the assumption that the *Ajax* is the last, or almost the last, play in the first style; the *Antigone*, on the other hand, represents the second, or "pungent and contrived" style, a phrase which Professor Finley takes as descriptive of the sharp antithetical mode of composition that prevailed throughout the second half of the fifth century and is most notably associated with Gorgias, Antiphon, and Thucydides.[4] Assuredly the *Antigone* abounds in antithetical devices. The verse has a tight, clean-limbed neatness nowhere else to be found in Sophocles. Even in its ideational structure as a whole, it betrays the intellectualistic milieu of the early Sophistic. A certain abstractness, visible in the balanced antithesis of characters and whole scenes, such as those between Creon and Antigone, Creon and Haemon, Creon and Teiresias, seems to indicate the growth of conceptual thinking out of mythic thinking, a process which began to take place about the time of Protagoras.

The priority of the *Ajax* thus inferred, however, has been challenged by various scholars.[5] Jebb and others assert that certain metrical liberties, such as the anapest in the first foot of the trimeter, trimeters divided between two speakers, together with a greater number of resolved feet, exist in the *Ajax* and are absent in the *Antigone*; their conclusion is that the *Antigone* is therefore more archaic, in that it is metrically more like Aeschylus, and therefore is earlier than the *Ajax*.[6] It has been recently proved, however, by H. D. Kitto, that metrical statistics in the case of Sophocles are misleading and false, so far as any attempt to date by them is concerned.[7] He points out that if we were to arrange the plays in the order of increasing resolution of feet, then the *Electra* would have to be by far the earliest play — a notion which nobody would care to defend. Sophocles was master of these devices, and used them at will and to his purpose; on purely metrical grounds at least, no consistent development can be made for him, as has been done with eminently sound results for Euripides.[8]

Certainly in all other ways, it is the *Ajax*, not the *Antigone*, which recalls Aeschylus. Jebb himself lists an impressive number of words from the *Ajax* which recall Aeschylus,[9] though these "heavy compounds," as they have been called,[10] tended to become part of tragic speech generally and never entirely passed out of vogue. More important, perhaps, though less tangible, is the matter of imagery. Sophocles digested his model well, and the Aeschylean flavor, far from standing out in patches, is diffused throughout the play in a kind of picturesqueness in word and stage business, an instinct toward the grand tableau, which is totally lacking in the somewhat austere *Antigone*.

In her first speech, Athena says to Odysseus:

> You stalk, keen-scented as Spartan hound,[11]

and Odysseus replies that her voice is

> Like an Etruscan trumpet, brazen-belled.[12]

In such knotty, brief, and somewhat recherché similes, one can still hear the rich loftiness, the geographical breadth,[13] the quick and extraordinary concreteness of the earlier poet. More examples could be quoted.[14] But in the matter of stage technique, too, it must be admitted that such scenes as Ajax with the bloody whip talking with Athena, Ajax sitting among the slaughtered herds, Ajax departing with the drawn sword, Ajax planting the sword, then death on the stage, the searching chorus, Tecmessa's scream, and finally the long, fierce, puny debate over burial while the great man lies in state — these scenes inevitably make it a drama of astounding effects (ἔκπληξις), and astounding effects were the special forte of Aeschylus.[15]

There are still other reasons for believing the *Ajax* to be the earliest play. The second half, for instance, with its whole new set of characters denotes a certain lack of skill in constructing the single play, for it contains the sort of trial and judgment scene, with its consequent assignment of rights and prerogatives, which we find often in Aeschylus; in the *Eumenides*, for instance, and in the fragments of the *Danaides*.[16] The *Antigone* and the *Trachiniae* also divide in two, but the division is not so sharp, and the second part grows steadily shorter and of less significance to the play itself. The problem of the third play of the trilogy was slowly being solved and disappears forever in the *Oedipus Rex*. It is possible that the actual model of the *Ajax* was the *Niobe* of Aeschylus,[17] whence the archaic style and structure,[18] the scantiness of plot, and the general form of "annihilation-tragedy."

The *Ajax* is not an immature work, but it does lack perfection of dramatic technique. In its stead, the *Ajax* possesses a sonorous grandeur which derives from Aeschylus and does not reappear in the other plays. Finally, this is the only play of Sophocles whose catastrophe is motivated, superficially at least, by the traditional formula of offence against a deity, and punishment.[19] In all probability, therefore, the *Ajax* was produced before the *Antigone*.

The date of the latter is almost unquestionably settled as 442. In 440, Sophocles was a general in the expedition against Samos, and ancient tradition has it that he gained that post through the popularity which the *Antigone* won for him. Political and military positions were not, of course, obtained in this way, but the story could hardly have been invented unless the *Antigone* had been produced shortly before its author's appointment. It is a case of *post quod, ergo propter quod*. The generally accepted date is either 442 or possibly 441 for the *Antigone*, which thus gives a *terminus ante quem* for the *Ajax*.[20]

Any more exact dating than this must rest upon slim evidence indeed, but it is possible that some reflection of the political situation at Athens forms the background of the play. It has been suggested that the fate of Ajax had its roots in the life of Themistocles, on the ground that Themistocles and Ajax both fell into disgrace after brilliant careers.[21] But the characters of the two men are not merely unlike, but mutually repellent. Also, unless we choose to regard the *Ajax* as earlier than the *Oresteia*, the burial of Themistocles could hardly have been a very lively issue at the time of composition.[22] If any Athenian lies behind the character of Ajax, a more probable candidate is Cimon, whose simple, aristocratic virtues were famed and beloved and consist well with the dignity of Ajax. Since the battle of Mycale, Cimon had fought barbarians with unflinching zeal; at the revolt of the Helots, for whose suppression he had volunteered Athenian assistance, Cimon had received an undue insult from the Spartan commanders and incurred ridicule and ostracism, a situation which may be dimly reflected in the passage where Teucer declares that he and Ajax did not come to Troy as vassals of the Peloponnesian overlords, Agamemnon and Menelaus, but as friendly allies.[23]

For the last ten years of his life, Cimon was steadily eclipsed by the radical Pericles, who must have seemed fully as untrustworthy and obnoxious an upstart to the conservatives as Odysseus seemed to Ajax; yet, toward the end, a kind of reconciliation took place, and Pericles was finally glad to admit and make use of Cimon's abilities in concluding the Five Years' Truce in 452. Sophocles knew both Cimon and Pericles, perhaps intimately, and that fact alone could account for a particular interest in the antinomy between them, and even a mythic conception of them in terms of the two old heroes of the Judgment of the Arms, whose names had already become bywords for the aristocratic and popular factions.[24] Cimon died in 449, and the *Ajax* would have been a fitting funeral speech for a dramatic poet to make for his friend, for it did honor to both the dead man and his rival, who was nobler than was expected,[25] and it pointed an accusing finger at Sparta. Finally, it is perhaps significant that Cimon belonged to the clan of the Philaidae, who claimed descent from Ajax through his son Philaeus.[26]

This is, of course, all the purest hypothesis, but the coincidence is surprising, and there is a peculiarly political ring to the second half of the play which somehow wants to be accounted for. Menelaus and Agamemnon are pretty transparent oligarchs; Teucer, the bowman, is a man of the people; Ajax is an aristocrat of the old school; [27] and Odysseus finally emerges as a reconciliator, as an enlightened and democratic champion of the "city as a whole," to use Thucydides' phrase.[28] This is not to say that the *Ajax* is a political allegory. Ajax remains Ajax, not Cimon, and in a later chapter the more vital moral and spiritual purport of the play will be examined. But the political scene may well have given it its peculiar bias. Some date shortly after the death of Cimon, therefore, seems likely; perhaps 447. This year also corresponds nearly with the great shift in policy which Pericles made from the extreme radical position of the previous campaign for land empire, to the moderate stand which successfully promoted the maritime efforts of his later life and earned him the esteem of Thucydides as the one man who represented the citizen body as a whole.

TRACHINIAE AND OEDIPUS REX

There is a wide divergence in the proposed dates for the *Trachiniae*. Internal evidence suggests that it was written under the influence of Euripides, but doubtless the scientific positivism with which German scholars of the last century tried to pin this evidence down was misguided.[29] The verbal parallels which Wilamowitz discovered [30] between this play and the *Heracles* of Euripides (produced between 423 and 420) failed to prove that the *Heracles* was Sophocles' source, nor could it be definitely shown which, if either, of the two poets did the borrowing. In this case, the final analysis seemed to reveal Euripides as the more likely borrower,[31] but the passages in question consisted chiefly of clichés which are the common property of tragedians.

Another question that called forth a great deal of philological acumen was raised by the scene in the last part of the *Trachiniae* where the dying Heracles sleeps on the stage. This too was supposed to be derived from the *Heracles* of Euripides, and Dieterich, who developed the point from a hint given out by Wilamowitz, erected an elaborate history and theory of sleep-scenes, treating not only these two, but other similar ones in both Sophocles and Euripides. But this whole structure fell when the great Polish scholar, Thaddeus Zielinski, explained the real motivation and meaning of the scene in the *Trachiniae*, and freed it from its supposed dependence on Euripides.[32] The whole debate was brilliant, but fruitless.

On the other hand, to deny Euripidean influence altogether is a little perverse.[33] To associate this play with the structure and spirit of either the *Ajax* or the *Septem* of Aeschylus is certainly to miss the point. The *Trachiniae* is a tragedy of peculiarly undeserved, one might almost say meaningless, suffering, and as such is closely connected with the *Oedipus Rex*. More than that, its criticisms of the gods and reflections on an inexplicable cosmos point, if not directly to Euripides, at least to the restless and questioning character of his generation. If the play is episodic, or carelessly composed,[34] that fact also might well be due to the increasing looseness of the later drama.

Most important of all, it seems impossible that the character and treatment of Deianeira owe nothing whatever to Euripides. Not that she is by any means a borrowed portrait. Even Perrotta, who believes the play was produced as late as 409 or 410 under the strong influence of Euripides, nevertheless can say that no Euripidean heroine ever had the "profound tenderness" and "restless sweetness" (*dolcezza inquieta*) of Deianeira.[35] It might be added that few have had the heroic stature either. Deianeira has a freedom of movement comparable to the great ladies of the *Odyssey*, Helen, Arete, and Penelope. Her gentle grandeur sets her apart from the contemporary Athenian ladies with whom Wilamowitz would associate her,[36] and even a shade above the great Alcestis, who, when she parts from her home and children, is not above mentioning the wealth she has enjoyed and boasting a little.[37]

But certain details of Deianeira's portrait — the candor with which she reflects on love, her own fading beauty and Iole's freshness, the intimacy with which she reveals herself to the chorus, and her remark about noble words coming from the low-born [38] — all have an unmistakably Euripidean flavor. The resemblances, indeed, have more to do with personality than character, more to do with the surface impressions than with the inner similarity. Deianeira's tragedy is her own. She does not fall by an internal conflict of passion, like the Phaedra or Sthenoboea of Euripides, but by a fatal nexus of events, the mysterious and thoroughly Sophoclean web of action and suffering.[39] There is no reason, therefore, to think the play is dependent on the *Medea*,[40] or on any other of Euripides' early works about distracted women. Sophocles' charming and dignified heroine cannot have been modeled on any of these.

Nevertheless, the extreme difference in flavor between this play and any other of Sophocles implies that here he was making an experiment. Even the prologue, with its direct expository narrative preceding a little genre scene of mother, son, and faithful nurse, gives a homely and thoroughly Euripidean picture, having little to do with the main action.[41] This prologue is not stiff or archaic; it is only a little inorganic, a fact which must be traced not to a general immaturity about prologues, but to the impact of Euripides' new kind of effectiveness with small scenes which Sophocles had not yet entirely adapted to his own manner. Later these little intimacies are used more lightly and do not disturb the characteristic texture of the play, but intensify it.[42] The very prominence here of these Euripidean touches would imply that they were still new to Sophocles' hand; at least, in no other extant play are they so distinct, though Sophocles saw more and more of his rival's work.

The suspicion arises therefore that the *Trachiniae* may have been written when Euripides was still fairly new, and that such an extraordinary sudden spurt of Euripideanism in the already middle-aged poet can best be explained by his having been tremendously impressed by some individual play. To ask which play admittedly leads to guesswork; yet no product of Euripides' early years would have been so likely to impress Sophocles as the subtle and graceful *Alcestis* of 438. Indeed, in spite of the blindness from which poets traditionally suffer with regard to the poetry of others, it is hard to imagine how Sophocles could have judged this work with anything but the enthusiasm shown by posterity in general. Also, it happens that of all the verbal parallels which have been found, or invented, between the *Trachiniae* and various plays of Euripides, only the parallels with the *Alcestis* will really bear examination.[43] Zielinski is at great pains to prove that these are as worthless as the parallels with the *Heracles*, and that the *Trachiniae* preceded the *Alcestis* by a year or so.[44] This answer is, of course, within possibility, and it is tempting to think that Sophocles is indebted to no one for his portrait of Deianeira. But then one must explain the other Euripidean elements, as well as the fact that this play alone has such an abundance of them.

In short, the *Alcestis* seems the only likely *terminus post quem* to be found.[45] To find a *terminus ante quem* is not so easy. No play of Euripides can really help us here, unless we can regard the poisoned-robe episode of the *Medea* as inspired by the shirt of Nessus. It is possible that the ode on love in the *Hippolytus*[46] reflects the episode of Iole in Sophocles. But the myths were far too common property for such arguments to avail. Only one thing is certain, and that is that the superb mastery of the *Oedipus Rex* cannot have preceded the experimental *Trachiniae*.[47] It remains, therefore, that the *Trachiniae* stands third in the order of extant plays and was produced at some time after, and probably rather soon after, 438 and before the *Oedipus*.

Far less controversy exists over the date of the *Oedipus*. With a few exceptions, scholars are agreed that it probably belongs to the early years of the Peloponnesian War and that the pestilence which threatens Thebes in the play, and which did not belong to the original story,[48] was introduced to commemorate the Athenian plague that broke out in 430. This assumption is reasonable enough, although it must be admitted that the description of the plague in Sophocles is not very detailed, so that it is hard to know if it is a firsthand account from a recent observer.[49] Still, the general psychological situation — the temples crowded with suppliants, on the one hand, and on the other, the steadily increasing fear that the gods and their oracle may be false — these have their echoes in Thucydides.[50] The words of the chorus, "Why should I dance?"[51] coming after a reflection on the unavoidable blasts of the gods — compare Thucydides' reference to the plague as an "act of God" (*daimonion*) — are a kind of threat to give up life entirely, with its forms and beliefs, in the face of the obvious immorality of the cosmos; and again, such an attitude is described by the historian as a result of the Athenian plague. All the moral norms were given up, lawlessness was rife in the city, and men became reckless in the face of a danger for which there seemed no reason and no defense.[52] Indeed, it may well have been the peculiarly irrational kind of god-sent evil such as the plague — an evil which struck good and ill alike, and so prompted men to regard it as all one whether or not they reverenced the gods — which led Sophocles to treat the problem of evil and fate as he did in the *Oedipus*. For nothing is more difficult than to see how Oedipus could have deserved his fate, or how by a greater piety he could have avoided it. His fall is as irrational as the plague, and as he staggers under the successive stages of its revelation, he too begins to lose his traditional piety and faith in oracles.[53] Perhaps at no other time was the air of Athens so charged with just the psychological attitude toward evil which we find in the *Oedipus;* and this is perhaps the most compelling ground possible for putting the play in this period.[54]

Zielinski goes even further and declares that the date was 429.[55] The plague began in 430, he argues, and in 428 Euripides imitated *Oedipus Rex* in the *Hippolytus*. The latter assertion rests solely on some passages, common to both plays, but apparently more at home in the *Oedipus*.[56] These parallels again seem to be commonplaces, even the longest and most convincing one, which contains what is clearly a ready-made sophistic argument in defense of a charge of conspiracy, and occurs again and again in Euripides.[57] Nevertheless, it must be admitted that the argument is wholly in keeping with the situation in the *Oedipus*, while in the *Hippolytus* the hero seems a little absurd to bring it up. These parallels indeed may bear some weight, but Zielinski's point is hardly established beyond doubt. The best argument for a date around 429 still remains the moral and psychological assumptions which lie behind the play, and which were most appropriate and fresh in the years of the plague.[58]

ELECTRA

Between the *Oedipus Rex* and the *Philoctetes* of 409, there is a gap of about twenty years, during which it is generally supposed that the *Electra* was written. Few scholars have offered a definite date.[59] Its position in the series is therefore relatively undisputed. A correct interpretation of the play, however, depends in no small degree upon the tormented question of whether the *Electra* of Sophocles preceded or followed that of Euripides. A review of this argument may clarify it somewhat and narrow the dating possibilities a little as well.

Ulrich von Wilamowitz raised this question in 1883 with an article which claimed priority for Euripides.[60] It would be vain to recount all Wilamowitz' reasons for this theory, the more so since in 1899 after Hugo Steiger's brilliant article, *Warum schrieb Euripides seine Elektra?*,[61] Wilamowitz acknowledged the latter's insight with a gracious compliment and accepted correction.[62] There, no doubt, the matter should have ended, but both sides of the dispute had called forth already an extraordinary number of partisans, some of whom did not give up so easily. Bruhn in particular, in his introduction to the *Electra*,[63] continued his assertion that the Sophoclean play was a defense of the Delphic Oracle against the attacks of Euripides, with the result that the younger Wilamowitz felt called upon once more to defend the priority of Sophocles.[64] Since that time the argument has cooled, but that it is by no means settled is apparent from Perrotta's date of 410, and Pohlenz' feeling that the first of the two to resurrect the old myth must have been the one who had the strongest inner compulsion to do so. According to him, this was Euripides, whose interpretation differs more radically from Aeschylus'.[65] Such a statement is due principally to a basic misunderstanding of the Sophoclean *Electra*, an assumption, namely, that Euripides habitually wrote for a serious ideational purpose, while Sophocles by contrast wrote the "sacred stories" only for their own sake. A similar objection, which existed long before Pohlenz, was that if Sophocles had come first, Euripides would have written his play as a polemic against him rather than against Aeschylus.[66] But the fact seems to be that this is exactly what he did do. The "polemic" against Aeschylus is in the nature of a genial if ironical smile, while that against Sophocles is deep and bitter, and rooted in disgust with the "sacred stories" of the Olympian and Delphic religions, which Euripides, like most of his contemporaries and all posterity, apparently thought were the stock in trade of the "pious" Sophocles.

Certainly Sophocles, whatever his purpose in writing drama, was no reformer. His insight into the nature of evil was too deep, especially after writing the *Oedipus*, for him to be able to give himself to an out-and-out humanitarianism, or to social or political reform. Evidently his refusal of all such hopeful answers stamped him as reactionary even in his own time. He seems to have been roused to no polemic efforts in self-defense or to a counterattack on contemporary views; in all probability he was not averse to many of those views, however he kept his poetry free of them. It was Euripides, the restless one, who, finding all wrong with society, probed not so much the essential nature of evil, but rather fixed on the abuses at hand and defined them, applying the standards of a mind which, though despairing, had at least found the satisfaction of being free from superstition. It has often been asked how Euripides could have dared to write an *Electra* after Sophocles; but it is more reasonable to ask, how could he not have written one? Where could he have found a more likely affront to his sensibilities than a play in which a matricide is hailed as a god-sent deliverer, and at that, after all that Aeschylus had done to clarify the tangled morality of the tale? Even if Euripides saw what Sophocles' real purpose was — and certainly it was not the justification of matricide in general! — how could he resist attacking a play in which such a justification was even incidental?

Steiger's careful study of just how and where Euripides attacked his rival is so conclusive and important for the interpretation of both *Electras* that it will bear being restated. Steiger asserts that Euripides felt a strong moral and religious compulsion to correct the impression that such a murder could be commanded by a god — that is, a real god.[67] We know from the quiet sarcasm of the *Ion* [68] what he thought of Apollo, and from the *Iphigenia in Tauris*,[69] a play written in these same years, what he thought of Orestes.[70] It is not hard to find passages in his play which openly criticize or refute the savagery of its predecessor. For instance, Electra's hesitation about mistreating, or even boasting over, the corpse of Aegisthus is sufficiently pointed to be a clear reproof to the bloodthirstiness of Sophocles' heroine.[71] The direct condemnation of Apollo in the last scene of the play is equally unmistakable.[72]

Moreover, in order to meet Sophocles squarely and write a play no less effective, Euripides took up the gage in the matter of dramatic technique and tried to outdo this unequaled masterpiece of suspense.[73] There is an obvious reworking, by inversion, of many Sophoclean motives: the brilliance of the great narrative in Sophocles is challenged in the hair-raising account of the murder of Aegisthus; [74] if Sophocles' Electra was drawn heroic and hard, Euripides could do it too, and worse, so he makes her actually participate in the murder of her mother. Most important, all the devices and sentiments that Sophocles had used to blacken the character of Clytaemnestra are transferred by Euripides to Aegisthus, in order to make it seem that by his death alone the children are released from danger.[75] So it is that in the later play it is Aegisthus rather than Clytaemnestra who dreams the frightful dream and tries belatedly to propitiate the gods; it is Aegisthus who tortures Electra, while Clytaemnestra is a weak and passive observer. Yet even Aegisthus, if only that he may contrast with his Sophoclean forerunner, is made sympathetic in his death by the sheer description of his agony. Euripides' almost petulant denials of the conception offered by Sophocles, justify the feeling that he marred his work in more than one place by an overinsistence on polemic and travesty.[76] Thus line 230 in Euripides, where Orestes says he will not keep Electra in long suspense, is a clear deflation of the dramatic agony of Sophocles' long recognition scene.[77] Similarly a reproof of the battle of words between Aegisthus and Orestes in the last scene of Sophocles' play is to be found in Euripides' at line 883.[78] There are many other passages which betray a like origin.[79]

The Euripidean *Electra* grows on its resistance to the Sophoclean, and cannot have preceded it.[80] Euripides' is a play which shows the coming change in the subject matter of drama: the old stories can no longer be interpreted, for the contemporary view is the only view; the old symbols are no longer understood or wanted. The Athenians were getting ready for the new comedy, which is even more clearly heralded in Euripides' *Iphigenia* and *Helen*.

The *Electra* of Sophocles therefore must have been produced before 413, the date of Euripides' play, and probably not very long before. Such an attack is less effective the longer it is delayed, and it is reasonable to assume that Euripides did not delay his answer too long. Furthermore, the style and astonishing virtuosity of Sophocles' play proclaim that it belongs to the time of his fullest maturity of genius. This is the first extant play in which the tension continues to rise until almost the last line. There is no falling action, in the usual sense of the word. The actual murders may be done with less fullness of expression than are the scenes connected with the coming and recognition of Orestes, but there is no abatement of intensity. It is the complete triumph of the single play as art form, and, if anything, is a better unit than the *Oedipus*. However, it seems impossible to say at just what time after the *Oedipus* Sophocles would have become capable of this mastery. But there may be a hint of the date in the actual *mise en scène*.

It will be remembered that Aeschylus laid the scene of the *Oresteia* not in Mycenae, the traditional location of Agamemnon's capital, but at Argos. Professor Bury suggests that the reason for this change may have lain in the alliance between Argos and Athens concluded in 460 B.C., just two years previously.[81] Now in 420 Athens had allied herself with Argos again; but after the collapse of Alcibiades' Mantinean Confederacy at the battle of Mantinea in 418, Argos abandoned her Athenian alliance in favor of one with Sparta. Hence perhaps it becomes significant that Sophocles now laid his play in Mycenae [82] which, already in ruins and half mythical, stood outside the increasingly painful sphere of foreign affairs. At least, it is interesting to note that in the prologue of both later *Electras*, the word *argos* occurs as a common noun in the rare sense of a "watery lowland," not as the name of the city.[83] It is possible, therefore, that the play was written after the break with Argos in 418, which would narrow the date of composition to some time between 418 and 413, and probably nearer the latter. Thus it falls in Sophocles' latest years and nearer in time to the *Philoctetes*, with which it has certain moral affinities, than to the *Oedipus Rex*, to which it is almost diametrically opposed.

The order of the plays, then, seems to be as follows:

> *Ajax* (*ca.* 447)
> *Antigone* (442/1)
> *Trachiniae* (*ca.* 437–432)
> *Oedipus Rex* (*ca.* 429)
> *Electra* (*ca.* 418–414)
> *Philoctetes* (409)
> *Oedipus at Colonus* (401)

The dates of the *Philoctetes*, and of the *Oedipus at Colonus*, which was posthumously produced by the poet's grandson, rest, as stated earlier, on the undisputed evidence of ancient authorities.[84]

PART TWO

TRAGIC ARETE

ἀρετῆς βέβαιαι δ᾽ εἰσὶν αἱ κτήσεις μόναι.
— *Sophocles*

IV

THE MATRIX OF HEROISM: AJAX

THE Greeks invented, among their other contributions to culture, the concept of heroism. Rather say, they invented heroes; for there was no initial concept to which the Homeric Achilles was drawn. The state of mind which produced such a figure embraced a certain group of associations and convictions — pictures, attitudes, and beliefs — rather than a philosophic estimate of the nature of man. These pictures and beliefs grew into a kind of religious vision, a vision which demanded at least a certain solemn respect, however vague its outlines were and however its very existence seemed to impose on the assumptions by which the ordinary man can live. The vision, for such it is, rather than a concept, was typically Greek — and by "typically Greek" is meant simply that such a vision did not occur in the mythologies of other people. Beowulf can swim eight days and nights in armor, slaying "whale-fishes" all the way; Thor can eat three whole oxen and wash them down with four or five barrels of mead; when the heroes of the Kalevala bleed, prodigious floods ensue; and in a similar vein, Firdausi's Rustum, at the age of eight days, toddles out of his crib and slays a bull elephant with one blow of his fist. Not to deny these myths their significance and beauty, it must be said nevertheless that they contain an element of sheer megalomania which may have appealed to Carlyle as essentially heroic, but which is, on the whole, absent from the Greek vision. Where it does occur, except possibly in the case of Heracles, it is peripheral rather than central to the hero's character.

There are two qualities deeply rooted in the Greek view of heroism which make it different from all other views, and these are qualities of the hero himself. The first is self-destructiveness. The hero is primarily, in most mythologies, the man whom nobody can destroy; but in Greece he was the man who had to destroy himself. The nor-

mal assumption, perhaps, would be that Achilles, with his superhuman
strength and speed, his divine armor, his immortal horses, and the
Pelian spear, would almost inevitably live to an advanced age. But
it is precisely the opposite. The necessary condition (*aisa, moira*)
of these supreme gifts is misery and an early death. Achilles is the
saddest man at Troy.[1] But his grief and death are not foreordained
by an external fate; they are foreordained by that innermost quality
known to Homer — arete. Achilles had his choice between long life
and greatness;[2] he chose greatness, and therefore was Achilles. His
greatness, however, was a kind of continual spending of himself, and
Achilles was already on his way to self-destruction long before he
slew Hector. For the self-destructiveness of the hero hinges upon a
certain excess, an ability to outdo not only everyone else, but especially
himself, for whom he has no regard except as the receptacle of certain
supreme standards.[3] There are exceptions, of course, the most notable
being the adroit Odysseus; but a surprising majority of Greek heroes
stride grimly into ruin.

The other quality of the Greek hero is intimacy with the gods.
Odysseus is perhaps a better example of this than is Achilles, for
throughout the *Odyssey* Athena stands by him with unintermittent
vigilance. But there are many passages in the *Iliad* also which describe
the function of a god in close connection with a hero. The god either
directly assists the hero to do something, as Apollo helps Hector slay
Patroclus,[4] or motivates some act or idea. Of the latter there are many
examples besides the well-known ones of Athena's restraining Achilles
from killing Agamemnon and Zeus' sending the deceitful dream.[5]
In some cases this interference is simply accepted as a matter of course,
but in others the question does arise as to who is really responsible.
So Patroclus assures Hector that not he but Apollo slew him;[6] and,
in a most interesting passage, Priam tells Hecuba that he has had a
divine dream bidding him go and ransom Hector, and then asks if
she thinks it is just his own desire speaking to him.[7]

The well-known "double motivation" of Homer, however it be
explained, implies that to some extent the poet is unable to distinguish
between the divine and human forces at play. The action of the god
does not detract from the hero's own greatness, but accentuates it,
and gives us some idea of what is meant by the epithets "dear to Zeus,"

"godlike," and so on. Achilles would be very much himself in any case, but he is very much more himself by virtue of the care lavished upon him by Thetis, Athena, and Zeus. And the fact that these divinities are anthropomorphically conceived and enter the action by coming down from heaven does not prevent them from acting in a psychologically appropriate way; that is, they operate in character with the hero they affect. Both methods of divine operation, the external assistance and the internal motivation, remained dear to the Greek soul. Of the former, we may see examples in sculpture, such as in the pediment at Corcyra, representing Perseus slaying Medusa, while Athena stands behind the hero; and, even more strikingly, in the great Atlas metope from the temple of Zeus at Olympia, where Heracles strains every muscle to uphold the sky, while Athena, the image of divine repose, with one graceful and relaxed arm makes the miracle possible. It is a commonplace to say that such paradoxes illustrate the gap between man and God; the truth is, they show where the boundaries of man and God begin to merge. The very puzzlement, the very question, "Who is doing it?" is the whole point. For such a mysterious interplay between the divine and the human hints broadly at the assumption of divinity in the human, and this assumption receives its fullest expression in Sophoclean tragedy.

Ajax, son of Telamon, the "bulwark of the Achaeans," as Homer calls him, received heroic worship, both at Salamis, whence he came, and at Athens itself.[8] This fact may have imparted to Sophocles' drama a certain regional, religious intensity, for the local heroes were deeply revered. Perhaps also, the recent death of Cimon may have suggested to the poet that peculiarly political mode of treatment, which was certainly not demanded by the myth. But neither the political nor the anthropological backgrounds can be considered more than tangential to the central idea. Behind these more superficial levels lie the beliefs and associations that are the mainsprings of both politics and cult-worship. Behind the hero-cult lay the vision of the hero and behind the aristocracy lay the long tradition of the aristocratic credo, the credo of self-mastery, honor, and arete. It is the poet's business to pierce the upper levels and find the bases of association and religious belief — to find, in short, back of all that can be said of him, the hero himself.

The plot of the play comes from the so-called Epic Cycle,[9] stories about the Trojan War which never were fitted into any true epic scheme but always remained dramatic episodes — genre-scenes, perhaps, peripherally attached to the larger heroic saga. The poets who preserved them could not make real epics of them: they were by nature framed for tragedies,[10] for their purpose seems to have been to delineate the character of the hero around whom they grew. Thus, for instance, there are tales which are little more than pictures of the ruthless Pyrrhus, the overweening conqueror Agamemnon, or the weak and shallow Menelaus. From these stories even more than from the *Iliad* and *Odyssey* is derived our traditional idea of the heroic figures before Troy, with a few exceptions such as Achilles. Ajax is indeed recognizably characterized in the *Iliad*, but we know him best from his behavior on the occasion of the Judgment of the Arms.

When Achilles died, his miraculous armor was left to be the prize of the hero who had rendered the next greatest service in the war. The two claimants stand out in high relief — Ajax, the man of strength, versus Odysseus, the man of stratagem. The arms went to the man of stratagem, and one cannot help suspecting that the episode was invented in a partial spirit; certainly the sequel — Ajax' jealousy and madness and the whole sorry fit in which he slew the flocks and herds, thinking them the Greek leaders — did little enough in the original tale to sustain the dignity of the great warrior in his disappointment, and did much to gain him the reputation of a "beef-witted lord."

Sophocles' play begins in the middle of the fit of madness. Like Samson, Ajax had fallen victim to the combination of his own passions and his enemies' cleverness; and like Samson he more than redeemed himself by the manner of his death. When his madness was over and he came to himself, he debated briefly what he must do. Then, stating that he would wash away his crimes in the ocean, he went out, sought a lonely spot on the seashore, and fell upon the sword which Hector had given him as a chivalric token after their duel. Later, we learn from a messenger that Calchas had prophesied that if Ajax remained in his tent for one day, without going forth, he would be purified and live; if, however, he went out, he would die. Hearing this, Tecmessa hurries out with the chorus to look for him, and finds the body. The play concludes with the funeral of Ajax, but only after a long and bitter dispute between Teucer, his half-brother, and the leaders of the host, Agamemnon and Menelaus, who wish to take vengeance on the hero by leaving him unburied.

Such is the simple plot. Sophocles, far from condemning the excessiveness and unruliness of Ajax, immediately throws the sympathy on the hero's side in the opening scene, where Athena, ostensibly in the guise of an avenging goddess, encourages Ajax in his madness and plays with her victim so cruelly that even his enemy Odysseus is revolted and crushed. Throughout the following scenes, where Ajax comes to himself, debates his case, and dies by his own hand, we are given the strange spectacle of a man whose criminal insanity and uncompromising estimate of himself tower over a world of sensible people and emerge in some sense justified, or perhaps better, glorified. The play is in a way the inversion of all that we commonly hold to be Greek: immoderation rises to grandeur; an overweening excess stands forth finally as a kind of righteous pride; the body of a mad, would-be murderer is buried in the final scene with such pomp and orchestral sonority that no one can disbelieve in the hero's greatness. It is an apotheosis without rationale, a tour de force of the sheer human spirit.

From a purely formal point of view, the *Ajax* is imperfect. The death of the hero divides the play into two almost equal halves, involving a change of scene and a long epilogue which seems superficially like a mere post mortem. This scene is often thought cold and undramatic. Sophocles was struggling here with the problem of evolving a single play out of the trilogic form used by Aeschylus, and had only succeeded so far in reducing the parts of the action from three to two. Aeschylus' three plays had been the *Judgment of Arms*, *The Thracian Women*, and *The Women of Salamis*. In Sophocles, the parts are perhaps mechanically ill-joined, but there is no disunity of meaning. Actually, it is only in the second half of the play that the moral problem finds full expression and the originality of the poet reveals itself. Sophocles may have been still partially dependent on Aeschylus for framework, but his purpose was already his own; through the many obscurities and difficulties which arise in reading the *Ajax*, it is possible to trace a single vision that even at this early date is clearly Sophoclean.

In Aeschylean tragedy, it has been rightly observed, the moral interest is centered in the kind of action, the character of the deed involved.[11] But for Sophocles the character of the hero is the core. Hence the violent acts of Ajax, though not condoned, are not specifically analyzed; they are left to be what they are, while the man himself creates the drama. Ajax is the first full-length portrait of a tragic hero in Western literature, and it is by no mere coincidence that both he and Achilles, the first epic hero, find themselves in identical situations. Both isolate and destroy themselves in the struggle with their own offended honor.[12] Much has been written about the tragic character, but it has not perhaps been sufficiently noticed that the tragic character is first the heroic character; it is so, at least in origin, and it remains consistently so in Sophocles. The real ancestor of tragedy is the epic, and the character of Ajax stems from the tradition of Achilles, the man of a compelling inner excellence. Both represent a kind of aristocratic self-conception, which is in strong contrast to the supple adjustments of Odysseus. The antinomy is finely expressed by Homer in many a passage, the best, perhaps, being the scene in the underworld where Odysseus meets the shade of Ajax and approaches it with friendly words; he is conciliatory, sensible, and sorry about the whole affair of the arms, which he terms a "god-sent woe." But Ajax is utterly unrelenting, even after death. He utters not one word, but stalks away in eternal resentment.[13]

For all his association with the democracy, Sophocles appears to have had a profound sympathy for the aristocratic tradition. Neither Aeschylus nor Euripides created such truly aristocratic figures as Ajax, Deianeira, and Neoptolemus. Of the fifth-century poets, only Pindar shows a similar concern with the standards and ideals of the old and rapidly fading nobility. In the *Ajax*, as the chorus assembles to investigate the dreadful rumors of madness and bloodshed, their first utterances characterize the hero immediately by touching upon a set of ideas regularly associated with the education of accomplishment, discipline, and breeding. Ajax, sing the choristers, is great of soul, but he is therefore the more subject to slander and envy; to a hero, loss of reputation is terrible, yet the great man is indispensable and imparts his own worth to those who are around him; if Ajax would show himself, the petty carpers who are saying he is mad would disappear in fright, but if he hides in his tent, the rumor will become worse.[14] These ideas form the framework within which the greatness and fall of Ajax are to take place. His very life is rooted in the self-mastery which brings achievement and the achievement which brings glory. Beautiful from without, as they appear in Pindar, these attributes are nevertheless the deadly stuff of tragedy, when viewed from within by Sophocles. They mean more than they say: they imply a standard which will not relax one jot of its requirements in the face of any circumstance.

Odysseus, on the other hand, is shown throughout the prologue as the man of prudence and common sense, who is greeted with approval by Athena in her first speech. He is also a talker, and responsible for the evil rumors which surround Ajax.[15] The contrast between the talker, or man of reason, and the doer, or man of heroic standard, corresponds, of course, to the contrast of guile and strength in the Judgment of the Arms. But it has other overtones which stretch all the way from Homer down through the fifth century. Sometimes, indeed, in the *Iliad* both talents are equally respected, at least by the poet. But between the individuals themselves there was usually tension, and some hostility, for already there existed a social gap between the two which only the venerable but valiant Nestor could bridge. Odysseus and Achilles are, on the whole, polite enough about it to each other.[16] But there is often the intimation that the true gentleman holds himself above reasoning matters out; he preferred to fight them out. Hence reason, debate — all, in fact, which the Greeks summarized as *logos* — slowly became associated with the democratic outlook. It seems to be no accident that Hector's companion in the *Iliad*, Polydamas, though far the wiser of the two in council, is of humble birth and therefore gains little attention or honor from the princely man of deeds, Hector.[17]

In the course of the fifth century, the antinomy between these two types became acute. We see it from the aristocratic point of view in Pindar. Thucydides is a more impartial witness, who, though democratic at heart, understood the excellence and limitations of each, and saw in their opposition a symbol of the two great ideologies which

clashed in the Peloponnesian War.[18] Behind the oligarchies at Sparta
and Thebes lay centuries of aristocratic culture with its strict discipline, stability, and rigid standards of performance. Athenian democracy, on the other hand, rested upon a faith in every kind of
enlightenment, and in human nature itself; discipline might relax, for
intelligence would carry the day; the social system might relax, for
anyone might be intelligent. But always there were dangers; the unruliness of individuals, the fickleness of the sovereign people, the possible failure of intelligence on any given occasion. The true Spartan
regarded all reasoning and debate as a tricky, suspicious business, and
slightly *déclassé*; the Athenian, always ready to discuss anything for
as long as possible, admired Spartan strength, but looked pityingly
upon its naïveté and repressive bigotry.

By the early forties of the fifth century, these attitudes were completely framed. The intellectual and political stage was already set for
the *Ajax* of Sophocles to appear. And yet, the play is no mere contrast of political types. Odysseus, for instance, though characterized at
first as a typical talker, a casuist and an opportunist, emerges in the
end as a man with a kind of ideal and universal intelligence, quite
above mere party politics.[19] Ajax too transcends the contemporary
scene.[20] By the end of the play, it is not he but the two sons of Atreus
who typify the Spartan pattern of thinking, while Ajax himself looms
larger and larger in the light of his own personal heroism and dwarfs
the other characters. In the last analysis, the keenest contrast for
Sophocles is not between oligarch and democrat, but between oligarch
and true aristocrat, or better still, between humanity in general and
the self-slain greatness of a hero. At this point it becomes clear that
the political analogies were only a means, a point of reference, whereby
Sophocles might reach his audience. His greater purpose was to present a hero, the eternal hero, who was for him a divine paradox, and
the central mystery of all life.

Kierkegaard once wrote in the *Unscientific Postscript*, "It is really
the God-relationship that makes a man a man." For the Greek tragic
character, it is also the "God-relationship" which destroys a man;
and in the particular case of Ajax it is not too much to suggest that the
two processes were one, that Ajax' relation with divinity made him
what he was and destroyed him. The metaphysic of such heroic moral-

ity, however, is always difficult to explain, and in the case of Sophocles'
play, the use of the divine figure of Athena in the prologue has
greatly obscured the issue. The goddess appears and summons Odysseus, who is skulking by Ajax' tent, to come and witness the humiliation she has inflicted on his enemy. She then calls to Ajax, and
mercilessly encourages him in his madness. When he departs, to continue his slaughter of the sheep, Odysseus, shattered by the whole
experience, and pitying Ajax, says gloomily:

> Well I perceive that we are nothing more
> Than images, we living — weightless shadows.[21]

Athena then pronounces what is apparently the moral of the play:

> Let this example teach you to beware
> To speak profanity against the gods.
> And if perhaps in riches or in power
> You seem superior, be not insolent;
> For know, one day suffices to exalt
> Or to depress the state of mortal man.
> The wise and good are cherished by the gods,
> But those who practise evil they abhor.[22]

This traditional warning against hybris and presumption is often,
indeed always, taken as the moral of the play. Ajax in his insanity and
violence has been made light of by Athena, but the question is, who
is Athena? Readers have always been shocked by this heartless divinity
who mocks in one breath and moralizes in the next, and scholars, in
the effort to save the character of a prominent Olympian, have interpreted her as everything from the "spirit of sophrosyne" [23] to a kindly
savior who has prevented Ajax from killing the Greek chiefs by allowing him to commit a lesser crime.[24] As if to clarify the dubious situation, Sophocles inserts a passage later on in the play, which implies
that Ajax' murderous plan was not his first offence. It seems that twice
before he had offered insult to Athena, and this, as the seer Calchas
points out, is the reason why the goddess took this opportunity to
drive him mad:

> This day alone, he said, Athena's wrath
> Would last against him. . .

                                              Thus spoke
        The prophet, and long since was Ajax deemed
        To have a mind disturbed: when first he left
        His native soil, "Be conquerer, O my child,"
        His father said, "but conquer under God";
        Impious and proud his answer was: "The worst
        Of men," he cried, "assisted by the Gods
        May conquer, I shall do the work without them."
        Such were his boastings; and when Pallas once
        With kind assistance urged him to the fight,
        Dreadful and horrible was his reply:
        "Go, queen, to other Grecians lend thy aid,
        'Tis needless here; for know, where Ajax is,
        The foe will never come." By words like these,
        And pride ill-suited to a mortal's power,
        Did he offend the vengeful deity.[25]

Unfortunately, this explanation only makes matters worse, with its
confused doubling of causes. The story of these two insults to Athena
occurs nowhere but in Sophocles, hence it has been thought that he
invented them in order to inject meaning into the *fabula sacra*.[26] But
that is not how Sophocles worked. The myth already possessed meaning on many levels, and Sophocles labored to express the profoundest
one. He may have invented the insult-stories, but in a spirit akin to
Dante's prose explanations of his sonnets, to satisfy those who cared
to look no further and to warn the more curious that the answer was
not so simple. Hence he put a moral of sorts in the prologue, but
then in his apotheosis of the hero denied its meaning. He invented
a story about insults to Athena, but made no clear connection between
this story and the Judgment of the Arms, which was the real cause
of Ajax' wrath.[27] He let it be known that Ajax had conceived his
murderous designs before Athena intervened and turned them against
the sheep, so that no such explanations were necessary anyway.[28]
Murder was hybris enough. Finally, he made the goddess limit the
punishment of Ajax to one day [29] — a strange procedure. The usual
Olympian method in cases of mortal presumption was far more simple
and direct.[30]

If all this be taken in the least literally, simple chaos follows. Given similar material, Aeschylus would have taken great pains to unravel the complex causes and establish their nexus. All these proud words and bloody actions would have been the structure of his plot. For Aeschylus, crime itself was tragedy; he gave his hybristic figures a tragic grandeur in the very monstrousness of their actions, or more exactly, in the moral ambivalence involved in their actions. So they reflect the moral duality of the world in which Zeus works his mysterious justice through time. Men learn in time, the world improves, and the curse is at length cast out. Likewise in Herodotus, the story of Croesus and Cyrus shows how a man, relatively sinless, but verging on hybris through the mere possession of wealth and power, may learn modesty through a god-sent affliction. The formula of hybris and punishment spelled for the Greeks a kind of grim optimism about the world, which is not very apparent in Sophocles. Croesus suffered, but repented and was saved; Orestes won his case at the last and lived happily thereafter. But it is all very different with Ajax. He learned no lesson, or if he did, he perished before he could profit by it.[31]

It is clear, however, that Ajax does not learn his lesson, and that the so-called moral of the prologue, the stories of insulted goddesses, hybris, and punishment, are all part of an old framework which Sophocles has here used, partly perhaps, through imitation of Aeschylus, but entirely in his own way. The proud words of Ajax and the strange prologue with Athena no longer reveal the bones of the tragic structure. They are modes of characterization and are only meaningful as such. The hero's haughtiness and crimes are symptoms of something deeper in the man himself, symbols of a greatness which antedates, survives, and all but obliterates their criminality. They are used as highlights upon a tragic scheme which is internal and psychological. Athena is a particularly subtle figure. Far from being an actual epiphany of the Olympian deity, or the embodiment of divine law, she is powerless to act except through some mortal's character, if she can be said to act at all.[32] She motivates nothing; she acts through no direct line of events; and the whole latter half of the play is devoted not to a justification of the gods, least of all Athena, who disappears entirely. It is Ajax who is justified, and nothing is said in favor of Athena's apparent "justice." The supposed *fabula docet* of the prologue is utterly forgotten, and Odysseus himself defends the fallen hero.

But if she motivates nothing, Athena illustrates much. In the prologue she is a kind of spirit of the hour, a catalyst without whom the scene would have been impossible. She illustrates what has happened and what can happen, but she does nothing to further the action. She merely confirms Ajax in his madness and Odysseus in his sanity. As patron goddess of both men, but especially of Odysseus, she is appropriate to the scene, for she stands for a vision of life which Odysseus accepts, but which Ajax has always rejected and still rejects. Thus she represents the sanity of the one in her calm and warning words to Odysseus, and yet reflects the wild mood of the other during that terrible cat-and-mouse game which seems so shocking. But she tells no great truth and exhibits no great power. She is limited within the capabilities of Ajax himself, and Odysseus' estimate of them. It is wholly in keeping with the plasticity of Greek polytheism that the figure of Athena can be used here to symbolize the inner being of the two men, painted large and timeless at the beginning of the play.

Later on she is used more narrowly. Ajax' refusal of her aid in battle, which Calchas accounts the origin of his punishment, is nothing but a device for characterizing the heroic nature. His father's warning and Athena's offer were both wishes for his safety. But Ajax, like Achilles, cared nothing for his safety, and laughed at both. Herein is the essence of the self-destructive heroic spirit. Its action may be folly and pride by the world's or even by the gods' standard, but by its own, it is simply arete. Arete includes consciousness of arete, and with such consciousness Ajax knew well where the real valor lay. The "help of the gods" was irrelevant to the man who knew himself; the gods for him were in himself.

Similarly the one day's punishment is the most transparent symbolism: if Ajax can be forced to endure one day of disgrace quietly at home, where his friends can look after him,[33] of course he will live on for any number of days. He will have done the sensible thing — reason things out, yield honor lost, and reckon life worth more. The gods need no longer afflict him, because, no longer being Ajax, he will no longer afflict himself. Athena's command for him to remain in his tent for one day is simply a mode of saying that Ajax cannot endure one day's disgrace.

In his later plays, as he grew more and more independent of Aeschylus, Sophocles found symbols which invited less confusion, though even in the late *Philoctetes*, it is easy to be too literal about the sudden appearance of Heracles. As the single drama of the single hero gradually evolved from the trilogy, it found its own way through the psychological difficulties which arose, and could abandon old formulas. But in the relatively early *Ajax* the character of the hero himself, in his opposition to Odysseus, demanded a symbol which could span both men and somehow reflect light both on the heroic nature, with its superhuman pride and self-sufficiency, as well as on its more sane but less heroic antitype.

As for Odysseus, he behaves with perfect civilization and decency throughout. His reaction to the sight of Ajax mad is that of a sane man before the spectacle of a great soul mocked. He yields, so to speak, to Athena, and admits the supremacy of the gods — a lesson easy for him who felt that way in any case. When he says that human beings are mere empty shadows, he is not saying anything new or great; least of all is he acting here as the channel for Sophocles' own belief in the nothingness of man and the almightiness of the gods, a doctrine which has often been stated as the central philosophy of Sophocles.[34] Those lines express merely Odysseus' view of life at the moment. He is the sort of person who draws lessons from life shrewdly, and before the play is over, he draws the more important lesson that there is a value to be set upon humanity over and beyond that which appears — beyond the "images" and the "shadows." In the final estimate, it is not his own prudence which is exalted so much as Ajax himself, the man "good in all things, and second to no mortal." [35]

Odysseus is a character who deserves admiration, but it is a mistake to assume, simply because he is so attractive and understandable, that he is a pattern of virtue, by whose standard Ajax must be condemned for wicked pride.[36] Odysseus provides no yardstick by which to measure a hero, except through contrast, as Sophocles intended. It is the contrast between the man who yields to what he feels to be necessity, or "the gods," and the man who yields to nothing because his own arete is for him the only divinity which can control him morally.

How right can such a man be? Can the gods make light of all men and turn them into empty shadows, or does a great individual sometimes seem to defeat the malignity of the world and fortune? As Pindar says:

> Man is the dream of a shadow,
> Yet, whenever comes the god-given gleam,
> A bright light shines upon men, and their
> life is sweet.[37]

And thereupon he invokes, not Ajax, indeed, but heroes of the same blood and breeding, upon whom the god-given gleam shone — Peleus, Telamon, Achilles. The old aristocracy believed in this gleam, this arete, and measured the value of human life in terms of it. Most humanity was shadow and dream, but once in a while there came a hero, and with him it was different. For the lyric poet it was natural to say the gods shed light on him. The tragic poet, who searched for the organic nature of everything and saw that virtues were immanent in humanity, conceived that light as shining from within, perhaps even in defiance of the gods, and constituting a kind of standard which its possessor could not deny or fail. Sophocles has thrown all the sympathy on the side of Ajax. Be his faults whatever they were, and they were grave, he nevertheless emerges from his bloody trial greater than ever, and for sheer magnanimity puts everyone else, Athena included, to shame. The *Ajax* is anything but a demonstration of the nothingness of man. It is a hymn of moral triumph.

Traditional Greek morality would interpret the fate of Ajax simply as hybris and punishment. But it should be remembered that when the Greeks meant, "This man came to a wretched end," they often said, "The gods sent wretchedness upon this man." From there it was but a short step to find a perfectly good reason why they should afflict him. The man was dead and couldn't prove there was no connection between what he did and what the gods did to him. It is a poor compliment to Sophocles' intelligence to say, as some scholars have done, that Sophocles wrote the *Ajax* because he piously wanted to honor a local hero, but that because he believed in sophrosyne, he showed that hero's egregious failure therein and consequent punishment. Ajax' attempt to murder the Greek chiefs was hybris, but it is not the point of the play. His slight to Athena was not hybris, but it symbolizes the point very nearly. Ajax was, and knew himself to be, inwardly stronger than all the external forces which might either help or threaten to destroy him. He could trust himself to be noble. But to the small people of the chorus, such self-sufficiency looks like hybris. They naturally fear such an attitude, for they do not trust their inner selves, and in defense they ally themselves with those elements in the world which try to make men less self-sufficient, and they term those elements "the gods."

The danger of hybris was always associated with greatness in the common mind,[38] but there are kinds and degrees. Sophocles seems not to have interested himself in the simple folly of Croesus, nor in the sheer malign criminality of Clytaemnestra, on whom vengeance was bound to fall. It was the answer of an older generation that behind every great man's fall lay the anger of some external god. Sophocles probed into the evil which comes of good, and it is in this category that the so-called hybris of Ajax belongs. Ajax was "the greatest single hero of the Greeks who came to Troy, except Achilles,"[39] and in that very greatness lay the necessity to behave as he did. His whole relationship with Athena illustrates merely the standard which Ajax held higher than safety. This was the really divine, daemonic force at work. The heroic assumption means precisely this — the possession of a standard which becomes a kind of fatal necessity that drives toward self-destruction. It is this which made Achilles "godlike" to Homer and which prompted the *Ajax* of Sophocles. The long-continued Wrath of Achilles might by some be called hybris, but it is also a defense of arete. It seems excessive and culpable only if one's standard is life and common sense; if one's standard is arete, it is an inevitable course. The true Greek hero raises the standard of his own excellence so high that he is no longer appropriate to life.

It was with no little insight that Professor Reinhardt fixed upon the isolation of the protagonist as the key to Sophoclean tragedy.[40] But this isolation is not due to the gap between man and the gods. It is not because of the hero's helplessness and blindness that he cannot "yield" to the world order. Rather it is his own clear vision which isolates the hero and creates a gap between him and the rest of humanity. His standard, his vision of himself, brings him near to the gods — near, and even into conflict with them. Indeed he is isolated, for he stands near the center of the world order, and far from the comrades who try to advise or comfort him. In Homer, Achilles' intimacy with the gods and their participation in his life constitute a kind of ratification and eternization of his character.[41] In Sophoclean tragedy the two distinctive features of Hellenic heroism merge into one: the attendant deity becomes a symbol of the indomitable standard; or, perhaps better, the standard, too high for life, becomes an inner god. The result is a colossal tragic unity, whose essential characteristic is the greatness of man.

This, and no other, is the force which drives Ajax. It is this divinity he fosters when he spurns Athena. Once the heroic way is chosen, there can be no turning back, no yielding. In fact, for Ajax to take the chorus' advice, yield, stay in his tent and save himself, would have been the uttermost betrayal of his own best ideal and the most abysmal depth of moral defeat.

Hence it is unthinkable that Ajax really "yields" in the great speech on time and its changes.[42] This passage, with its stunning eloquence and its vast panoramic view of the world of phenomena through the eyes of the hero, is one of the rarest and most beautiful in all Greek tragedy, but it has been subjected to some odd interpretations. The first wild passions, when Ajax discovered what he had done, are now over. He had sworn immediately to kill himself, but Tecmessa, his concubine, and the chorus of Salaminians have momentarily prevented him. Their hope is to restrain him from any desperate acts. Ajax, now in an apparently mild, controlled mood, says that Tecmessa's pleas have touched his heart, and he implies that he has given up all thoughts of suicide. He will bury his sword, purify himself, and yield to the gods:

> All that's strong
> And mighty must submit to powers superior.
> Doth not the snowy winter to the bloom
> Of fruitful summer yield? And night obscure,
> When by white steeds Aurora drawn lights up
> The rising day, submissively retire?

The roaring sea, long vexed by angry winds,
Is lulled by milder zephyrs to repose,
And oft the fetters of all-conquering sleep
Are kindly loosed to free the captive mind:
From nature then, who thus instructs mankind,
Why should not Ajax learn humility? [43]

Why not indeed? The Salaminian sailors should have known their man better, if they wished to save him. Ajax talks of humility as only a proud man is able: he leaves it to others. He is now so firmly intrenched in his own conception of himself that he no longer feels any obligation to explain it. He leaves his words to those who will understand their meaning, and cares not whether any do. Yet Ajax has all but said that he has agreed to live. How could he utter all these sane and commendable intentions, and then proceed to dispatch himself as deliberately as possible?

In order to clear Ajax of this apparent lie, some commentators [44] have involved him in a far more complex dishonesty, by saying that he tells no direct lie but words his speech so that he cannot but be misunderstood. Jebb, for instance, alleging that "the change of purpose is feigned, but the change of mood is real," points to the humility of Ajax at this point, a humility "brought about through the human affections." He now wishes to die in recognition of his sin and be reconciled with Athena. [45] But none of this is in the play. Ajax does not propitiate Athena in his death scene: he prays to Hermes for a quick death, to Zeus for decent burial, and at greatest length to the Erinyes to curse and blast his enemies, the Atreidae. [46] The rest is invocation and farewell, but not even a mention of Athena. The change of mood seems only to be the change of a man who first thought he had to commit suicide, but now knows he must. His milder tongue [47] is due to the finality of his decision.

Various other answers have been tried, [48] but the simple one is the right one. Ajax had to deceive his friends in order to get away and die unhindered. [49] Only so could he remain himself. Not for a moment could he consider living in a world where his glory was no longer esteemed, where he had been mocked and made light of by the gods. The only possible way for him to save his dignity was to set it off in the perspective of eternity. So he makes a speech about time.

Being no longer a part of time, or nearly so, he can view it as if from
without, and whole, and dismiss its phenomena forever, albeit with
a certain tenderness. Yes, he will wash off his stains; he will rid himself of the ruined parts of his honor. He will bury his sword, he
does not say where. Indeed he deceives his followers, though if they
had been greater men they would have seen through the deception.
But he is already so isolated in his eternal being that he cannot reach
them. They miss the point completely. The lie is neither deliberate
nor indeliberate. Ajax simply tells them who he is, with his sorrowful
irony about humility, and his quiet dismissal of the world. He will
be pure, he says; and so he takes his sword and goes.[50]

Ajax slays himself to rectify his position for all time, to let his
arete appear untrammeled by the outrages of his last days. The grief
of the chorus when his body is found, Teucer's gallant defense of his
right to burial, and finally Odysseus' appearance as his champion prove
that his position is actually rectified in the eyes of all but the carping
and pusillanimous generals, Agamemnon and Menelaus. The latter
should be a caution to those who prefer to find the "fault," or hamartia,
of Ajax, instead of seeing his greatness. His suicide is a moral act in
defense of his arete, a fact which we are in a better position to recognize than his own companions were. We need not be deceived by the
speech on time. The passage on the yielding of the seasons one to another, of storm to calm and sleep to waking, is very beautiful, but is
only the world of time, change, and becoming, and it is clearly a view
of the world which Ajax by his next action rejects as violently as
possible.[51] He belongs to no such world-order. Supreme arete is "in
the world, but not of it." It is an aspect of being; it never becomes,
and it cannot adjust. The hero is a law unto himself, but in what a
different sense from the robber-barons of the Middle Ages! There
may be a touch of the robber-baron in the Homeric Achilles, but in
Ajax the intuition for inward law and self-mastery is already a full-
fledged moral consciousness.

In his first real exposition of himself, Ajax views death as a moral
recourse, not as one in wild despair or fear, but as one who has a certain knowledge of death's meaning for him.[52] After a brief review of
the facts, in which he reasserts his claim to the arms of Achilles — a
claim incidentally which not even Odysseus denies — Ajax speculates

on his fate and future. But all recourses in the land of the living are
filled with shame:

> No more of this. No, I must seek a way
> Whence I may try to show my aging father
> My nature, born of him, is not a coward's.
>
> .   .   .   .
>
> I'd buy that mortal for a word — for nothing! —
> Who flatters and warms himself on empty hopes.
> The nobly born must either nobly live
> Or nobly die.[53]

This is not pride, or if it is, it is the right kind of pride, necessary to
virtue.[54] It is an attempt to evaluate mortal life by means of moral
reasoning based on moral faith. Ajax is measuring himself against his
inner law. Tecmessa's arguments are directed entirely toward his
pity,[55] and she touches his heart with them, but she cannot change his
mind.[56] He breaks all the rules of usual piety in his firmness and even
rejects Tecmessa, who kneels to him as a suppliant, with the supremely
impious words:

> Can you not see that I
> No longer am a debtor to the gods?[57]

His final word on the subject puts all external influences, human as
well as divine, in their place:

> You are a fool to hope to educate
> This late my nature [ethos].[58]

"Ethos is man's god," said Heraclitus, and it is true of Ajax. Ethos
is a man's inward being; to this god, this daimon, Ajax owed everything, and nothing to the external gods (theoi). And he was right.
In the whole latter half of the play, Sophocles underscores the triumph
of Ajax' faith in the law for which he died. His suicide is not weakness,
or stubbornness; it is the supreme self-mastery.[59]

The final estimate of Ajax as a person rests on the second half of
the play, which, though less poetically rich,[60] is morally all important.
Without this scene, the play would be like the Oresteia without the
Eumenides. Formally, it is the defense of Ajax and his right to burial,
but morally it is the defense of the ultimate value of a great individual

in the face of whatever claims society may have against him. And it proves that if the man is really great, society's claims must be modified; the small people must bow to the man of true standards.[61] Sophocles achieves this point by a favorite method, that of contrasting characters. Here Ajax, the aristocrat of the heroic ideal, is contrasted not with the man of the people, Teucer, nor any longer with the enlightened Odysseus, but with what Aristotle would call the real opposite of the aristocrat, the oligarch.[62]

The distaste with which an Athenian audience in the middle forties would receive the sentiments of Menelaus, with his insistence on class, his distrust of human nature and belief that it must be ruled by fear, in short his plain Spartanism, must have been intense.[63] Agamemnon is perhaps even more offensive, but he does not condescend to explain his position so fully, contenting himself for the most part with Horace's *Rex sum*.[64] But he shows his oligarchic conception of authority when he says the great ox can be controlled with the little whip.[65] The irony of this remark is that it is exactly what Agamemnon could not do. Ajax had not been controlled, and it begins to look as if, in the presence of the corpse of the great man, even Teucer, the mere bowman, will not be controlled either. The whole oligarchic assumption breaks and is humiliated, but it is allowed to depart peaceably through the kind offices of Odysseus. The end is the funeral of the hero, conducted by Teucer. Victorious over his enemies and over his own disgrace, Ajax enters history and sets himself up forever as a monument of moral triumph.

The *Ajax* embodies what was, in its time, a new kind of metaphysical conflict. It might be called the conflict of free will and determinism, but it is more accurate to call it the conflict of an inner moral standard with the external shape of life as a whole. As such, it became especially characteristic of Sophocles and took many surprising forms, and these in turn were always made a little obscure by the equivocal uses of the various Greek words for gods. Both sides of the conflict could equally well be regarded as divine. Thus Tecmessa and Teucer state firmly that the gods destroyed Ajax.[66] Quoted as they are from Calchas, these statements may be taken as mere ways of speaking, tragic clichés drawn from the traditional language. Indeed, Teucer and Tecmessa mean, no doubt, that Athena herself destroyed him; possibly even Sophocles, since he worked with symbols rather than with concepts, might have said the same. But the real truth is that the expression "the gods" can fit either of the conflicting elements, or both.

Divinity in Sophocles moves on many levels, often on several simultaneously. Thus in the *Ajax* we meet Athena as a somewhat neutral spirit of the hour in the prologue, whereas in Calchas' speeches she must be taken as the familiar Olympian deity. Besides Athena, there are also "the gods" generally, destroyers of Ajax, or governors of the natural world which Ajax describes in his speech on time and yielding. These are the symbols of life in the large, with which Ajax must of his own nature conflict. Finally there is the inner law of Ajax himself, a divine force that gives him his dignity and supremacy and compels his death. It is a token of Sophocles' individualism that of all these forms of divinity the most active is the last. It is the inner god that makes the tragedy and gives it motion. It differs from the divine attendants of Achilles in the *Iliad* and from the figure of Athena in the Atlas metope in that it is conceived as entirely Ajax' own possession, which may and indeed must conflict with divinity in less personal forms.

To call Sophocles an individualist, however, is to run once more the risk of labeling. Yet something of the kind must be recognized. Both the *Ajax* and the *Antigone* have been used to illustrate how Sophocles, himself a harmonious blend of mid-century independence with an earlier *Staatsverbindlichkeit*,[67] remonstrated with the lawless individualism of post-Periclean Athens. But it is once more the classic theory of hamartia which is responsible for the notion that these somewhat superhuman and highly individual protagonists of Sophocles, who go their own way so surely and directly,[68] are in reality confused, impious, and wrong-headed. The voice of the chorus is not the voice of Sophocles.

Rather, if the whole be taken as meaning more than the part, the *Ajax* reveals itself as one long paean of triumphant individualism. The *Antigone* is perhaps an even greater and subtler one. But this individualism is of a special kind, a heroic kind. It is not merely democratic; it is transcendental, and as such it has one root in the Homeric epic;

the other rests solidly on the deepest level of Athenian culture, and may be identified with that finely developed instinct for ideal types which has imparted to everything Athenian its humane and haunting lustre. For the Athenian mind, individual personality was a scheme of excellence, not a quirk. If the ideal failed in the Peloponnesian War, it never failed in Sophocles. Yet he would have done little service to the great tradition, had he descended to moralizing and polemic. Instead, to the end of his life, he continued creating the poetic likeness of heroic individuals and illustrating that kind of moral liberty which Thucydides in the *Funeral Oration* intimated was the cornerstone of the Athenian republic: "In regard to personal differences, there is equality for all before the law; and as for reputation, insofar as an individual grows eminent in any respect he is preferred to public honors, less for his rank than for his excellence [arete]." [69]

Similarly, the greatness of Ajax is vindicated over any mere nominal authority or personal animosity. It represents the triumph not of unleashed and unguided individualism, but of the disciplined individual whose guide is inner law, and whose infringement of other laws is only incidental to the enormous struggle he passes through in order to preserve himself as a type of noble behavior. Odysseus says he has been led to reconciliation by arete,[70] and it is generally supposed he means his own. It is doubtless Ajax' he means, but it does not really matter. In the final instance, the arete of heroes is a supra-political moral possession which they alone share and which can never be fully understood by lesser souls, or adjust itself to life. It is built upon an inward daemon of self-destruction. If it loses itself, it gains itself; if it becomes a shadow, it wins glory, and its tomb is kept sacred.[71]

V

MAN THE MEASURE: ANTIGONE

THE *Antigone* is by no means so difficult a play as the *Ajax*, nor on the whole has it been so misunderstood. The reason for this fact lies probably in Sophocles' own development. Some years had passed, during which he seems to have consciously remodeled his style in order to free himself from the atmosphere of Aeschylus which hangs so heavily over the *Ajax* (see Chapter III). The two plays contrast sharply in spirit. In the *Ajax* there is a dimness as of far away and long ago, but in the *Antigone* it is full day, and the outlines are unmercifully clear. There is a new ease of movement on the stage: dialogue and three-way conversations already are taking the center, where formerly the big scenes were set speeches.[1] If the monolithic figures of the *Ajax* recall the sculptures at Olympia and Aegina, in the suppleness of the *Antigone* we already see a foreshadowing of the Parthenon, then under construction. Yet a single tragic idea underlies the wide differences of the plays — the idea of tragic arete or self-destructive heroism. No two of Sophocles' works are really shaped alike, but he was led through many "winding ways of thought" by a single religious hope, the hope in the ultimate value of man. And at least in these early plays, the hope amounted almost to faith.

In ancient times the *Antigone* was always a favorite. Not only did it capture the prize, but also, on the basis of its excellence, Sophocles is supposed to have been elected to the generalship in the Samian War. Unlikely as the story is, it could scarcely have been invented, had not the *Antigone* touched some peculiarly intimate chord in the Athenian temper at the time. The writer of the ancient *Argumentum* attests his appreciation of the play, while another story, to the effect that Sophocles died while reading portions of it aloud to his friends, probably reflects at least some peculiar regard which the poet felt for this work. In it Sophocles seems for the first time to have emerged

entirely in his own person, and throughout his life he returned period-
ically to the house of Oedipus for his profoundest inspirations.

The house of Oedipus was to Sophocles, in some sense, what the
house of Atreus had been to Aeschylus. The latter's trilogy, composed
at the end of his life, is a rich paean of progressive humankind, evolving its personal and political morality under the imperious pressure of
time and suffering. The crowded lines lift the whole structure in an
almost Gothic splendor of intense aspiration, whose climax is the
redemption of Orestes. In the plain, square, diatonic music of the
final scene, the Athenian spirit, endowed as it was with the ability to
perceive in Orestes' position the direct mediation of divine justice, received its first worthy tribute, its first true mirror of itself. Under
Athena's hand, institutions shift their ponderous roots that the inspired
and innocent individual may stand upright. The city-state unites itself
in spirit with heroic man.

The Theban plays of Sophocles form no such trilogy; but in a
sense Sophocles begins where Aeschylus ended. The process of evolu-
tion is complete. In Oedipus and his daughter Antigone the heroic
individualism which Orestes achieved is already innate and functional.
It has passed from Becoming into Being, and therefore its tragedy
and triumph no longer require time — at least, not until we come to
the *Oedipus at Colonus*, wherein time again assumes a dramatic meaning. But in the *Antigone*, there is no temporal link between scene and
scene; the drama is complete in its every instant. The poet turns his
heroine upon the stage like a cut jewel and builds his scenes around
the igniting of her facets. And the historical starting point of such
a drama could only have been the transitional world of the forties,
when Athens, now at the fullest tide of empire and material wealth,
was no longer inwardly quite what she was fifteen years before. She
could still produce great individuals; she never lost that fertile art.
But the ever-increasing necessities of imperial policy were creating
a world where institutions and ideologies, not men, would soon be the
protagonists. Pericles himself was great enough to keep this world
one, but Pericles was mortal, and within another fifteen years both
he and the early Attic spirit vanished forever, except for the ideal
monuments of Thucydides and Sophocles.

Antigone, with her precise and unshakable perception of divine law, is the embodiment of the heroic individual in a world whose institutions cannot change but have usurped a right to existence apart from the justifiable interest of the citizens. For such an individual every moment of life is tragic, and Sophocles has chosen to show, not the steps in a process, but the bleakly irreconcilable issues, the fire and ice of bitter antitheses. After the death of Oedipus, his sons quarreled and Eteocles expelled his brother Polyneices, who in revenge gathered the armament known as the Seven against Thebes. When both contestants fell in the ensuing battle, the throne devolved upon their maternal uncle, Creon, as nearest of kin. So far the myth, with sundry variations. The story of the *Antigone*, however, may be Sophocles' own invention. In any case, we find it nowhere else, and so far, the search which scholars have made for its sources has proved quite vain. Creon's first public act, as king of Thebes, was to decree a magnificent funeral for Eteocles, who died a national hero defending the city; the corpse of Polyneices, however, was to be thrown out unburied, to be devoured by dogs and vultures. Such an interpretation of the roles of the brothers doubtless owed its origin to Aeschylus' *Seven Against Thebes*, where Eteocles makes a very heroic figure indeed, going to his death with full knowledge in order to redeem the curse which Oedipus had laid on both his sons and thus rescue the city.

For Sophocles, therefore, the point of Creon's decree is its orthodoxy. Anything derived from Aeschylus could be regarded as orthodox, so that no Athenian would be surprised at the relative evaluation of the two brothers' deeds. Creon by asserting Eteocles' cause gains an immediate air of patriotism, however reflection may cast a different light upon it. Later, in the *Oedipus at Colonus*, Sophocles deliberately made Polyneices the elder brother, in order to give his claim weight (see Chapter X).

Nothing, however, is said to indicate whether this is true in the *Antigone*. Aeschylus' view of the two brothers is simply allowed to stand as the basis for a long patriotic speech by Creon about the interests of the state. The chorus acquiesces, somewhat ambiguously, and Creon becomes the state.

But Creon had reckoned without Antigone, who did not hold the orthodox view. With her it was no question of mere political right, but of human right; the political structure had shown itself indifferent to the claims of humanity. The dead deserved their tomb, and it was a sister's duty to give Polyneices his. Nor was there any conflict in her mind: love and duty were one, not to be questioned for an instant. Here the state's hindrance could be no hindrance. No punishment could be worse than a betrayal of both her duty and her love. At first she calls upon her sister Ismene to help her, but Ismene is not so high minded. Gentle and timid, she refuses, though with shame. Antigone spurns her angrily and buries Polyneices alone. The story of her defiance and death is familiar. Creon, behaving according to his announced intention, walls up Antigone alive in a rocky cave. Only when he is warned by the blind seer Teiresias that the gods are angry does he yield and attempt to rescue her. But he is too late. She has already hanged herself with her girdle, and Creon's son Haemon has slain himself on her body. At the end, Creon is left to mourn over these corpses as well as that of his wife Eurydice, who dies by her own hand in grief for Haemon.

One hardly need look for a source, though the story probably rests on some old tale. Antigone herself bears so unmistakably the stamp of Sophocles' central passion that it is not surprising that the whole myth has been attributed to him. The scenes wherein she defends herself before Creon, and presently meets death with that sure step that marks all Sophoclean heroes, are evidence enough of the religion of human heroism to which Sophocles devoted his powers. The criticism which has turned him into an institutionalist defending the state against such unbridled individuals as Antigone can only be wondered at.[2]

More than any other ancient drama, apparently, the *Antigone* roused the great spirits of the *Klassik*; from its sharp antitheses and its white-hot debates Hegel evolved his famous interpretation that the conflict is between the family right and the state right and that neither can be said to be wrong or entirely justified.[3] This interpretation was at first followed implicitly, and later gave rise to different but equally schematized views: that Antigone represents "magnanimity" and Creon "self-restraint," [4] or that the play shows the conflict between religion and the state.[5]

Reinhardt was the first to protest against the existence of any such conceptual antinomy in the play at all.[6] The *Antigone* should not be considered merely an "idea" play. It may have pertinent bearing on all such ideas, but its meaning, if so limited, cannot be appreciated historically, or in the full sense, morally and poetically. It may furthermore be questioned whether these pairs of neatly balanced irreconcilable "rights" really exist. The evidence for Creon's rightness, for instance, is hard to find. His self-styled statesmanship, which sounds so promising in his first speech, by the end of the play has more of the appearance of a sham. If any conceptual contrast fits the *Antigone*, it is the contrast between true and false authority, between the ideal citizen and the lawless ruler.

Antigone's nature has done much damage to her, even as Creon's specious talk has done much to give him dignity, in the eyes of readers. Given a situation in which a high-minded young girl buries her brother in defiance of a royal decree, it would have been easy for Sophocles to make her pathetic. But Antigone is not pathetic. Sharp-tongued, contemptuous, almost ferocious in her declarations of her right, she fights fire with fire. She is at war from the minute the play opens until her death. Such a challenging piece of ungentle womanhood may have been more immediately intelligible to antiquity in the context of an heroic past; to modern minds it has presented a puzzle. Antigone is a woman in serious danger, and yet she talks like an empress. She must be wrong, or at least improper. She ought to have realized her place and urged the tender weakness of her sex; instead, she calls King Creon a fool to his face. Her very harshness has tended to throw some sympathy on Creon's side and raise the presumption that the king had a right to decree what he would regarding the burial of traitors. If Antigone denied that right, Creon at least was the king, not she, and he must enforce obedience. But at once we are plunged into the question of the justice of the law, the legality of authority. It is Antigone's claim that a higher law delimits the temporal authority of a king, and that if there is conflict, the king's law must yield:

CREON
And darest thou then to disobey the law?

ANTIGONE
I had it not from Zeus, nor the just gods
Who rule below; nor could I ever think

> A mortal's law of power or strength sufficient
> To abrogate the unwritten law divine,
> Immutable, eternal, not like these
> Of yesterday, but made ere time began.
> Shall man persuade me then to violate
> Heaven's great commands, and make the
>   gods my foes? [7]

It has occurred sometimes in history that rulers are called upon to justify their authority before a tribunal which represents transcendent values; in this case, Antigone is the balance in which Creon is weighed, and found wanting.

Surely Antigone is excessive in her manner, not only before Creon, but also to her sister Ismene. Ismene is as passive and obedient as a world of men could wish her to be; she is too sane to join in such a reckless and defiant plan. She tries lovingly to dissuade Antigone, but her efforts meet with only hatred and scorn. Ismene is in and of this world; Antigone is not. It seems scarcely credible that Antigone is actually betrothed, least of all to Haemon, a young man almost romantic in his passions and at the same time moderately gifted with a political deftness which appears in his attempts to handle his father. Ismene intimates that Haemon and Antigone are made for each other,[8] but it is hard to believe her. Sophocles permits no scene between these lovers. Only at the end, through a messenger, we hear how Haemon clasped Antigone's body in his arms, and then slew himself. The picture has significance beyond its pathos, for it emphasizes the enforced separation of Antigone from simple, human love, the impossible isolation of her soul. Haemon loves her, but can neither save nor reach her. She belongs to a different world from any of the others in the play, and it is not until the coming of Teiresias that the two worlds are set off clearly. Teiresias has the shadow of institutional as well as divine authority upon him, whereby he can prevail with Creon; his blind seerdom bridges the gap between the active wills of Antigone and the king.

As Goethe long ago observed, the most natural commentary on the *Antigone* as a whole is the last act of the *Ajax*.[9] The painstaking care with which Sophocles shows that Ajax deserved sepulchre makes it impossible to believe that Creon had any moral right to issue his decree against the burial of Polyneices. In a similar way the political types which conflicted in that last scene make it equally impossible to mistake the values so strongly contrasted in the *Antigone*. Odysseus, it will be remembered, appeared in the scene as a reconciler of politically opposed units represented by Ajax, Teucer, and the Atreidae. It is even possible to see in Odysseus' strong, moderate stand the germ of that virtue for which Thucydides makes Pericles famous, the ability to represent the city as a whole.[10] Yet, Odysseus showed no hesitation in taking Teucer's side against the Atreidae, the side of an individual against the vested authority of the king. The best interests of all, which Odysseus claims to serve by this action, would seem therefore to involve the respect of individuals, particularly of their personal and religious claims.

The belief that any individual potentially contains valid insight into justice, divine and political, was specifically Athenian. Such insight was a kind of arete, the kind of arete peculiarly appropriate to a citizen.[11] On the tacit assumption of this virtue in her citizens, Athens built her democracy, and her justification therein can be seen in her performance during and after the Persian wars, when the close cohesion and released energy of her men made her, overnight and almost without intention, the inevitable mistress of Greece. The arete of individuals became a function of the *polis*. These men felt they had perceived divine law — witness the *Eumenides* of Aeschylus; Apollo could come directly to Orestes with his commands, and the city's institutions could grow to meet them. No less could any Athenian shape his city through his own arete. Both in thought and in action, the gods seemed near. Order was not imposed, but organic and rooted in each man's mind.

If we are to believe Thucydides, Pericles, whose political influence steadily grew from about 460 until his death in 429, was the last Athenian leader who conceived the city in such terms, and he had his difficulties with a populace already growing confused and wayward with the swiftly changing times. Nevertheless, in the Age of Pericles, arete was still political arete, and the *Antigone* is a truthful picture of it. But unlike Orestes, the heroine stands no longer in a world which believes in her. She is isolated, and her moral insight is not rewarded but punished by the almighty lay-figure of state. As one who saw the subtle changes taking place in Athenian society, Sophocles represented the divine laws as existing for the heroic soul alone, or perhaps better, as gaining real operative existence only through the action of the heroic soul. For him the problem abstracts itself, however. He writes no social document, or political allegory, and it would be utterly impossible and absurd to look for Creon and Antigone in the Athens of 442. It is simply the tragedy of arete again, only this time it is the political arete of the mid-fifth century.

The theory of Wolfgang Schadewaldt, that Sophoclean tragedy presupposes a divine cosmos corresponding to the social one of the polis, more nearly applies to the *Antigone* than to any other play. But of course, Antigone herself does not conflict with that cosmos. She it is who perceives its laws and defends them with her life. And for that matter, neither does Creon conflict directly with the divine world. He conflicts with Antigone, and with that part of the divine world which she carries in her will. It is important to realize this point, for it means that the "divinity" which is involved is not a static and external entity, but an organic constellation of inner standards supported and given weight by Antigone's own will and sacrifice.

Antigone's great speech on the divine laws shows her as the prototype of the perfect citizen. Many critics to the contrary, there is no overbearing or overemancipated individualism in Antigone; indeed, her self-discipline is the most apparent thing about her. Like Ajax, she chooses to die well rather than live badly,[12] which is not generally considered the mark of an undisciplined personality. In Ajax, however, the inner law that compelled him to destruction was entirely personal — his own vision of himself which he preferred not to outlive. Antigone has this quality too; much of her action proceeds from her sense of heroic superiority to Ismene, her own duty to the love she bore her brother, in short, her knowledge of her own difference.[13] The glory of her deed urges her on, and she will not let Ismene rob her of any of it.[14] She has the full measure of self-destructive heroism. But she has more besides. Her political arete, her vision of the divine law on which every true government must be formed, give her a new dimension. Ajax is great and mighty; but Antigone is of colossal grandeur. She combines the virtues of Ajax and Odysseus in a chiseled magnificence that even Sophocles never surpassed. The

inner moral light is so universal and the extreme to which she follows
it so heroic that she is necessarily unique. Of course she is harsh to
Ismene. How could anyone possessed of such a burning moral faith
be anything but harsh, in the moment of action especially, to those
whose standards vary with circumstances? [15] And yet Ismene is neither
a fool nor a weakling, but a very amiable girl, and we pity her beside
Antigone, who is too grand for pity. She is a norm with which we
could find no fault,[16] were it not for the context wherein she is placed.
Yet there she is, and one can only wonder why, except for her sweet
disposition, she wins so much approval from chorus and critic alike.

Antigone has been blamed not only for her transgression of the
norm as represented in Ismene but also, more surprisingly, on the
grounds of her disobedience to Creon. There has been a good deal
of hairsplitting over this point. Wilamowitz, for instance, says, rather
mysteriously: "The people approve of what she did, but they do not
approve of the fact she did it." [17] Aside from the obscurity of this
remark, it should be noted that the people (chorus) are very bad
judges in general.[18] Frequently enough, their commentary is unwittingly ironical. At one point, for instance, meaning to reprove Antigone, the choristers really state her case as her own actions had stated
it, and as she would defend it: "Your self-willed nature has destroyed
you." [19] Her self-willed nature had indeed destroyed her, but whose
will could she rely on except her own? The chorus has failed to
reckon the moral destruction Antigone would have met had she obeyed
the decree. In a similar vein, Schadewaldt says the decree of Creon
was wrong, but Antigone was wrong to disobey it, although her
deed was right.[20] It is impossible to follow such reasoning, and retain
an honest mind. No matter who pleads it, Creon's case fails, and his
decree was violence. For those who seek hybris in Greek tragedy,
it is an excellent example. Any violent misuse of power is hybris, and
by any Greek standards, it is violence to deny burial to the dead and
to murder a near relative.

Creon is the new version of the Atreidae. He is more subtle, but
he is still the illegal ruler. One remark suffices to place him in the
camp of those who believe the oligarchic doctrine of iron control:

> Spirited steeds, I know, are brought to heel
> With a small bridle.[21]

Thereupon, in the next line, he addresses Antigone, his own niece and the daughter of his former king, as his slave. There is no need to redouble examples. The character of Creon has been admirably summed up as that of the typical tyrant.[22] His quickness to wrath, his rejection of criticism, his suspicion of corruption among the people, his resentment of women, and his demand for utter servitude [23] all find their parallels in the familiar habits of the great Greek tyrants. But it should be added that he is a tyrant who cloaks himself in the oligarchic watchwords of "good order" and "obedience to law." There can be no talk of a conflict of two rights. No Athenian, in the zenith of the Periclean Age, could grant a point to a man who behaved like a tyrant, and talked like an oligarch, however he sometimes prefaced his real sentiments with fine-sounding doctrines about the stability of the state. The famous stability of the Spartan government meant repression, control from above, and suspicion; and in this kind of stability Creon is fully versed. No wonder that he and Antigone speak constantly at cross purposes and mean different things by "love" and "hate." [24]

It is therefore clear that Antigone's famous stubbornness, the fault for which she has been so roundly reproved, is really moral fortitude. She does not go "too far." How far should one go in resisting the tyranny of evil? Given real political arete, how much allegiance can one give to an illegal master? It is useless to speak of the defects of Antigone's qualities; there are no defects. Nor need there be any fault whereby her fall is justified. It is as foolish to try to justify it as it would be to try to defend the legal murder of Socrates. Indeed, Sophocles' drama was to be played in grim earnest in 399.

On the other hand, many, recognizing Antigone's innocence but misled by the Aristotelian prejudice that behind a fall must lie a fault, have tried to prove either that Creon is the real tragic hero, or that at least the moral of the story lies in his fate.[25] Indeed, he illustrates pride going before a fall, but there is nothing tragic or even morally interesting about him. Whether we find Creon thoroughly hateful or merely pitiable, his plight brings little satisfaction. He is puny. What remains amid this puniness is the ineradicable remembrance of Antigone's supremacy. In a world of hollow men, she is real. In a world of petty, grievous individuals, she, the greatest individual of all, emerges as the pattern of the universal unconsolable grief.

The famous first ode of the play is a speculation on this tragic essential in man,[26] who dares all and conquers all except death, whereto his genius leads. The poem recalls the spirit of Prometheus, the great inventor, master of all devices and arts, who wears out his years chained to a rock. Man, the most marvelous thing in nature, crosses the sea and yearly ploughs the earth; he can capture for his purpose bird, beast, and fish; by his intellectual skill

> He has taught himself speech and wind-swift
> Thought, and the temper that rules in cities;
> Shelter from frost and shafts of rain —
> Resourceful man; resourceless though he goes
> Into the future in vain. From death alone
> he will not find escape.

He possesses wisdom and undreamed-of art, sometimes for good, sometimes for evil; but he lives within a moral scheme and must reverence law and the gods. Therewith the chorus prays for safety from the godless and lawless man.

It has been a fairly general assumption that the end of the poem, with its reference to the transgressor, refers to Antigone. Rather Antigone is described in the first part, under the heroic type of humanity, limited by mortality and moral law, but unlimited in the scope and daring of her soul. The poem rises in a surge of humanistic fervor, and turns tragic as the very qualities which give man his dignity reveal their destination, the end which is death, and which alone makes them wonderful.

As to the little pietism at the end, it refers neither to Antigone nor Creon, but is typical of the chorus itself. The chorus, in contrast to the heroic individual, ordinarily chooses safety. Its members have no moral position. They may sympathize with Antigone, but they blame her as Creon does. They bow to Creon's will, albeit coolly.[27] Theirs is a detachment without judgment, a moral receptivity without moral will. True, when Creon consults them, they advise him to yield to Teiresias, as the safer course. But not until Creon is crushed do they decide that he was morally wrong.[28] One suspects the chorus in Sophocles of being an intentional symbol of the inadequacy of everyday morality to judge the ultimate questions.

In her scene with Creon, Antigone seals her fate; she is condemned to be buried alive. The king had originally assigned death by stoning as the penalty for burying Polyneices, and the commutation of the sentence is, of course, due to Creon's desire to avoid the formal pollution involved in actually killing one of his kin. In the *Oedipus at Colonus*, Creon will again reveal his peculiar concern with the external forms of religion, while ignoring all the profounder meanings. Such superficiality is part of his nature. The ancients may indeed have regarded formal pollution as a fairly serious matter, at least at times; but Sophocles could distinguish quite well between the spirit and the letter, and it is not without careful intention that he contrasted herein the superstitious and specious sophrosyne of Creon with the harsh-spoken and reckless inward religious fire of Antigone. The latter, indeed, embodies a kind of sainthood, whose intensity and ferocity, perhaps even more than her actual deeds, brought about her martyrdom. Creon's sophrosyne regarding the execution of his niece is a small but characteristic example of his religious temper.

As long as she is before Creon, Antigone is unrelenting in her self-mastery. When the guards are leading her away, however, her tone changes.[29] In the great lyric dirge, and the long mournful speech which follows it, she laments her early death and for the last time defends her position. The speech especially presents difficulties, for in it she seems to doubt herself a little. Somewhat like Ajax, in his "yielding" speech, she apparently softens.[30] But only her tone has changed, not her mind; she is still proud of her deed, but since no one is present to defy, she is no longer defiant. There is no evidence that she doubts her rightness. Suddenly, however, in the midst of this speech, she begins to reason, in cold-blooded terms, about the relative value and availability of husbands, brothers, and sons, and her conclusion is that she would have acted thus only for a brother; in the case of a husband or a son (either of which could be replaced by a new one) she realizes she would not have been justified in defying authority. A more disillusioning passage could scarcely be imagined, but fortunately it can be safely expunged as spurious. No more glaring example of an actor's interpolation exists in ancient tragedy, and it is only the fact that the reasoning here resembles a passage in Herodotus that has prevented scholars from rejecting it unanimously.[31]

Once this passage is removed, the scene is intelligible and not in the least out of character. It is one of those passages where the protagonist pours out his full consciousness of the evil into which he has fallen. It is an attempt of the lonely heroine both to reach the world in purely human terms, and to consider herself *sub specie aeternitatis*, in the light of her own *kleos*, that heroic glory which constituted a kind of historical immortality. Illustrative of the strange interplay of human with superhuman in her character is the way in which Antigone embraces this kleos, and almost in the same breath rejects it as a mockery of the sympathy she yearns for. It is the very humanity of the Sophoclean protagonists which makes their superhumanity so tragic. The two natures of Christ were never more subtly disputed by medieval theologians than are the two natures of Antigone (which are indeed one) set forth and interlaced in this lyric scene. As Ajax, when his mind is made up, can afford to pity Tecmessa, so Antigone, now that her fate is settled, can afford to pity herself, to regret her broken betrothal and destroyed youth.

But her impassioned outpouring is not only a lament; it is also a prophecy of her own greatness. For she compares herself to Niobe,[32] who seems to have been a peculiarly significant figure for Sophocles.[33] In the *Electra* too, the heroine compares herself to Niobe, and says she counts her a goddess.[34] And here, in answer to Antigone, the chorus says that Niobe was a goddess. Now the whole point of the Niobe story was that Niobe was a mortal, and a presumptuous one, who incurred the wrath of Leto by boasting about her children. Hence, according to all usual standards, Niobe should be regarded as a guilty and impious woman, duly punished for her presumption. Why does Sophocles in two places make her a goddess?

Aristotle considers the case of Niobe, and while he does not call her a goddess, he makes her an example of an "excessive good." [35] Such excesses are no doubt unfortunate, but they are not morally bad; and, he continues, "There is no incontinence involved in them, for incontinence is blameworthy, and these excesses are not." In short, Niobe is an example of "good incontinence," of which Sophocles' Neoptolemus is another example; [36] for "good incontinence" seems hardly distinguishable from "an excess without incontinence." Thus Aristotle, taking his examples from tragedy, exonerates of moral guilt Niobe, the time-honored symbol of pride. And a hundred years earlier, Sophocles looked to her as an ideal of steadfastness in affliction. True, as Electra says, her steadfastness lay in weeping forever, as Electra does; but therefore she is divine. The answer is that like Antigone and Electra, Niobe followed a blameless love to excess, and in that excess found ruin but no reason for repentance, and her steadfastness itself — that continued excess — made her in very truth divine. The excess of arete may drive one "to share both in life and in death the lot of those equal to the gods." [37] Antigone sees herself like Niobe, therefore, and the chorus, caught up as usual in the play of the moment, admits there is the shadow of divinity about her. Thereat Antigone cries out that they are mocking her; her mind is confused between her own humanity and superhuman strength. Yet it was she who first brought up the comparison. It is the vision of eternal kleos, the dearest hope of the heroic soul.

The falling action of the tragedy is not without its puzzle, for with the entrance of Teiresias, presumably, a whole new set of agents appear. These are, of course, the gods, whose presences are felt in the person of the seer. He has little character outside of the specific message he brings: that Creon must reverse his decree and save Antigone, for the gods are angry. At face value, this seems a little melodramatic, an eleventh-hour arrival of rescue. The common assumption is that the gods here assert themselves in the interest of justice. Yet if one interprets the Teiresias scene thus, the conclusion inevitably follows that the gods, who are supposed to be justifying their existence, are either malign or hopelessly incompetent. By the time they move, the holocaust of self-destruction has already taken place. If this is indeed the gods' action, their sudden appearance is a little like the proverbial coward who boasts about a battle for which he came too late. On the other hand, if they merely wished to punish Creon, there was no need to send Teiresias, or do anything at all, for the steps in the human action are all perfectly self-sufficient: Creon kills Antigone, Haemon in despair kills himself, and Eurydice, who enters solely to add her drop of gall to Creon's cup, takes her own life in sorrow for her son. One may or may not take this as a lesson from the gods and a sign of their justice; the chorus certainly does.[38] But if it is the gods' doings, then the gods have hidden themselves in tragic masks and acted wholly through the actors. Why does Teiresias come, and why are the gods involved at all? Taken literally, neither their justice nor their omnipotence appears from the closing scenes, but rather the opposite.

The answer seems to lie, once more, as in the *Ajax*, in Sophocles' use of the gods — that is, the Olympian deities — as symbols. By letting them speak only after the action is complete, he carefully divorces them from any suspicion of causation or interference. But they still, of their very augustness, bear witness, for the world at large, to the truth and significance of the heroic action. Thus no responsibility is removed from the actors, and their psychology is not violated but magnified by reference to figures out of eternity. Such divine or semidivine persons, who are themselves outside the action, picture it for us whole.[39] They show no more than the action has shown, but they give it a cosmic setting. For Teiresias, the blind seer, the sputtering of the altar flames and the shrieking of the birds are signs of heavenly displeasure, of a time out of joint. He senses an unholy crime and hastens to tell his fear. In so many words, he states that it is a sacrilege to invert nature, to leave the dead Polyneices unburied, and bury Antigone alive. But it is for Creon to act. Teiresias confirms Antigone's rightness; but he could not have done so without her death. It was her standard, her moral belief from the first, which has now become the concern of life in the larger sense; if it was divine in her, it now returns more universally divine, under the guise of "the gods." But nothing new has happened, except that Creon is now able to look in a mirror large enough and authoritative enough so that even he cannot mistake the fatal outline of his own deed and the justice of Antigone's. Had Teiresias come sooner, or had Creon's change of heart been sufficient to rescue the innocent, we might say that the gods came down from heaven and interfered. But they meant no such thing. They intended neither justice nor a display of power when they refused the sacrifice; they meant only to show how things were.

Choice, action, suffering, and death are the domain of humanity. The gods do not enter it — at least, not in Sophocles. All motive comes from within the actors, and only in the sense of an inward moral standard, which is itself a kind of divinity, can any god be called responsible for Antigone's death. It is she who drives the action and wills her death. Similarly, Creon's actions rise exclusively from character, the character of a tyrant, and in the end he suffers not for a standard, but for a loss. He devises his own punishment, as Antigone devises her own glory.

One must be wary with Sophocles. The express approval or disapproval of the gods, introduced directly into the action, may seem to mean more than it does. We did not need the gods to tell us Antigone was right, though doubtless Creon did. Moreover, the approval of the gods upon her deed lends no hint in this play as to who the gods really are, or what sort of divinity has set its seal upon her moral position. In the last analysis, the gods whom Teiresias represents, though presumably in some sense the governors of the universe, remain in the midst of their inscrutable secret, and serve only to illuminate once more the greatness of Antigone. As in the *Ajax*, they are mere symbolic coefficients of the human sphere. More real theological thought lies in the comparison between Antigone and Niobe, for therein a recognizable though inward divine element moves — the eternal aspect of human arete. But it is impossible to determine as yet the nature of the larger divine world which swings partly into view in the final scene, nor is the relation of this larger world to the godlike dynamic inner force even dimly broached. But already in the *Antigone* it is possible to observe the kind of heroic action through which the poet hinted at this relation for many years before he was able to define it more fully in *Oedipus at Colonus*.

"His being appears only in his destruction," says Reinhardt of the Sophoclean hero.[40] The statement is preëminently true of the first two plays. In both of them the sheer excellence of the protagonist compels his fall, for it makes him no longer appropriate to this life. He is ready to become a god, like Niobe, through persistence in a noble excess. The case is especially clear in the *Antigone*, where no crime can possibly be alleged as a moral justification for her fall. In the *Ajax*, there is still some dependence on a formula of sin and punishment,[41] though it is used in a new symbolic way and the point lies wholly in the greatness of Ajax. The particularly startling feature of both these plays is the immediacy with which both protagonists find justification in death. Both pass instantly into a position where their superiority can no longer be questioned by any, except possibly by such petty souls as the Atreidae.

Antiquity's association of greatness with a fall is well known.[42] There is much confusion, however, about the actual reason for the fall, for sometimes guilt was involved, as in the case of Aeschylus' Agamemnon and Clytaemnestra, and sometimes not, as in the case of Croesus in Herodotus. Solon and Aeschylus [43] drew, on the whole, clear distinctions between greatness which the gods strike because it is guilty and greatness which is innocent and deserved. It was consistent with their theory of divine justice that they should make such a distinction and correct the earlier superstition that all greatness brings a fall. How surprising it is, then, to find in the *Ajax* that Calchas reverts to the old doctrine and says that "overlarge and useless bodies fall at the gods' hands with heavy misfortunes." [44] Sophocles could not have thought this of Ajax, but Calchas and others did; in writing so, the poet is clearly making use of a familiar frame of reference, and no more. To Sophocles, the pride of Ajax is identical with his best self, and if he had been less proud he would have been less good. To the everyday man who believes in getting through life as easily as possible, supreme arete often looks like mere pride, folly, and even hybris. But the quality which Sophocles saw exalting man from within has none of the irresponsibility of these sins. It is discipline, through and through. The arete of Ajax involves so stern a discipline and so great a belief in his own dignity that it destroys its owner and makes him more like the gods than like humanity.

The contrast with Euripides is immense. All the passionate and irrational conflicting forces which that humane and suffering poet felt at work in human nature lie far below the level of Sophocles' gaze. He can touch them if he will, but they are not his theme. It is commonly said that Euripides is a psychologist, because he sees man torn from within; but Sophocles is no less a psychologist, in that he sees man led from within. Euripides saw the many small conflicts of men. Sophocles concentrated on the one great conflict of man — the conflict which comes of trying to sustain the moral and spiritual value of life itself. Euripides was only superficially a rationalist;[45] underneath he believed in the meaningless compulsions, the Dionysian throb of a misled and unhappy world. In Sophocles we find steadier thinking about the problem of evil; but perhaps for that very reason his results are more mysterious than those of Euripides. Those who believe that Sophoclean heroes are faulty have puzzled embarrassedly over the passage in Aristotle's *Poetics* which quotes Sophocles as saying that he made men as they ought to be.[46] Should people be proud, like Ajax, or stubborn, like Antigone? The answer is yes, if they can really be like them.

The two younger tragedians illustrate well two very opposite results of the Sophistic Enlightenment. Sophocles, in fact, seems particularly to reflect the change which the Sophists brought about in the method of treating the problem of divinity.[47] Aeschylus tried hard to establish the shape which deity took in relation to the life of man; Sophocles, in the early plays, looked away from the inscrutable question of the gods themselves. If we remember Protagoras' agnosticism about the existence of the Olympian gods,[48] we may understand how Sophocles can be so cryptic about them and why the actual motivation of his characters is so strictly human. To Euripides on the other hand, the devaluation of the Olympians meant the devaluation of life, and he frequently identified the gods with the most destructive passions of human kind. To Sophocles, devaluation of the Olympians meant revaluation of human life from within. He returned to the roots of religious thought.

Sophocles was not a reactionary who hated the Sophistic movement and refused its every assumption. His plays show certain elements which could only come from Sophistic sources.[49] It is very surprising to find such scholars as Pohlenz and Perrotta, asserting that Sophocles raised himself in opposition to the new "heretical" doctrine of Protagoras that man was the measure of all things.[50] This doctrine could not have been so new as it sounded; for the very anthropomorphism of the Greek gods gives clear indication of how the earliest Greeks measured all things. The Hesiodic tradition of Divine Justice had done much to obscure the fact, but Greek thinking remained anthropocentric. Protagoras' statement conflicted with Aeschylus, but not with Homer. In the case of the two younger tragedians, it was merely a question of which kind of man was to be the measure. Euripides might exalt a kind of straightforward morality, and write:

> If gods do evil, they are not the gods.[51]

Sophocles' answer lies not in the fragment usually cited in this context:

> There lies no shame in what the gods direct. . .[52]

His answer is diffused throughout the heroic morality of his plays. Euripides asserts that the gods must behave in accord with man's morality in order to retain the divine title, but on the other hand he treats man as a weak and passion-driven creature: is it by this standard that he would measure all things? Sophocles asserts merely the divinity of the heroic soul. The hero had always been near to the gods; in Sophocles he is nearer than before. Only so can man really be the measure of all things, if the divine idea is in himself.[53] The little man, who is the man of Euripides, can measure nothing. The great man is the real standard of the fifth century.

PART THREE

TRAGIC KNOWLEDGE

Hell is for the pure; that is the law of the moral world. . . Thus it is arranged, and hell is certainly inhabited only by the better sort; which is not just. . .

— *Thomas Mann*

VI

LATE LEARNING: THE TRACHINIAE

As an example of that form of tragedy in which the hero achieves moral vindication in death, the *Antigone* could hardly be surpassed. The process of justification, which in the *Ajax* had required a long scene of debate, is drawn organically within the principal scheme of the *Antigone* by means of an elaborate technique of antitheses, which mark off and define its issues clearly by the time the catastrophe comes. Arete, self-destructive but triumphant, was the keynote of both plays. But Sophocles, though now about sixty years of age, had by no means reached the end of his poetic fertility. The gloomy change which appears in his next two plays is a puzzling one, for we know of no circumstance either in his own life or in the history of the middle thirties which would account for such an apparently sudden failure of the faith that gives the earlier works their reassuring brightness. Behind the *Oedipus Rex*, indeed, some historical relevancies may be discerned. But the *Trachiniae*, which assuredly is the earlier of the two, reads like the poem of a young man who has just realized the full cruelty of the world. Perhaps it is not unreasonable to attribute a part of the change, and therefore part of the inspiration of these next plays, to the influence of Euripides, who reached the first fullness of his power during the thirties. In any case, together the plays represent another large step in the metaphysics of evil, to which Sophocles devoted his life, and form a second period in the development of his religious thinking.

The stages of Sophocles' development in the art of tragedy have been all but completely ignored. C. M. Bowra gives passing notice to a difference in religious attitude between the last three plays and the earlier ones; [1] but on the whole, scholars seem to have felt that the extant works all represent the same fundamental outlook. Doubtless the fact that we possess no play written before the poet was fifty lends a certain justice to this conclusion.[2] Nevertheless, development is clearly apparent and offers the only answer to the variety of these works. The Greek dramatists seem not to have suffered any abatement of creativity because of old age: Aeschylus at sixty-seven or so produced the *Oresteia*, his greatest work, and Euripides in his mid-seventies the pulsating and vital *Bacchae*; at ninety, Sophocles had just finished *Oedipus at Colonus*, a play whose grandeur is matched only by its freshness. The age of fifty was only a little past the midpoint of life for Sophocles, and it opened his real period of inventiveness; up until then, it is a fair guess to say that he worked under the shadow of Aeschylus. The ancient tragedian served a long apprenticeship.[3]

The plays of Sophocles' middle period are bitter and destructive. Their atmosphere is poisoned by a kind of universal despair, which is equally noticeable in the works of Euripides in this decade. But whereas for Euripides the permeating evil of life comes — in the early plays, at least — from the chaotic human passions, Sophocles lays all the blame upon "the gods," leaving the term, as ever, to be understood in the sense of that broad Hellenic polytheism which could see all things as gods. For him, humanity still wears its jewel of arete, but no apotheosis, like that of Antigone, follows. These protagonists lose and lose terribly.

A quest for truth, leading to an *anagnorisis*, or recognition scene, which Aristotle treats as an essential of tragedy, gives the plays of the middle period their air of being all about knowledge. They might be called plays of tragic knowledge — tragic because in spite of all efforts to make it come in time, it always comes too late. "Learning too late" is nothing new in Greek poetry. Creon learns too late; so does Helen in the *Orestes* of Euripides, and Aeschylus' Clytaemnestra uses the phrase to threaten the chorus. Pindar describes the symbolic Epimetheus as a "late-thinker." It is regularly associated with affliction which brings one to one's senses and is therefore in frequent use in tragedy.[4] In the passages cited from the *Antigone*, the chorus and Creon associated it closely with the smiting of the gods. Thus it is merely an extension of the old idea, familiar even in Homer, but especially in Solon, that the vengeance of the gods comes late, but it comes.[5] It has to do with the whole Greek association of action–

suffering–learning, and it also bears closely upon the theme of life penetrated and illuminated by time, which made its first appearance in *Ajax* [6] and will become of the greatest importance in *Oedipus at Colonus*. It is, in fact, a well-worn tragic moral doctrine, but Sophocles is unique in his use of it.

Solon made the lateness of Zeus' vengeance an evidence of his slowness to wrath, and even the suffering of innocent children an essential part of his justice. Aeschylus found this aspect problematical and studied the inherited curse with special care. It is his great accomplishment that he weeded the superstition out, and evolved a rational theological scheme, showing how sin breeds sin, how evil creates its own necessity until suffering brings wisdom. These theologians persisted in the belief that sin lay behind punishment, that behind the lateness of knowledge lay the unwillingness to learn, *atasthalia*, or blind pride. The tragic force of many an Aeschylean character depends upon this supreme criminality, which, in its violation of justice, amounts to a violation of the world-order of Zeus. Sophocles too could create such a character, though his Creon is not drawn on such a large scale, and, as we have already seen, cannot properly be called tragic.[7]

But it is neither Creon's nor Clytaemnestra's kind of late learning which interested Sophocles as the basis for tragedy. Sophocles saw in the Aeschylean scheme of justice-in-time one or two features which left something to be desired by anyone whose primary conception of life was in terms of the individual. The justice of Aeschylus' Zeus, for example, sometimes required three generations, sometimes a few thousand years. Aeschylus was a tremendous man. For him, salvation was a cosmic, or at least, a racial matter. Not everybody lived long enough to see justice come or to benefit from it; what counted was the universe. So much might perhaps be deemed acceptable; but on the other hand, it appeared that men sometimes were destroyed without any real sin for cause, in which case divine justice seemed not only slow but decidedly lacking. The age of broad hopefulness had drawn to a close, and the larger vague visions had faded.

Sophocles did not rationalize these dilemmas. With the Sophistic Enlightenment in full swing and the Peloponnesian War already threatening, Sophocles turned to the theme of late learning, and he did so to illustrate the irrationality of the world. His heroes of this period, Deianeira and Oedipus, are not those who have been too proud to learn, but precisely the opposite. There was a Greek proverb, "The fool learns by suffering," and critics of Sophocles have tried hard to squeeze Deianeira and Oedipus into the category of fools. But it will not work. None of Sophocles' characters exhibit such sheer intelligence as these two, and none try harder to achieve good ends. Yet they die, or are disgraced, or both, and nowhere do we find a final estimate of glory settling its aura upon their excellence. They pass uncomforted and despised. All attempts to find faults or hamartiae in them have been, to say the least, of doubtful success, for Sophocles intended them as examples of high-minded humanity which wills the best and achieves the worst. In Deianeira and Oedipus, we are faced with the fullest bitterness of tragedy — evil unmitigated by any sort of victory and resulting directly from the most moral action possible to the protagonists.

These tragedies contain the fall of guiltless people, which Aristotle said would be revolting.[8] Yet, their virtue is not yet the virtue of the Lyceum or the Academy, but still the old heroic stuff, arete, not now Homeric, but of the Periclean Age. One of its mid-fifth-century aspects appeared in *Antigone*. In later plays more will appear. Still it remains a question why the middle plays, with their fever pitch of terror and their constant sense of irrational and inescapable malignity, satisfy as they do. Perhaps it is their unmitigated honesty. We meet the problem of evil pure. But there is perhaps a better answer, which is that the hero, though no longer vindicated and set up like a trophy of moral victory, still is not degraded to the rank of a fool and a knave. He loses himself, and he finds no greater self. But the motivating arete was true; its heroic willingness to accept destruction is no longer of such universal moral impressiveness; no one even hints that Deianeira's death makes her resemble the gods, nor does she think so. She is at best a very exquisite woman; at worst, a tool of meaningless forces.

In the *Ajax*, Sophocles was struggling toward what he expressed fully in the *Antigone*; in the *Trachiniae* we can see the seeds of *Oedipus Rex*. And as the idea of triumphant arete was talked about in the *Ajax* but became organic to the *Antigone*, so in the *Trachiniae*

we shall find many references to learning too late and the uncertainty
of knowledge; [9] in *Oedipus* there are no references, but instead a plot
built organically around the theme and masterfully developed.

The familiar wisdom with which Sophocles opens the most intimate
and touching of his works sounds at once the theme of the uncertainty of knowledge, the unsteadiness of life, the possibility of error
about values. Deianeira says:

> There is an ancient saying among men,
> How none can know this mortal life, if it
> Be good or evil, till it ends in death;
> But I, though not yet come to Hades, know
> My life is heavy and ill-starred.[10]

The same theme, but differently expressed, rounds off the nurse's
tale of Deianeira's death.[11] Thus all we see of the heroine is framed
by the darkness and danger of future events and the frightening impossibility of judging or foreseeing. In her quiet and somewhat Euripidean monologue, Deianeira relates how she became the wife of
Heracles, and how this marriage has brought nothing but lonely days
and nights of terror, while the mighty man was far away, performing
his colossal exploits. This prologue lacks the usual, well-molded dramatic naturalness of other Sophoclean prologues, and the action fairly
creeps at first. But Sophocles was devoted to no fixed method; his
art was supple, and in this play it bent itself to the lonely helplessness
of the heroine and the lyric emotions of her nature.

Deianeira tells how Heracles, in order to win her, had battled with
the river god Achelous, who wooed her in various monstrous shapes —
a folk-motif to which, in a later chorus, Sophocles adds a symbolic
touch. Heracles freed her from this danger, married her, and has for
years maintained her at Trachis, where she has borne him a son,
Hyllus, and other children. Yet she possesses no sense of comfort or
safety, because of his eternal absence and peril. He has now been away
for fifteen months, during which time Deianeira has heard only rumors
of him. There is also, on this occasion, further reason to fear, for
Heracles, contrary to his custom, made a will before he left, and
instructed his wife to execute it in accordance with a certain oracle

given by the doves of Dodona. As usual in Sophocles, the oracle is a little confused, a not-quite-direct statement of futurity: Heracles will either die on this expedition or else return after fifteen months victorious, and forever after live a life free from toil.[12] The supposed promise of the second alternative is, in Greek terms, little more than a disguised repetition of the first: only the gods live free from toil. However, another oracle — or perhaps part of the same one — said that Heracles would attack the city of Oechalia in Euboea, and that in this war he would either die, or else thereafter live the blessed life.[13] The same *double-entendre* stands in these lines, but with different contingencies.

A third oracle is also involved, though it is not mentioned till later, and is known only to Heracles, not Deianeira. This is that Heracles would never be slain by a living hand, but by someone already dead.[14] By the end of the play it emerges that this dead person is the centaur Nessus, upon whose story the main plot of the *Trachiniae* hinges. Shortly after their marriage, Heracles and Deianeira had to cross the Evenus River. Nessus, who took travelers across for pay, carried Deianeira while Heracles swam. Midstream, the centaur tried to violate her. Deianeira screamed and Heracles shot him with one of his arrows, deadly with the poison of the Lernaean Hydra. As he lay dying, the wily centaur told Deianeira to save a little of his blood, to use if she ever needed a love charm. The blood, of course, contained the Hydra's venom, and was to be Nessus' way of avenging himself.

Such is the complex antecedent history of this rather simple play. The wealth of oracular material only emphasizes the impossibility of knowing the future. It must not be interpreted as Sophocles' way of saying how easy it would have been for everybody to know better what he was doing. The supposed clarity and helpfulness of these oracles are deliberately confusing. They represent what hindsight, or knowledge free from time, might know, but which no one in the moment of action could conceivably know.

At the end of the prologue, on the advice of her old nurse, Deianeira sends Hyllus to verify the rumor that Heracles is already at Oechalia. Presumably Hyllus must meet him coming back, for in the very next scene messengers arrive announcing his victory and imminent return. The herald Lichas enters, bringing with him the spoils and captives from Oechalia, which he commits to Deianeira's care. Among them is the princess Iole, for whose love Heracles has sacked the city; but Lichas keeps this knowledge from Deianeira, hoping thus to spare her feelings. One of the messengers, however, in loyalty tells her, and in a resplendent scene she wrings confirmation out of Lichas. Deianeira is all gentleness toward her rival, whom she pities for her captive state and for the destruction which she has brought upon her own land. Nevertheless, she feels that she cannot live in the same house with a younger and prettier rival, and she prepares a robe, anointed with the love charm of Nessus, which she sends by Lichas as a gift to Heracles. Almost immediately she begins to have misgivings, and shortly afterwards, Hyllus enters cursing his mother for murdering his father; the blood of Nessus was a consuming poison, and Heracles is already dying in horrible agonies. Without a word, Deianeira goes in the house and takes her own life.

The remainder of the play shows Heracles' last moments. He is brought in, and dies heaping maledictions on his wife and wishing that she were alive that he himself might kill her. This scene is often considered weak and otiose; nevertheless, it has its desired effect. Hyllus, who has learned his mother's innocent intention, tries to defend her to Heracles, but in vain. Heracles is not interested in her. When he hears of the blood of Nessus, he realizes the meaning of the oracle about his being slain by one already dead; his only other thought is for the fate of Iole, whom he forces the unfortunate Hyllus to marry. Deianeira is forgotten. Heracles is borne out to his pyre, and Hyllus closes the play with those blasphemous-sounding lines which are so hard to reconcile with Sophoclean piety:

> Lift him up, friends, and yield me great
> Compassion herein, knowing the gods'
> Unmercy is great, such deeds they do,
> Who, breeding our race, and taking the names
> Of fathers, allow such sorrows as these.
> None can foreknow the future; but all
> That has come to pass for us is sorrow
> But shame to them,
> And most wretched for him who, of all men,
> Sustains such loss.

And you, maiden, remain not at home,
But come, and behold death new and mighty,
These many woes, unheard-of grief,
And nothing hereof which is not Zeus.[15]

It is significant that the plays of the middle period involve greater unlikelihoods in plot than the other works of Sophocles. The plot of *Oedipus Rex* has been assailed as incredible; and similarly that of the *Trachiniae*, with its magical involvement, may strike the reader as less dramatically effective than the simpler and more inevitable occurrences of life. Two facts must be observed. In the first place, Sophocles was in this period bent on dramatizing the off-chances, the unexpected and unexpectable, and hence deliberately chose the more fearful and terrible stories from the mythic corpus at his disposal. Secondly, it should be remembered that the likelihoods of antiquity differed from modern likelihoods: antiquity abounded in supposititious children and recherché love-charms, which not infrequently resulted in death. But the chief defense of these plots is their treatment, and the meaning which the genius of Sophocles drew from them. Man must act, if he acts at all, from likelihood. This fact the Sophists of the time developed not only in theory, but especially in the practical procedures of legal argument; [16] and once more, it is possible to see how Sophocles was affected by the Sophistic, but in his own peculiar way. He makes his characters act on the basis of likelihood, while the fatal dice are loaded hopelessly and irrationally in favor of the most unlikely event. Thus, in the split between the hoped-for likelihood and the unknown, unlooked-for facts, the plot of the *Trachiniae* becomes a long and painful search for truth, whose final discovery brings overwhelming despair. Hence Deianeira's great scene is not that in which she sends the robe, or where she kills herself, but that in which she finds out from Lichas who the captive princess is and why Heracles has brought her home with him. Later, she finds out what the results of the robe were: and after her death Heracles and Hyllus find out the answers to the remaining mysteries. The whole structure of the play is a quest to uncover certain truths, a quest which unravels against a constantly sounded contradictory motif of the uncertainty of knowledge and the impossibility of knowing anything but what is past. The famous irony of Sophocles here takes a new form: the characters constantly struggle to do what they constantly say cannot be done. Deianeira herself sets the tone for the whole piece in her opening lines, where she says first that life cannot be judged until it is over; but then, contradicting herself immediately, she says that she knows her life at least is miserable. Likelihood tells her that she is safe in saying that; but she has yet to learn how miserable she can be.

The commonplace of the opening lines, that only the past is certain, develops subtly through the first part of the text in preparation for the great main theme of knowledge. Musing in retrospect upon the battle which Heracles waged with the river-god Achelous, Deianeira, though she knows the contest came out well, or as she wished it, wonders now if it was really well:

> Anxious for him, I nourish fear on fear,
> As night succeeding night leads on a toil
> Succeeding toil.[17]

For a time, night itself becomes the motif of uncertainty, delicately at first, but significantly in connection with words that suggest wifehood and motherhood;[18] then, to round off the chorus, night appears as a full-fledged symbol of evil:

> Not even dappled night remains
> For mortals always, nor fate nor wealth,
> But all passes, joy and the end
> Of joy succeed each other. . .[19]

Finally Deianeira herself returns to it, saying that in the night's darkness and terror she has learned the lesson of maturity and the cares of being a wife.[20]

Then the idea temporarily fades into the background while the action proceeds, and all the uncertainty is gone at the approach of Heracles. But with the entrance of the captives, it comes again in a new form. Out of the uncertainty about who Iole is and what Heracles intends with her arises Deianeira's fatal insistence to know, as if knowledge were all-sufficient and had no dangers. In the scene with Lichas, Deianeira's "Why is knowledge terrible?" startles us.[21] We know why the knowledge is dangerous, even if Deianeira does not; yet she is so sane, as Lichas admits, that she deserves frankness:

> Dear lady, for I now perceive you know
> That you are mortal and not witless proud,
> I'll tell you all the truth. . .[22]

But the desire to know is like the desire to do: resolution must follow clarity, and the next time we hear the theme of knowing, it is with the idea of action. Deianeira tells her plan of the robe, and asks the chorus if they approve. The leader says, naïvely: "You must do it to find out."[23] One only knows what one has done. Act and suffer, suffer and know.

Then come the revelations. One after another, Deianeira, Hyllus, and Heracles all find out too late. Deianeira might have known the charm was poison, as she says,[24] but her words are hindsight. Hyllus might have guessed his mother acted unwittingly; Heracles might have guessed the meaning of the oracle.[25] Probabilities collapse before the truth which can be known only after the event. But of all the broken figures at the end, Deianeira alone is tragic, for her will is the only one involved. It is she who wills the good and works the evil, and it is she who gives the play a horizon of meaning broader than the mere irrationality of the world.

The *Trachiniae* is a love story. According to an anecdote in Plutarch, as well as by Sophocles' own admission, he knew his subject well.[26] If he left it to Euripides to treat the most undignified details of love, he himself could handle its most tragic and most beautiful aspects, and at least hinted at the rest. Deianeira herself is drawn *con amore*. Doubtless she owes something, no one can say how much, to Euripides' Alcestis; but she is quieter, nobler, and sweeter. Certainly there are enough specially Sophoclean features about her to make it possible that Sophocles was here fully original. He had already sketched something of her in Tecmessa: both women have in them that paradoxical quality of yielding strength, not a weak but an intelligent and heroic submissiveness which is so characteristic of Shakespeare's heroines — a kind of genius for human things. Certainly Euripides never even intended quite so much. Alcestis has become the everlasting prototype of a noble woman; she saved her husband, where

Deianeira destroyed hers. Nevertheless, there is a touch of restrained, heroic grandeur about Deianeira that makes her infinitely more the *ewig-Weibliche* than Euripides' graceful, but self-conscious lady. Deianeira is all love; she is probably the only completely dignified picture of a passionately devoted woman extant in Greek tragedy; we must go back to the Homeric Andromache or Penelope for her like. The latter, the faithful house guardian for an absent husband, is an obvious model.[27] But Penelope seems equal to her trials, and those trials are never so intimately galling as Deianeira's. What would have been the great queen's chagrin, had Odysseus brought home Nausicaa? What did Medea do?

Deianeira preserves her dignity amid these humiliations by her profound sympathy. It constitutes a kind of basic sophrosyne, not only toward Heracles, but also toward Iole, and even toward the old nurse.[28] Her hard discipline keeps her voice low. When there is reason to rejoice, she rejoices, but guardedly, because the future is obscure, but even more because the suffering of others awakens her pity and fear.[29] As she looks at the captive girls, she instinctively notes Iole and questions her impulsively, out of the very depths of compassion and human intelligence.[30] This same compassion and intelligence make her free of all jealousy or spite. She receives the girl kindly, and with a modesty delicately designed to avoid any slightest unnecessary embarrassment, she sends her love to Heracles:

> What else then might you say? I hesitate
> To have you tell too soon of my desire
> Until I know if he too yearns for me.[31]

Her love has a universal breadth that does not stop merely with Heracles but makes her sensitive to every human stimulus, and gentle as no other Sophoclean protagonist, and almost no other Greek character, is gentle. It is a kind of supremacy of gentleness, a kind of arete. Whatever Sophocles learned from Euripides, he did not learn from him this mystery of an individual so molded to a certain kind of perfection that the individual includes a universal. Arete which surpasses the norm becomes an ethic fact of greater issue than the norm, and Deianeira is as great in her special perfection as Antigone is in hers.

Antigone's way may be more heroic, but Deianeira's lacks nothing of itself; in her we may see the beginning of a whole new concept of character in Sophocles, a more modeled and many-sided character, whose supremacy is closer to humanity than that of Ajax, but in the end, no less supreme.

Needless to say, the fault hunters have not neglected Deianeira. The fault most commonly attributed to her is "ill-advisedness," [32] which is as much as to say, she had a plan, but it went wrong, which is apparent. Hamartia of this intellectualistic sort says nothing about the person involved but is really inherent in life. The question of whether Deianeira's use of a love-philter renders her morally guilty closely resembles the nineteenth-century feeling that the love-philter of Tristan and Isolde freed them from charges of adultery. The philter is not so crucial; it merely embodies the sorry recourse to which Deianeira is driven. A modern version of the play would use a different symbol without changing the moral position of the heroine in the least. Legally Deianeira would probably have been regarded as innocent.[33] The chorus never once reproves her for using the potion, nor does Hyllus, after he finds out. Not even Heracles in his terrible wrath makes anything of it. Whatever the courts would have said, Sophocles did not wish the use of this love potion to be considered criminal.

Perhaps the least understandable charge which has been leveled at Deianeira is the one grown venerable in the annals of tragic criticism — pride. Professor Bowra says her real guilt lay in her effort to dominate her husband, and he lists a great deal of Athenian law to prove that the virtuous wife owed it to her lord and master to bear patiently with his concubines.[34] Deianeira, he avers, had sophrosyne at first, when she accepted Iole. But when she had recourse to magic, she ceased to be a good wife, and was trying to control her husband. "Her decision," he says, "shows an unexpected and deplorable pride." [35]

The recourse to magic is anything but prideful. The psychology behind the use of love-magic has been thoroughly studied by Thomas Mann in *Joseph in Egypt*, an almost clinical report on the breaking of the last agonizing threads of self-respect in a sensitive and intelligent woman.[36] Deianeira is no Mut-em-enet, nor is she reduced before our eyes to the ruin Mann paints. What she suffers is said simply in two lines addressed to the chorus:

> Conceal this deed; for if you suffer shame
> In secret, you will not fall in disgrace.[37]

The philter is shameful because of what it means to her own worth. She is no longer, as she explained earlier to the chorus, able to sustain her attractiveness in Heracles' eyes by her beauty, which is fading, nor does Heracles apparently feel much obligation to remain faithful.[38] Obviously she does not want her humiliation published. In this act she swallows the last of her pride.

Deianeira has no hamartia, unless it is a fault for a woman to contest the case for her husband's love with another woman. From all that might be culpable — recrimination, anger, jealousy, or any Medean violence — she holds herself free. She acts only upon her unquestionable right to retain what is hers. The psychological awareness of the twentieth century bids us make a point of understanding with a degree of sympathy the terrible compulsions that move Medea; but it requires no effort to sympathize with Deianeira, since she does nothing to repel us. It is heroic to maintain innocence in a situation such as hers, and if her innocence is denied, the play loses the meaning which regularly distinguishes Sophocles, the heroic humanist, from the psychologist, Euripides.

Nor is Heracles' new love for Iole in any sense a "marriage of true minds," which Deianeira might respect or leave alone, but something quite different. Throughout the play there are numerous scattered references to the destructive power of Eros. The messenger says, "Love alone of the gods inflamed him to make this war," and "for love of this girl the whole city lies fallen." [39] Lichas, when he finally breaks down and tells the truth, does so in similar terms,[40] and the chorus, after the death of Deianeira, sings a bitter ode, ending with an accusation of Aphrodite.[41] But Deianeira three separate times refers to Heracles' passion as a disease; [42] and says that therefore she cannot be angry with him for it. Later, however, when the poisoned robe has been delivered and Heracles is dying, Hyllus, in his passionate

narrative, uses the theme of disease again,[43] so that one suspects
Heracles' new illness of being only a continuation of the old one. Such
a morose dwelling on the evils of lust is odd for Sophocles, and reminds
us that Shakespeare too in his darkest tragedies and sonnets was moved
to dwell upon it with terrible earnestness and frankness. Sophocles is
not so outspoken, but the problem of lust is present. Deianeira knows
whereof she speaks. The description she gives of Achelous the river
god prompts the later song of the chorus, where the contest of the
monster with Heracles for Deianeira's hand is pictured as a bestial
combat urged on by Eros, while the pitiful prize waits.[44] There was
also the meeting with Nessus.[45] Deianeira knew the "disease" to her
sorrow.

Here is no allegory of sacred and profane love; yet the contrast
between the diseased Eros and the compassionate universal love which
is Deianeira's arete stands clear. Nothing is said to characterize her
side of the antinomy directly. It is part of her isolation and self-abnegation that no positive value is set upon her existence by anyone. Yet the
excellence she exhibits is the excellence of her love, and it is this
which throughout she is unwilling to betray. There is no law, either
moral or Athenian, which could justly compel her to respect the
"disease" more than her own honest devotion. And it is this conviction of the moral reasonableness of her position that makes her act,
for all her sophrosyne, and for all her wise caution about the future.
In a way, her sophrosyne itself urges her, for nothing could have been
worse moral folly than to yield to such a situation.

Deianeira's moral position is an intuitive one; she is not like Antigone who reasons loftily. But her intuition is sound, and it brings her
to a conviction of justice as personal and individual as Antigone's,
though less sweeping. It is her own possession and depends upon the
feelings which make up her nature, and the inner law of genuine love
which motivates all her acts. The speech in which she tells the chorus
she cannot live under the same roof with Iole lacks all rancor and
petulancy, while at the same time, the moral potency underlying it
brings her nearer and nearer to action.[46] Earlier, the same moral intuition had given her the strength to unmask the falsehoods of Lichas.

This unmasking scene, as it has been sometimes called, is the core of
the play. In a controlled but passionate speech she begs Lichas for
the truth:

> By Zeus that thunders through the sheer ravines
> Of Oeta, I beseech you, do not lie!
> No low or evil woman hears your tale,
> Nor one who does not know of human life,
> That it dwells not in changeless joys forever.
>
> . . . .
>
> If you have learned
> Your lies from Heracles, your learning's low;
> If you have taught yourself, beware, for when
> You'd be a good man, then you'll seem a villain.
> But tell me all the truth!
>
> . . . . . .
>
> And if you feel some fear, it's not well feared,
> For not to learn the truth — that tortures me.
> Why is knowledge terrible? Has not Heracles
> Had many wives before? Yet not from me
> Has any one of them heard curse or blame.[47]

What arrests us in this speech is the unquestioning conviction that
the truth, however hard, is more bearable than a lie. Uncertainty,
darkness, night, the inability to judge — these are the sources of
Deianeira's fear and misery. The truth cannot terrify her. In this quest
for truth is the germ of the *Oedipus Rex*, and in the irony of Deianeira's
question, "Why is knowledge terrible?" the poet's tragic motivation
is visible. Men die of knowing the truth. All the more impressive
therefore is the courage of those who seek it.

Deianeira's great speech has been sometimes badly misunderstood.
A fruitless comparison with Ajax' "yielding" speech has led to the
notion that the two are spoken in a similar spirit, and that Deianeira's
appeal for truth is a lie elaborately designed to get the truth out of
Lichas. She is supposed to pretend to yield to her fate, as Ajax pretends.[48] Some have thought that the array of former mistresses which
she attributes to Heracles is an invention of her own, to convince
Lichas that she will treat Iole well. One scholar even distinguishes a
"saga-Heracles" who had mistresses, from the "tragic-Heracles" who

did not.[49] If the women had existed, Deianeira would have used the philter before; on the other hand, if she was really so restrained about Heracles' amours, why did she use it at all? A great many of these philological angels dance drearily on their pinpoint. But to the Athenians, Heracles was Heracles, whether in saga or tragedy. His carnal appetites were famous, and no one would have disbelieved in his mistresses for an instant. If Deianeira's words were false, Lichas, who was privy to his master's secrets, would have known it; and in any case, she need not have repeated her stratagem to the chorus.[50] The speech could never have been understood as a lie by the audience, and if it was meant to be, it would be extremely bad theatre.[51]

The unmasking scene is a portrait of Deianeira's will. It is her first real action, the first function of her arete. Active and assertive, she begins to weave her fate, and when she sends the robe to Heracles, her deed is only the result of what she finds out here. The quest for truth entails action, and action entails suffering; for the hero, self-immolation. In spite of the basic contradiction of trying to know when only the past can be known, Deianeira tries, and she acts, where no action is safe.[52] She knows Heracles all too well; yet she fights for the integrity of her love. It is the familiar tragic tension between the desire for safety and the necessity for action.[53] The hero will rise to meet that necessity, though the chorus may recommend safety. In the attempt to act, the attempt to know, Sophocles saw the splendor of humanity. Human sight may be limited; Deianeira may arrive in one sense only at greater darkness. But in another sense she achieves through action the rounded and timeless knowledge of the oracle, blasting as that knowledge is. Her tragedy is not in her failure, but in the nature of the truth she uncovered.

In the end, she is entirely destroyed. Justice is never done her. It is impossible to feel that the revelation of what she had done brought her to a true estimate of herself, or that the self-loathing which drove her to suicide was in any sense the judgment she deserved. Aside from a half-hearted defense by Hyllus, she remains unredeemed; her very name, "Husband-slayer," reflects only her criminal record and none of the charm and devotion which Sophocles gave her. Certainly she has not the great self-knowledge of Antigone, nor is her way laid out so surely by principle and rationale. Where Ajax and Antigone sacrificed themselves, she punished herself. Her virtue, instead of emerging transfigured, remains locked and secret in herself. Yet her death, like theirs, is in its own way a defense of her arete. The nature of love is to lose all dignity for the beloved, if necessary. This she had done, and when it worked only harm, it was purely and simply the standard of love which she embodied that drove her to self-punishment. In injuring the beloved, she had done the unforgivable. For her, the cause was lost, and she never even hints that she is dying well because she can no longer live well.

The character of Deianeira has full heroic equipment, and though her goodness works her destruction, as did Antigone's, yet there seems to be no eternal correlative for her. She negates herself, and vanishes. All the brilliant faith of the earlier plays, the faith that human arete could ultimately justify itself, is gone from the bleak close of the *Trachiniae*. And if human effort fails to justify life, it remains unjustified, for in the world of Sophocles, there is no such thing as an act of grace, except from within man. The spectacle of the most benignly loving nature effecting results that hate could scarcely contrive comes home as horrible, but true. Not always, even by self-destruction, can the human spirit exalt itself. Sophocles has gone beyond the *Antigone* into a realm of disillusion, whose bitterness comes not from knowing that man can be low and mean, but that he can be noble and magnanimous to no ultimate purpose.

This grim attitude is further accented by the character of Heracles, who enters at the end. It would have been easy to let Heracles, the great and generous, hear the whole story and forgive his wife, as Euripides' Hippolytus forgives Theseus. But Sophocles does not want such a quiet ending. He does not want us to have that much comfort.[54] He presents us with a fantastically gross Heracles, interested solely in himself, and unshaken by the faintest self-doubt or hesitancy in his passions.[55] The long final scene is a planned cruelty in order that Deianeira, who has been alone throughout, may still be alone, and unloved. In his abysmal selfishness and furious ravings, Heracles is consistent with the picture formed during the play of a man consumed by a disease. He has been made appropriate to the shirt of Nessus.[56]

Early in the play the chorus said that Zeus would take care of his offspring, meaning Heracles,[57] but this pious hope is not fulfilled. It is emphatically and sarcastically denied by the last speech of Hyllus, wherein the unmercy of the gods is pointedly contrasted with the compassion of mortals, and Zeus is directly blamed for the evils which have befallen.[58] It is in vain that scholars try to torture the line, "No man knows the future," [59] into a tacit reference to the coming apotheosis of Heracles,[60] or, with equal vanity, assign the last four lines of the play to the chorus, as a correction of Hyllus' impiety, with the meaning that if we yield to the gods, all will be well.[61] Hyllus, who is completely crushed, has no choice in the matter; and if Sophocles had wished to refer to Heracles' apotheosis on Mount Oeta, he could have done it more clearly. Instead, he studiedly suppresses it. Heracles is no matter for an apotheosis, and the line is only another reflection on the old theme of the insufficiency of knowledge. With greater justice, Perrotta writes: "[Sophocles] doubts that divinity is just. His religion hinders him from looking to the bottom of his own thought; he suffers with his doubt. But not being able to say that divinity is good and just, he says merely that divinity is powerful, and that we are nothing but instruments in its hands." [62] And this seems nearly the truth, except that Sophocles has no religion which prevents him from looking to the bottom of his thought. That is exactly where he has looked, and indeed he cannot say that divinity is good and just. But the conclusion is no Euripidean criticism of the Olympian gods. They go by the board with Sophocles. Here "Zeus" is something organic and functional in life which prevents man's best from being of any worth. Had he said "fate," it would have meant no more and no less; but Zeus, as the father of Heracles, is more symbolically appropriate, and more bitter.

This seeming impiety is no new thing in Sophocles: Teucer, standing by the dead Ajax, spoke of the gifts of enemies, the sword forged by the Erinys, and the devices by which the gods, and the gods alone, bring man to ruin.[63] The scruple of speaking ill of Zeus is more the scruple of scholars than of Sophocles.[64] It is treason to force any kind of piety into these despairing lines, in order to bear out the theory that Sophocles was pious. The closing lines in any case are not particularly impious, for the Greeks might equally praise or blame the gods; if Aeschylus asserted that Zeus was always just, he was not defending a creed. He was only trying to prove something which was not always apparent. Sophocles was free to differ, so long as he did not profess atheism, and here he differs violently.

In the two early plays, if the gods seemed unjust, it hardly mattered, for humanity was of such stature it filled the universe with moral fact and value. One could afford to allow them their heedless or malign behavior. But in the *Trachiniae* all is doubt and suffering, and the outcry against the insufficiency of the gods arises most directly from the sense of the insufficiency of man.

VII

IRRATIONAL EVIL: OEDIPUS REX

THE issues of the *Trachiniae* stand clear; the injustice of the gods — and the gods, in this instance, are presumably the forces which govern life in the large and the external fates of man — is bitterly accused. Cast in these religious terms, whereby circumstance is itself conceived as a form, a framework of divinity, the tragedy of irrational evil is more than a complaint against life; it assumes the proportions of a quasi-theology, whose keynote is despair. All the knowledge which the best of good will can attain is too late, and the only truth is, we know no truth.

But the mythological subject matter which lay at the disposal of the Greek poet was infinitely rich and was destined to provide Sophocles with an even better vehicle for the theme of knowledge. Sophocles regularly allowed himself to be led by the myth which he had in hand and refused none of its implications. He "corrected" no stories, as did Pindar. He injected no special meanings, as did Euripides. Such elements as he is thought to have invented — the hybris of Ajax, for example, or the plague and the oracle in the Oedipus story [1] — are all elements which might well have been there; they imply nothing read in. They serve merely to symbolize action, accentuate character, or point a meaning which existed in the myth from the beginning. It is not surprising therefore that Sophocles, after writing his version of Deianeira's story, turned to the even more pointed one of Oedipus and found in it a fuller expression of the insufficiency of knowledge and the irrationality of evil.

Oedipus was proverbial for two things — sagacity and atrocious misfortune. Greek popular wisdom had it that if a man were careful and prudent, he would avoid trouble. Of all men, Oedipus should have succeeded, but of all men he particularly did not. Oedipus remains a type of human ability condemned to destruction by an external insufficiency in life itself — as if knowledge were possible, but the objects of knowledge, to use Plato's phrase, were somehow illusory, or at least evil. Such is Oedipus in the Sophoclean version, and such he must have been always. The myth is ultimately its own best interpreter and needs no *fabula docet*. It is for form's sake alone that the *Oedipus Rex* closes with the same old Herodotean saw which opened the *Trachiniae*:

> Let mortals hence be taught to look beyond
> The present time, nor dare to say, a man
> Is happy, till the last decisive hour
> Shall close his life without the taste of woe.[2]

These closing lines have been thought to be the moral, but if this were all, there hardly needed to be any play, not to mention the chaotic masses of critical material which it has occasioned.

The *Oedipus Rex* passes almost universally for the greatest extant Greek play [3] — an assumption based, no doubt, on Aristotle's preference. This judgment might perhaps be questioned since it does tend to thrust other monuments of the Greek theatre into the background and narrow our conception of what tragedy "should be." But it is more pertinent to ask how the *Oedipus* has sustained its reputation in view of the interpretations put upon it — particularly those interpretations which treat the play as a vivid proof of Sophocles' simple faith and pure piety.

The terrible old story of how Oedipus unwittingly slew his father and married his mother, and of how the consequences of the act fell upon his whole house thereafter, had already kindled the imagination of Aeschylus. Of his trilogy, *Laius, Oedipus,* and *The Seven against Thebes,* only the last survives, an eloquent though static and archaic portrait of the patriot-king Eteocles, and we can only vaguely conjecture how Aeschylus disposed the earlier and more intensely dramatic events of the plot. Knowing as we do, however, from the *Oresteia* something of his attitude toward the god-sent, congenital criminality which haunted the doomed houses of his tragic scheme, it is at least plausible to suppose that the trilogy displayed an ever recurrent, irrepressible streak of hybris, breeding evil upon evil, and stemming ultimately from Laius' disregard of the oracle which had warned him against having children. In the end the noble self-sacrifice of Eteocles cancels the curse, and Thebes is delivered at once from the Labdacids and the destruction threatened by the expedition of the Seven.

For Sophocles, however, the tale has deeper though less clearcut implications. Something of the fiery character of Laius, as it is hinted at in the *Oedipus Rex*, is perhaps derived from Aeschylus. But Oedipus himself illustrated two great dilemmas: first, like Orestes, he was the unwilling instrument of crime, and second, he was at once the emblem of shrewd wisdom and utter blindness. Aeschylus must unquestionably have dealt with the first of these dilemmas, and it is probable that he believed that Oedipus, in some degree, deserved his sufferings. But it is with the second dilemma that Sophocles is concerned. In the *Oedipus Rex*, he passes over the question of whether or not Oedipus is morally guilty of parricide and incest and concentrates wholly on the extent of his knowledge. Later, in the *Oedipus at Colonus*, Sophocles reverted to the other dilemma, and made old Oedipus defend his moral innocence in several spirited harangues, but the whole matter of moral guilt or innocence is never broached, even for an instant, in the earlier play. Nevertheless, it can be demonstrated simply from the character of the king himself in the *Oedipus Rex*, that Sophocles never considered him morally guilty. He was, from the first, the man who contrived his own fall without deserving it. And to this bitter fact may be added the even bitterer one that the means by which Oedipus destroyed himself was not his folly but his keenly intelligent moral conscience, which led him to take every possible step to avoid the unspeakable pollution that had been prophesied for him.

As he tells us himself,[4] Oedipus thought that he was the son of Polybus, King of Corinth; but once, after being twitted by a drunken companion about his origin, he consulted the oracle and was told that he was destined to kill his father and marry his mother. Horrified, he avoided his supposed parents thereafter and made his way through Phocis, where his real father, Laius, met and attacked him at a crossroads. In the fight which ensued, Oedipus slew Laius and all but one of his companions, and then proceeded to Thebes. So far, if we make allowances for the bloody practices which travel in the wilder districts sometimes enjoined upon the wayfarer of the heroic age, Oedipus had behaved with a good conscience. At Thebes he found the "riddle-singing Sphinx," the pest of the land, which by his sagacity he destroyed. He was rewarded by the grateful citizens with the hand of the recently widowed queen, Jocasta. And so for some years he reigned and bred sons and daughters, a happy and revered ruler, until the coming of the plague, at which point Sophocles begins his play. The plague, we are told, had been sent as a punishment because the city was polluted by the unavenged blood of Laius. And now, apparently for the first time, the question arises: who is the murderer of Laius?

If Sophocles had wanted us to consider the problem of right and wrong, he would have dramatized the scene at the crossroads. Instead he has dramatized the search for the murderer; the whole action is therefore devoted to the effort to draw truth out of the uncertainty and ignorance which at first center around the plague and later begin to gather more and more ominously around the king himself. In their fear and helplessness, the pestilence-ridden people turn to Oedipus as suppliants. He greets them with what must be taken as surprise at the supplication, for his questions cannot indicate that he has not noticed the plague. He asks why they have come to him, the "famous Oedipus, so-called," [5] for in such a crisis to sit as suppliants before the palace instead of before the temple is a little unusual. Then the priest explains, and we see why Oedipus is great and glorious. It is not just that he is king:

> Not that we hold you equal to the gods,
> But we your children sit upon your hearth
> Judging you first of men amid the ills
> Of life, and in your dealing with the gods.[6]

He then recalls how Oedipus relieved Thebes of the Sphinx:

> And that by no advantage gained from us
> Nor learned, but by assistance of some god,
> Your name and fame is, you have saved our life.[7]

The appeal of the priest, with its moving yet dignified description of the general suffering, is especially remarkable in that it is an inversion of the usual situation, in which the secular ruler consults the priest or seer about divine things, as Oedipus later consults Teiresias. Here the priest consults the ruler, but less as ruler than as a person of special gifts, whom the gods have dealt with in former times for the public benefit. The priest recalls to Oedipus not his duty as king but his ability as a man, and begs help on that basis. Indeed, he may say, with formal piety to avert envy, that Oedipus is not the equal of the gods; but the fact is that he and the people treat him as a god, by coming with suppliant boughs and asking him, out of his sheer mental gifts, to stop a plague. Here, then, is a hero receiving the most remarkable tribute to his arete, which in Oedipus's case is of an intellectual nature. We perceive that the rule of Oedipus rests upon this arete, that he is in fact the "first of men" in the sense that Pericles was, for his pre-eminence is a result of his innate intelligence.[8] Significantly enough, the first words which Oedipus returns to this appeal have to do with knowledge:

> O my unhappy sons, too well I know
> Your sad estate; I know the woes of Thebes.[9]

And he continues to say that he has not slept, but has "wandered the ways of thought," and he ends his speech with that association of knowledge with action which occurred also in the *Trachiniae*:

> The noble Creon went by my command
> To Delphi, from Apollo's shrine to know
> What must be done. . .[10]

The man of heroic stature is once more before us. To one who has recognized them in the earlier plays of Sophocles, these emblems of the tragic hero are the clearest heraldry of what must come, and they are differenced only by details of the individuality and by the kind of arete involved. Oedipus has a special affinity with the gods, by which his personal arete works wonders; he chooses action instead of safety; all that remains is for him to destroy himself, which of course follows. As he dismisses the suppliants, he summarizes himself and his position as principal in the tragic action: he will solve this new riddle, as he had solved that of the Sphinx (theme of knowledge); he will vindicate the land and the god (theme of action and closeness to divinity); he will not spare the murderer even to help himself (theme of self-destruction).[11] From the prologue alone we can recognize

Oedipus for what he is. Aristotle to the contrary, he is "of superior virtue"; the people regard him nearly as a god for his intelligence, and Oedipus himself recognizes his birthright at once and his responsibility when he accepts the challenge to act in the face of a *daimonion* — a "divine" affliction.

One of the most striking features of Sophoclean dramaturgy is the symbolic appropriateness of the prologue to the drama as a whole. As scene upon scene unfolds, Oedipus adheres, with ever rising intensity, to the heroic moral purpose which he declared in the opening tableau. And as the consequences loom larger and darker, Oedipus is the more confirmed in his consistent loftiness of character. Foreknowledge of the end of the story tends to prejudice the reader's opinion of him, and must have done so even in antiquity. But as Sophocles wrote his text, there is no evidence of moral delinquency in the hero. It is the myth, not the play, which raises such questions as, "Was Oedipus wrong to slay or marry anybody after hearing the prophecy?" Or, "If Laius believed the oracle, why did he have children, and if he did not believe it, why did he bother to expose Oedipus?" It is almost as irrelevant to criticize the play in the light of these questions as it would be to analyze the *Iliad* on the basis of the justice of the Trojan War.

Nevertheless, these questions continually recur. The moralist, seeing a man destroyed, assumes that he somehow deserved destruction, and the fact that Sophocles never directly says so — in fact, never even hints so — ought to have caused greater embarrassment than it has. True, the *Oedipus* does not accuse the gods as explicitly as does the *Trachiniae*. But the whole action, insofar as it is subtler, and the character of the hero, in that it is determined by a more conscious and uncompromising moral fibre, constitute what is perhaps more forceful than even the passionate lines which close the *Trachiniae* — in short, a detailed picture of the irrational and unjustifiable evil inwrought in the texture of life, against which the greatest natural and moral endowments struggle in vain. The lack of any real counterpoise between sin and punishment, such as Aeschylus believed in, has made the play bewildering, but that is exactly Sophocles' purpose. He assumes here a darker background than in any other of his works. Even at the end of the *Trachiniae*, we almost feel that the gods might have answered Hyllus' outburst if the play had not ended; all was not said, all was not proven. But the *Oedipus* is complete: if the whole Olympian court entered via the machine, there would be nothing they could possibly say.

Karl Reinhardt is one of the few scholars who have not taken the question of Oedipus' guilt or innocence as the point of departure. Reinhardt states clearly that the main theme is not guilt or innocence, but truth and seeming.[12] Yet "truth and seeming" hardly sums it up, for this is a formula which might apply to any play involving recognition and reversal; it recalls, for instance, the motif of shadow and substance in the *Ajax*, and it will reappear in later works. Sophocles was peculiarly sensitive to the dividing lines of the real and unreal, of truth and seeming, and there is often a quiet interplay of the two which lends his poetry an atmosphere of flickering mystery, of major keys veiled suddenly in minor. But in this play "truth and seeming" alone says little of the moral essence which exists in Oedipus himself. It tends to shelve the moral question a little too completely and neutralizes the full bitterness of the drama; for the innocence of Oedipus, though not the chief problem of the play, is certainly one of its most important assumptions.

It is unfortunate that it can no longer be an assumption to the modern reader. *Oedipus Rex* is, by this time, buried under so many layers of critical acumen, that anyone who dares believe in the innocence of Oedipus must answer formidable philologists and prove his mettle. Indeed, to those who consider Oedipus morally guilty of parricide and incest, there is little that can be said, for of course he committed these crimes, however unwittingly. Although Aristotle, who distinguishes carefully between the willful act and the unconscious act, would surely disagree, it might be urged that Oedipus' crimes are more in the religious than the purely legal or moral context, and that therefore, whatever his motivating intention, Oedipus himself is just as "hateful to the gods" — in the eyes, at least, of the ancient chthonian religion, with its blood-for-blood law, defended and exalted by daemonic hosts of Furies, with their attendant spirits, the *Alastores* and *Miastores*. But although this old religious attitude may have still prevailed among most Greeks of the time, it is doubtful how far and how simply Sophocles could have believed in the shadowy bloodhounds of murder in the middle of the Periclean age of reason. In 458, the Athenian public had witnessed the trial scene of the *Eumenides*, and had seen Orestes acquitted in the final court of appeal; and if Orestes, why not Oedipus? But there was no orthodox creed in these matters. Even if the gods themselves were supposed to hold Oedipus guilty (and apparently they did), Sophocles was free to differ. In fact, it was the office of the tragic poet to hold his own values and to use these, not the plastic figures of the gods, as his moral standard. That perhaps is the crux of the problem: in popular belief the gods were supposed to hate and punish Oedipus for what he actually did; Sophocles, on the contrary, has painted him as a man willfully innocent, passionately honest in motive, and full of heroic arete. And if he did so, he must have thought so, and he could not have concurred with the judgment of the gods.

It is precisely this difference of opinion between the gods and the poet, corresponding as it does to the disproportionate disposal of sin and punishment in the myth, which has made it so hard to adjust the apparent piety of Sophocles to the unmitigated pessimism inherent in the action of the *Oedipus*. To try to reconcile these opposites and draw therefrom a salutary lesson in sophrosyne is likely to lead to self-contradiction.[13] The gods cannot be just, if Oedipus is morally innocent. Yet, as the hero's character stands, this seems to be the case. The implications are so gloomy, and so different from the traditional picture of Sophocles, that it has been proposed that Sophocles must have had some compensating thought in mind, and that the play must be a treatise on either the nothingness of man, the necessity of religion, or sometimes both.[14]

Two other ways out of the dilemma have been suggested: predestination [15] and the hamartia theory.[16] To lift the burden of guilt from Oedipus, however, by saying that his fall was predestined by the gods is to destroy his innocence as well.[17] He becomes a cipher, and falls back into the theory of the nothingness of man. Besides, there is no evidence that such extreme fatalism ever existed among the Greeks until Stoic times.[18] The subtle interplay of divine and human character in the Homeric poems cannot be summed up as predestination; for throughout all classical Greek literature possession by a daimon indicates, as in the case of the Atlas Metope, not the annihilation but the illumination of individuality and moral responsibility.[19]

On the other hand, the theory of the tragic flaw, it is usually taken for granted, seems especially applicable to this play.[20] Yet, whenever it is applied, the familiar difficulties appear: one finds either too much or too little wrong with Oedipus. If he is wrong to have killed or married anybody, then his "error" or "failing" is hardly a trifling one, considering whom he killed and married; he becomes a considerable sinner. But if his only real failing is a hot temper, which no one could possibly call criminal, the degree of calamity to which it leads is as repellent as if Oedipus were entirely innocent. Either way, there is little moral satisfaction.

As was stated earlier, Oedipus was proverbial for sagacity and misfortune — for a fatal disequilibrium between inner gifts and outer circumstance. The effort to explain the latter by means of a tragic flaw has even led some critics to deny the sagacity of Oedipus. It has been said, for instance, that a god may have helped solve the riddle of the Sphinx and that if so Oedipus was not so clever as he thought.[21] But to a Greek, to say that a god helped him was only a way of saying that he was superhumanly wise; and that is exactly what the prologue symbolizes. Similarly, there seem to be no grounds for saying that, in dealing with the question of Laius' murder, Oedipus gets all the wrong answers.[22] To his sorrow, Oedipus gets all the right answers, and cannot be deterred from seeking them.

Yet his dominating characteristic is supposed to be a fiery spirit which corrupts his mind and destroys him.[23] Indeed, the character of Oedipus is complex, highly so; it involves extremes of gentleness or ferocity typical of heroic ages. Yet the fierce intensity of Oedipus must not be mistaken for mere rash violence. In the scene with Teiresias, the blind man of insight enters the stage at the king's summons and declares under pressure that Oedipus himself is guilty of Laius' blood. Oedipus instantly suspects a plot between the prophet and Creon to overthrow his rule, and the wrathful accusations which follow are incisive and violent.

Now in the *Antigone* it was observed that Creon's hasty suspicion of corruption was symptomatic of a tyrant. Oedipus too is a *tyrannos*, and the heat of his anger and his dire threats may do him little credit. But he is not therefore mentally corrupt. Why should he believe this preposterous statement about himself? Teiresias offered no proof for what he said, but based it simply upon his prophetic art, which is not sufficient in this case to convince even the naïve chorus.[24] The suspicion which rises in Oedipus, though wrong, is in no sense unnatural. The state was suffering from a curse, a religious pollution, which provided adequate opportunity for disorder and revolution.[25] If Creon had wished to assume the controls, he could have chosen no better time, and no better instrument than Teiresias to break the reputation of Oedipus, whose power was not hereditary but rested on his arete. Destroy his glory, and his rule is destroyed. No better conspiracy could have been formed; even the reluctance of Teiresias to speak could be interpreted as a conducive subtlety. From the king's standpoint, since he had as yet seen no real evidence for connecting himself with the crime, it was clearly a case of collusion.

Granted, however, that easy access of suspicion is in the character of the tyrant, Oedipus shows no other tyrannical features, as Creon does in the *Antigone*. He can be wonderfully gentle, and the people are devoted to him. His deep respect for Jocasta is completely untyrannical.[26] He never once, as Creon does when pressed, identifies the state with himself but, quite the opposite, pledges himself as a responsible and god-fearing ruler to its aid.[27] One of the proofs of the skillful dramatist is the ability to show the tension between the habitual behavior of a character and the unexpected traits which he betrays under the strain of the dramatic moment. Although Sophocles conceives Oedipus throughout as capable of considerable ferocity, the extreme outbursts at Teiresias and Creon are exceptions to his usual behavior. No one in the play ever generalizes about the king's dangerous temper. If the suspicion which causes these outbursts is a shade tyrannical, it is even more in keeping with clearheadedness and shrewdness.[28] Oedipus, as is characteristic of him, puts two and two together very quickly, and wants to know immediately whether Creon or he, Teiresias, thought up this plan.[29] Later, in the scene with Creon, the latter defends himself with the ready-made arguments on the undesirability of power, arguments which were already well known in Athens, and already under suspicion.[30] Sophocles has built the scene so subtly that Oedipus, although mistaken, violent, and unjustly angry, commands respect, while Creon, who happens to be innocent and telling the truth, sounds like a hypocrite. The king indeed threatens ominously, but he lacks the sheer arrogance of power characteristic of a real tyrant and unquestionably present in the Creon of the *Antigone*. And in any case, as has been pointed out,[31] Creon and Teiresias depart unharmed and in the end Oedipus even apologizes to his brother-in-law.[32]

The famous hamartia in actuality is a part of Oedipus' central virtue, as Ajax' pride and Antigone's stubbornness are parts of their virtue. These are not defects of their qualities, but evidence of their qualities, and the way in which they differ from other men. The very fact that they are different, and are meant to be, necessitates a certain degree of misunderstanding. They will not always ingratiate themselves as polite society would have them do. The hero is always a little difficult to live with. If a man is a law unto himself, society will probably conclude that he has no law. And that is sometimes true. But it is also true that the usual standard of man in general is not primarily law but living; and if the hero cares nothing for the rules of living, he is never able to make his inner law comprehensible to those who do.

The other faults that Oedipus is sometimes accused of, such as oversophistication and distrust of oracles, raise the whole question of impiety in the play. It has been stated again and again that the *Oedipus* was Sophocles' protest against the decay of religion and morality in the Periclean Age.[33] But in actuality, this belief had its origin in a misunderstanding of the character of Jocasta, for it is she who is primarily supposed to be a victim of these failings.

Jocasta exercises a curious charm over the reader of the play. Strictly speaking, she is unnecessary to the plot, for the actual information which she gives about the murder might have come from any source. But aside from the obvious fact that it is natural for her to be in the play, and that she greatly increases the tragic pathos by her presence, she occupies a special position in her relation to the hero. She completes him, and only toward the very end of the play does he free himself from a certain emotional dependency on her. Similarities appear between Antigone and Electra, Ismene and Chrysothemis, Tecmessa and Deianeira; but Jocasta is unique. She is queenly without being in the least heroic; womanly and warm, but without the yielding sweetness which we find in Deianeira. She has a suave and compliant way, but at the same time she is highly influential with Oedipus and commands deference from all. Not merely in word is she the wife and mother of the king; she is both and behaves like both simultaneously, with the profoundest ease and grace. It is almost as if she knew her own terrible secret.)

Her attitude toward religion has caused considerable worry. Her obvious skepticism about oracles of course exposes her to the suspicion that Sophocles, who supposedly believed in them, must have shaken his head as he wrote her lines.[34] On the other hand, when she is frightened by Oedipus' extreme agitation, she brings an offering to Apollo,[35] an act which led Wilamowitz to dismiss her as merely frivolous.[36] To doubt the veracity of an oracle is not, however, to be an atheist; nor does Sophocles seem really to have disapproved of his heroine. Indeed, it is far more likely that he shared her view, at least to some degree. In 429 B.C., Athens was far too full of fraudulent, beggarly oracle-mongers for any educated man to be utterly naïve in the matter.[37] Yet, superficially at least, Jocasta's attitude seems to be reproved. After the great scene in which she has successfully convinced Oedipus that Creon is guiltless of treason, Teiresias in all likelihood simply mistaken, and oracles always open to doubt, the chorus sings an ode which has been almost universally taken for a pronouncement ex cathedra by the poet himself:

But if any man walks haughtily in deed or word, with no fear of Justice, no reverence for the images of gods, may an evil doom seize him for his ill-starred pride, if he will not win his vantage fairly, nor keep him from unholy deeds, but must lay profaning hands on sanctities.

Where such things are, what mortal shall boast any more that he can ward the arrows of the gods from his life? Nay, if such deeds are in honor, wherefore should we join in the sacred dance?

No more will I go reverently to earth's central and inviolate shrine, no more to Abae's temple or Olympia, if these oracles fit not the issue, so that all men shall point at them with the finger. Nay, king, — if thou art rightly called, — Zeus all-ruling, may it not escape thee and thine ever-deathless power!

The old prophecies concerning Laius are fading; already men are setting them at nought, and nowhere is Apollo glorified with honours; the worship of the gods is perishing.[38]

These lines supposedly contain Sophocles' warning against the weakening of morals in Athens during the Peloponnesian War and reveal

the "psychological impulse which drove him to remonstrate with his
beloved Athenians: 'Look, that is man and his luck; look, that is God
and His wisdom.' " [39] But no Athenian, faced with the plague and the
other catastrophic events of the year 429, would have denied that man
was weak and the gods irresponsible and mighty. The year of the
plague and Pericles' death gave little evidence that the gods cared to
do anything good for man. If Sophocles had wished to reawaken public
religion, he could scarcely have chosen a worse way than by preaching
the careless power of the gods and the nothingness of man — the very
beliefs, in fact, which were themselves the concomitants of the Athenians' lawlessness and moral decay. [40] Out of their sufferings a general
irreverence did indeed arise, a suspicion that the world was utterly
irrational and that human actions made little difference to Providence.
But Sophocles seems to have felt the pressure of irrational evil at least
as early as the *Trachiniae*, and if he did not altogether lose his faith,
at least he altered it, and wrote far more bitter plays.

The ode certainly reflects the temper of the times, but it is not
spoken as a reproof, either to Jocasta or to the Athenians. It should
be remembered that these same choristers, in a preceding ode, had
refused outright to believe Teiresias' words:

> Never shall I, till I see clear proof,
> Take sides with accusers:
>
> .   .   .   .   .   .
>   Therefore, in my mind,
> Never shall you [Oedipus] incur the charge of villainy. [41]

Now, indeed, though themselves troubled by the doubtfulness of all
"divine matters," the choristers are far from being shocked by
Jocasta's complete dismissal of the art of prophecy and are inclined
to agree with her, though at the same time they intersperse little
prayers that the fallacies of religion may not be the whole truth. They
profess no faith with fervor. They threaten Zeus and Apollo with neg-
lect and contempt unless the oracle does come true, [42] which is as
much as to say: "I believe this prophecy is probably true, but if I see
no evidence, so much for prophecies and the gods in general." Their
address to Zeus is typical of an ancient kind of prayer which included
not merely supplications but also threats, in the event the supplications were not heard. [43] And at the same time, poured into the old

traditional shell, is the disquieting current of real unbelief, that same agnostic despair which Thucydides says accompanied the plague, the feeling among the people that the gods who permitted the world to go as it did deserved no respect. "Wherefore should I join in the sacred dance?" The poem is a popular reflection, not a credo by the poet.

It is also a little strange that the chorus at this point should pray against Oedipus, when they cry out to the gods to make the truth of their oracles manifest. But this is only further proof that the chorus in Sophocles represents the somewhat confused morality of the bourgeoisie, who can feel that the times want stabilizing and can see well enough that Oedipus has been violent with Creon and that Jocasta has been high-handed about prophets, but who cannot see the real implications of the scene or understand the genuine intelligence that is guiding the king and queen. Sophocles could not have written the scene as he did, if he thought that all it meant was what the chorus sings. This is not to say that the ode is not one of Sophocles' finest. The popular attitude appears in a sympathetic light, but it is a confused attitude,[44] a passive one, and not particularly noble. It praises purity in word and deed, humility and avoidance of hybris, free competition[45] and fair dealing; it hopes that the gods will defend their prerogatives. It is all quite proper. But it omits the whole question of action, which is the business of those on the stage, in contrast to those in the orchestra. It overlooks the moral question of the play, the fall of an innocent man; more important, it overlooks the heroic inward drive of arete which motivates that fall. It reflects the atmosphere in which the play grew, but it does not give the play's moral.[46]

Aspasia's court, with its free thinking and loose morals, has been suggested as a source for the character which Sophocles gave the queen,[47] and more particularly for her remark, "It's best to live at random."[48] There may indeed be a touch of Aspasia about Jocasta, as there may be a touch of Pericles in Oedipus. Within the framework of the play, Jocasta qualifies as an intellectually gifted woman, with powers of argumentation, clear judgment, and reason, all of which Aspasia possessed to some degree at least.[49] But there is no evidence for thinking that Sophocles differed greatly from the ingrained skepticism of his fellow Athenians. Sophocles was no stranger to Aspasia's society, and he was a friend of Pericles. Besides, a dubious attitude toward the oracle was no new thing in the Sophistic Age. Well before the free-thinking movement, the Alcmaeonids bribed the Delphic Oracle; Peisistratus trumped up a goddess to escort him to Athens; and The-mistocles, on the eve of Salamis, manipulated a few signs and wonders to get the people out of Athens.[50]

The general remarks of Plutarch about the religious attitude of Pericles [51] and the little anecdote that he tells to illustrate it show clearly the "intelligent piety" of the Periclean circle, an attitude which the devout and moral Plutarch seems to approve. Signs and wonders may not be devoid of all meaning, but they must not com-mand our minds. The refined Jocasta, like Pericles, refused the super-stitions of professional divination, or *mantike*, but was prepared to believe in a real sign from a god himself.[52] In her attitude we can see very clearly the meaning of man as the measure; the human judgment was regarded as sufficiently dignified to discriminate in divine matters, somewhat indeed as it was found to be during the Reformation. There was no impiety in such discrimination.[53] As for the Delphic Oracle, it maintained its reputation in general, despite some well-known frauds and mistakes. It still could be right, and popular belief favored its pronouncements. But there was no creed or faith which bound one to its infallibility.

By no Athenian standards whatsoever are the king and queen god-less or sinful in their religious attitude. In their "intelligent piety," the emphasis is assuredly on intelligence, but that fact only signalizes the more the inwardness of Sophocles' idea of divinity for man. If Jocasta views her religion intelligently, Oedipus surely views his intelligence religiously. At least, it builds itself within him into a daemonic drive on which he stakes all, in the conviction that it is his duty to know. It is a kind of inspiration with him; and Jocasta, though unable to match him in ultimate tenacity, is fully his match in argument. The long scene in which the two of them hold the stage alone is one of the most skillful and mighty dramatic *tours de force* in literature. It would have been easy for the secret to come out entirely, or for the scene to fall to the level of mere conversation through the narra-tion of past events or the discussion of the value of prophecy. But Sophocles has successfully avoided this pitfall by making both characters speak every time from their whole beings; each keeps the secret dark because he does not know the secret. Each knows only what he knows. Thus the argument becomes more a revelation of character than a discussion of an idea. Both characters aim at perfect honesty. Yet each is so isolated within the limits of his own knowledge that only so much of the central secret of the story emerges as serves to pique Oedipus further and build the ever-increasing suspense.

The dilemma which Jocasta faces at the beginning of the scene is this: if Teiresias is telling the truth, Oedipus is lost; if he is lying, as Oedipus first thinks, there is likelihood of collusion between him and her brother, Creon. Jocasta must prove that neither of these possibilities is true, and she handles the problem in a masterly way. She begs Creon off for the moment,[54] and the chorus helps her in the lyric scene which follows. Then, when Oedipus is quieter, she questions him, and when he says that Creon sent the seer to make this charge, she quietly ignores the implication of treason, and by the effective method of example, shows that seers can be wrong without being necessarily corrupt.[55] Even Delphi had been mistaken; why should they fear Teiresias? The effect of Jocasta's argument is different from her intention, however, for the story she tells makes it look as if Teiresias may be right.[56] At least, Oedipus begins to think so, but Jocasta, who believes the story of the six robbers,[57] still sees no reason to put faith in prophets. She will fetch the witness, to humor Oedipus, but she is sure of what she knows.[58] Even if he changes his tale, it will prove only that Delphi was wrong, for Laius was supposed to have been killed by his son! [59]

Jocasta has argued very successfully. Creon is absolved and Oedipus is calmer, though — not surprisingly — still slightly confused. A course of rational action has emerged. But the queen has been more successful for herself than for Oedipus. In arguing against Teiresias, she has unwittingly brought up evidence for him, by casually mentioning the three wagon ways where Laius was killed. Oedipus remembers killing a man at a meeting of three wagon ways, and it is now his turn to begin to be clearheaded. Jocasta, however, has convinced herself fully — and why should she not? — that the prophet is wrong. In the later scene when the messenger reports the death of Polybus from natural causes,[60] she is only the more convinced, as Oedipus is too, that all divination is inaccurate. It all fits perfectly with Jocasta's views of the matter. The genius of this famous plot lies in the fact that the evidence on which the various characters draw their various conclusions leads truly to those conclusions. There is no element of blind folly, hybris, or unwillingness to learn.

The fact that Oedipus and Jocasta are both wrong does not mean that they are both fools, or victims of a reprehensible "free-thinking" movement. They behave with thorough intelligence throughout. If the oracle comes true, that does not make the chorus wise. For the chorus would never have found out whether it were true, had not Oedipus been willing to stake everything, his very rights as a human being, on the effort to know. Intellectually Jocasta is a fitting mate for Oedipus. Consistently with the rest of the play, she is characterized almost entirely by her mental traits: she first appears interfering in a political quarrel, and her effectiveness in that scene depends not on her emotions (in contrast to Tecmessa, for instance), or on her moral will (as is the case with Antigone and Electra), but on her opinion. Throughout, we are confronted with Jocasta's intellectual gifts, her skill in argument, her views on life, religion, and the world at large. She is accustomed to dealing with men, and she deals with Oedipus well. She stands beside him throughout his ordeal, or almost, and the same tragedy which overtakes Oedipus overtakes her. Both think fast and clearly, but find truth too late and too bitter for them. Both had been careful: Jocasta had exposed her child, Oedipus had left Corinth. Both are disillusioned, first in the gods, and finally in themselves. And both can bear disillusion with the gods, but Jocasta cannot bear disillusion with herself.

The quest for knowledge is only tangential to the tragic action of the *Trachiniae*, but in the figure of Oedipus, the man of supreme insight, or *gnome*, the quest for knowledge is itself the tragic action. Hence the wonderful unity of the *Oedipus*. Knowledge about the situation becomes, in time, the hero's knowledge about himself, and, by implication, man's knowledge of himself. For Oedipus is Everyman; but unlike his medieval counterpart Oedipus remains an individual. But every man is an individual, a point which the Middle Ages forgot; to Sophocles man was heroic man, and the hero is above all an individual. In the figure of Oedipus we see once more that exquisite balance between the general and the particular, the norm and the variant, which lies behind so much Greek art, whether it be the Homeric epics, or fifth-century sculpture, or the formal, but stoutly independent little men of the vase painter Cleitias. As the scenes of *Oedipus* unfold, the hero also becomes aware that he is really in quest of himself and that the quest is dangerous. But then he is only the more confirmed in it. The blaze of fury with which he repulses the accusation of Teiresias is no more intense than the terrible determination with which he pursues the truth after Jocasta mentions the three ways, and he realizes he may be guilty.[61] It was perfectly possible for him to abandon the search then and there, by seizing on the fact that Laius was supposed to have been murdered by a group of robbers. The only eyewitness had said so, and "he said so in public, so he cannot take it back," as Jocasta points out.[62] Oedipus had every right, it may be supposed, to take Jocasta's word for it, and be safe. But the honesty of Oedipus is heroic, and the hero's law is his arete and his place in history (*kleos*). How could he, the great solver of riddles, abandon the greatest riddle, or trust to any hearsay? He was not instructed in the case of the Sphinx, and he will not be now. He must find out himself, and so he chooses action again, though rather grimly, and insists that this eyewitness be sent for.[63]

The attainment of true self-knowledge may be the most difficult and lonely of all forms of heroism. Certainly the *Oedipus Rex* contains the bitterest findings in all Sophocles' search for the meaning of humanity. Deianeira cried, "Why is knowledge terrible?" though she knew that the knowledge would hurt. How much more courageous is Oedipus in his insistence upon knowing, after he begins to suspect how fatal may be the knowledge that he seeks! His demand for the eyewitness is not the only occasion on which he enforces evidence against himself. He always has to enforce it. Teiresias wished to spare him,[64] but his good will was met with denunciation. And when it comes to the final issue, when the truth of the whole affair hangs upon a single word, Oedipus' white-hot urgency alone keeps the drama in motion. All other wills are stopped. Jocasta begs him to seek no further.[65] Even the old herdsman refuses to speak until threatened with torture, and his horror is pathetic as he realizes he must say the fatal word:

> Alas, I stand on the dread brink of speech.

And Oedipus answers:

> And I of hearing. Yet it must be heard.[66]

The answer is tense and final; Oedipus knows well what he is going to hear, but his spirit does not desert him. The inner law works; the hero does not leave his task.

Because he really was a parricide, and incestuous, Oedipus can hardly emerge as a pattern of heroic virtue as Antigone does. But Sophocles has not forgotten to invest his hero with that kind of arete which the myth and his traditional sagacity afforded him. It is a kind of intellectual supremacy and honesty therewith, which cannot but recall Thucydides' view that the genius of a ruler lay in four things: "To know what is required and be able to interpret it; to be patriotic and above corruption."[67] Oedipus is not, as has been supposed,[68] a passive and suffering protagonist, in contrast to Antigone. The whole quest for knowledge implies action for Oedipus, as it did for Deianeira. Jocasta, near the climax, sees Oedipus' insistent search as action:

> Yet hearken, I beseech you, *do* this not![69]

In essence, the effect of these characters' intelligence on themselves is very similar to the effect of Ajax' arete on himself: they are betrayed and destroyed by it. Excellence, not failure, is the source of tragedy. It is not the confusion of Oedipus which leads him to the terrible secret, but his clarity. And this fact is what is symbolized in the curse which he lays on the murderer. It is the curse of self-destruction which every heroic soul endures. No symbol could be more apt or complete. Oedipus' keen consciousness recognizes his position the minute the truth begins to dawn;[70] the significance of the curse comes clear to him. True, as Bowra says, the curse is real, and Oedipus is his own victim.[71] But the curse is in character, and that is why it is real. A curse, like an oracle, is an expression of what is true.

In a similar way the supernatural factor in the motivation operates through character. There is no divine interference in the play; "Apollo knows the future, but does not create it." [72] The only difference between human and divine knowledge is that the latter is not limited by time, and therefore may see all things as finished. Time, in the later plays of Sophocles, plays the part of a mediator between the divine and human. In the *Oedipus*, however, time has no special function, except as the road upon which the mind travels in order to find out what is timelessly true: "Time has found you out," says the chorus, and one is perhaps justified in classifying time in this play as one of the numerous determinants of evil and earthly sorrow. But what really functions is the mind of man, and its success reveals its failure. The failure has been emphasized, in terms of human nothingness, the folly of human wisdom, the gap between man and the gods, the emptiness of human good fortune. But these facts were all well known before Sophocles. Rather the essential interest lies in the strength of Oedipus, the keenness of human wisdom which can find out its own secret, the function of a divine necessity within man which makes a standard of its own and holds the standard to be worth more than empty good fortune. The darkness and discouragement of the play, on the other hand, come from the bitterness of the truth itself, and the fact that the arete of Oedipus brings him no praise for the victory over his own mystery and no reward for his courage and intellectual integrity. The gods within man are at work, but such is the circumstance of man's being that they bring him no glory.

The action of the play itself, therefore, is motivated by the free will of the hero, which culminates in the act of self-blinding. Bowra tries to show that it is his daimon which drives him to this deed, in order to fulfill the will of the gods; [73] but there is no will of the gods, so far as Oedipus is concerned, except insofar as his own will possesses a divine force. The Olympians have not willed his fall; they have foretold it. To say that the gods are responsible, as Oedipus does, [74] means at most that they permit life to be as it turns out to be. The gods in the *Trachiniae* and *Oedipus* seem little more than the animated power of circumstance and symbols of the fatal nexus of limitations within which man acts and suffers. When Oedipus cries, "Apollo has accomplished these evils," he is referring to the whole concatenation of events, including the oracle that symbolizes his total fate. The ineluctable element is not a mysterious, far-off, causal Fate, or the will of Apollo, but life itself. Within the predestined necessity of living in this world, Oedipus has acted with a free will: "My own hand struck the blow," and he gives his own reasons.[75] He still has reasons, and he is free to treat himself as he will.[76]

Oedipus is crushed by what he learns, yet his learning is a kind of victory — a Pyrrhic one, of course, in which the victor suffers most. But in the moral sphere, a Pyrrhic victory is surely the greatest. Oedipus hoped the answer would be more cheerful, as Ajax hoped to win the arms. But ultimately Ajax strove to keep his honor unstained, at any price; with equal fervor Oedipus strove for clear sight. And in the end he has it; Ajax cries, "darkness my light" — and Oedipus says to his eyes, "in dark hereafter . . . see."[77] For both a veil has fallen. It is hard to say why Oedipus blinds himself, but the answer is not self-punishment. As Ajax seeks to manifest his true self by death, Oedipus seeks to know his true self by shutting out the deceptions of the outer world, which he has completely seen through. He is still seeking knowledge, as the dying Ajax sought honor. He would even stuff up his ears [78] that he might contemplate the more relentlessly the evil truth he has found. If his confidence about learning was overweening, he certainly does not repent, but rather, like Don Giovanni, he goes to hell affirming his life principle. He swore to know himself, and in the end he stands by that knowledge.

The kind of tragedy with which we have been dealing in the two middle plays must, if viewed squarely, give the death blow to the time-honored classicist conception of the simple, pious Sophocles. No amount of preconception can drive these two gloomy pieces into a shape consistent with a religious attitude of faithful trust in the justice of the gods. The chorus maintains its ground-bass of casuistical, popular morality, but the active and suffering souls play tragic variations upon it; and insofar as the gods appear or are mentioned at all, they contrive evil. But the gods as personages are not in the plays; they do nothing that life could not do. Whatever divinity meant to Sophocles, it was not summed up in the public religion of Athens; nor does the disillusion and sorrow of these two plays center around a fear that Zeus, Athena, or Apollo may not be perfectly just and well-disposed toward man. The gods — witness Athena in the *Ajax* — could be for Sophocles bleak symbols indeed. The fear is rather that human excellence, which has its own divinity, may not be sufficient to assert itself in the face of the irrational evil which descends without plan or justice, and whence no one knows. It is the fear that a man's very being may be taken from him.

The inner light of Ajax and Antigone preserves them like gods in their massive stature; perhaps in the earlier days of the Periclean Age man looked more essentially heroic. The most heroic, really supreme arete rose by its own compulsion to a height that made it larger than life and too large to live. It destroyed itself by asserting itself. Now a change has come. Man can still destroy himself; give him the heroic stuff and he must. But where is the power and the glory? Deianeira dies in disgrace, completely pitiable, but scarcely pitied. The great and noble Oedipus, who solved the riddle of the Sphinx by that divinity which attended his intelligence, becomes an outcast, hateful to the gods, and really was so from the beginning. In both cases the ugly truth was always there, and the knowledge of it comes too late. Some have urged that Deianeira might have thought better of the plan in time, but that is quibbling: some such catastrophe lay in the texture of the events and people anyway. The case is made even clearer in the *Oedipus*, where the hero could have been no better off for finding out any sooner. This is not melodrama. It is a revelation of the evil lot of man. Let him have all the equipment for glory and honor, let him deserve it by the best lights known to his heroic soul, the clearest knowledge he can come to is self-loathing, because of what he really is. The greatest effort to do good has ended in evil, and not merely the evil of self-destruction, which is bitter enough for Ajax and Antigone, but a new kind of evil — the evil of an unbearable self for which one is not responsible.

The *Oedipus* is the fullest expression of this conception of tragedy. Sophocles seems to have experimented often in this period with the problem of unwilling crime. Thus in the lost *Niptra*, which was probably composed about the time of the *Trachiniae*,[79] the plot seems closely to have resembled that play.[80] Odysseus, warned by an oracle that he would die by his son's hand, finds out too late that Telemachus is not his only son, but that the leader of the hostile invaders of Ithaca, against whom he fights, is really Telegonus, his son by Circe. He is slain by Telegonus, who is then revealed. It is impossible to say whether or not this play contained implications as broad as those of the *Oedipus;* probably it was of lesser scope and more like the *Trachiniae.*[81] The same kind of action was probably the subject of another lost play, the *Thyestes.*[82] On the basis of an oracle, Thyestes commits involuntary incest and is destroyed. Here is perhaps the germ of *Oedipus Rex.* The *Niptra* could have contained little sense of guilt unwillingly incurred; we have the innocent sufferer, but not the unbearable self. Thyestes, we may suppose, suffered the torments of the unbearable self, after he recognized his crime. Sophocles wrote two plays on this theme,[83] though what the other contained we do not know. But the problem of internal innocence and external guilt was coming to a climax, and only reaches a solution in *Oedipus at Colonus.*

In all the plays of this period there must have been much bitterness. The accusations against the injustice of the gods, which we find in the end of the *Trachiniae,* must have been echoed in other shattering scenes of recognition.[84] It seems hardly possible that Sophocles could have had a reputation in Athens for simple, serene piety between the years 436 and 429. Unfortunately, those years are less documented by any contemporary evidence than almost any others of the Periclean Age. Herodotus broke off long before, the work of the contemporary historian Hellanicus is in fragments, and it was not the business of inscriptions to record the leading dramatist's state of mind. Euripides' plays of this period are either chauvinistic or are about feminine psychology. The nearest thing we have to a commentary is Thucydides' description of the plague, whose psychological effect on the Athenians, as already pointed out, is a fitting background for the treatment of evil in the *Oedipus Rex.* The failure of all human and sacred recourses, and the resulting abandonment of faith and religious scruples in the face of the inevitable [85]— which seemed to the historian the worst aspect — point to a time when simple answers to the problem of evil are duly and necessarily put to shame, and a sensitive and intellectually powerful man must think it out anew.

Sophocles' interest in irrational evil antedated the plague. Indeed, it fascinated him all his life. But in the middle plays the problem is especially urgent, and in the *Oedipus* it is the central theme. Nevertheless, toward the end of the play there is a slight hint of a new theme, an unexpected turn which does not relieve the gloom — even perhaps intensifies it — but which later will become very important.

Sophocles always has his hands on a vast number of ideas which he interweaves as the poetic impulse seizes him, and whereas they may be orientated in one direction in one play, they may take a wholly new one in the next. In the end of the triumphant *Antigone*, we found, casually introduced in connection with Creon, the motif of learning too late, which dominates the *Trachiniae*, and becomes in the *Oedipus* a vehicle for the profoundest symbolism. Now, in the end of the *Oedipus*, for the first time, and very tentatively, is sounded the motif of endurance. It comes in the great speech which Oedipus gives just after Jocasta's despairing exit, a speech which the anonymous author of the *Treatise on the Sublime* might well have taken as a pattern of sublimity. This speech seems, and is generally thought to be, the climax of Oedipus' blindness. But there is insight in this blindness. A kind of reckless pride speaks, but it is a true and exalted pride, and proclaims man's dignity on the edge of ruin:

> Now let burst forth what will! But as for me,
> Though it be lowly, I will know my breed.
> She, womanlike, letting her thoughts run high,
> Blushes upon my low-born ignominy:
> But I, holding myself the child of fortune
> Who gives me good, I shall not be ashamed!
> She is the mother bore me; and my brothers
> In blood, the Months, have seen me small and great.
> Being so derived, I will not flee, nor turn
> Another; and so fail to find my race.[86]

This is the boast — like Deianeira's "Why is knowledge terrible?" — that man can endure the knowledge of his real fate. But from Oedipus it comes forth in a thundering challenge. All the threads meet here — the heroic search and its unflinching honesty; the contempt for all but the truth; man and his fate and the months of his life; the universe, in fact, seen whole and pedestaled on the most exalted dignity; and finally, the individual himself, who would not be another no matter what his fate, but boasts that he dares know all. It is the profession of endurance which concerns us. For it must be noted that Oedipus does not die, like Jocasta. He does endure his knowledge, and though he blinds himself to confirm that knowledge, he lives with it. Twice later he seems to refer to what he must and will endure,[87]

but his words are vague, and we are not meant to attach much significance to them. In the theatre they would count for little. The disgrace and grief of the end are unmitigated; but the motif of endurance is there, and it paves the way for the last stage of Sophocles'
development, with its resurgence of faith and its new evaluation of
the human spirit.

PART FOUR

TRAGIC ENDURANCE

E più e men che re era in quel caso.
— Dante

VIII

TRIAL BY TIME: ELECTRA

THE great speech of Oedipus, in which he calls himself the child of fortune, is the first trumpet call of a new attitude. There, on the brink of the disastrous knowledge which he had so sternly pursued, a new vista for a moment unfolds for Oedipus; it is as if the poet wrote beyond his intention and gave a glimpse of the longer view which Oedipus was to achieve in time. Sophocles could hardly have seen twenty-five years ahead and known the lines he would write in his last work. But he was growing with his greatest character, as Goethe grew with Faust, and he could not have failed to have some foreknowledge of his spiritual directions. These lines give only a glimpse; and it passes immediately, leaving the picture of the shattered king, whose godlike intelligence had brought him power and position, and had then taken away much more than it had given.

Yet Oedipus had declared his dignity. He boasted that he could endure complete knowledge of himself, and he was to make good that boast in time. Like Faust, he too had to become blind before he could say to the passing hour, "Yet, tarry, you are so beautiful!" To Mephistopheles, these words were ridiculous, for to him Faust's last hour seemed the poorest and weakest of his life. But Mephistopheles was a spirit of denial and did not understand the essence of moral salvation, which is the paradox of strength in weakness. In Christian theology, the devil loses the game simply because he has no idea of what the soul may achieve through humility, time, and suffering. The concept of Purgatory is the Christian answer to the irreconcilable poles of Heaven and Hell. There are stories of the devil in Paradise, in Hell, and in Heaven; but we never hear of him in Purgatory. In Purgatory, time, which can destroy the flesh, functions also as a weapon which the soul may use against the satanic universe.

Sophocles' last period is "purgatorial," in that it deals with the soul's use of time. The emphasis, however, is not on the purging of sin, for the characters are not sinful; the emphasis is on heroic endurance in the loneliness of heroic rightness. This new aspect of human strength, the ability to live morally in time, motivates the last three extant plays and rises to a climax in the *Oedipus at Colonus*. Compared with that tremendous apocalypse, the crown of Sophocles' work, the *Electra* and even the *Philoctetes* are mere studies.

These plays might be denied the title of tragedy; they begin with the shock which in the earlier works had been catastrophic. But tragedy means many things. In the *Ajax* and *Antigone* arete triumphed by a kind of phoenix death: out of the fiery ordeal arose an indestructible historic vision. In the *Trachiniae* and *Oedipus Rex*, although human virtue fulfilled its function without failure, life itself seemed an indignity no virtue could surmount. The three last works are very mysterious for all their brightness of atmosphere. Man's best has again begun to count. His inward divinity brings him closer to the gods themselves, or — since that phrase is perhaps meaningless — to a larger transcendent idea of the divine and eternal, which ratifies and seals the striving divinity of the human, or at least of the heroic sphere.

Looking back to Homer, Sophocles could see how much the *Iliad* differed in its basic assumptions from the *Odyssey*, supposedly the work of the poet's old age. The *Odyssey*'s greater detachment from life is only a symptom of the essential qualities of its hero, who is almost the opposite of Achilles.[1] To Achilles, life was a means to glory; he approached it like a citadel to be stormed; it would be complete at the moment he showed the greatest contempt for it — and that moment came with the slaying of Hector. But to Odysseus, life was an end in itself; it offered the eternally fascinating puzzle of experience and knowledge, and it would never be complete. Achilles is the One and Odysseus the Many: arete sums up the former, but Odysseus has many virtues, the two most important of which are constantly referred to in his two chief epithets — "full of counsel" and "long-enduring." The latter indicates a strength to get through life successfully, and the former an intellect capable of deciphering its problems and understanding experience. The association of knowledge with endurance is as fundamental to the *Odyssey*[2] as the association of heroism and early death is to the *Iliad*. The arete of Achilles underlay Sophocles' early tragic conceptions, Ajax and Antigone; in the last period, it is a new kind of arete, the arete of Odysseus, which endows the hero with greatness. Once more, the Greek word for this quality, *tlemosyne*, admits of no single translation embracing all its meanings of endurance, courage, skill, and self-control. In Sophocles, tlemosyne is all that Odysseus was, and more. The idea is developed in the later works with every possible moral subtlety.

The case could be argued that Odysseus has too much flexibility for a real hero, and true it is that he became in later times the prototype of the talker and shifty politician for those old-guard aristocrats who looked to Achilles and Ajax as the true types of ideal manhood.[3] The man who prefers to live to fight another day claims no special heroic posture; yet he does assert an indefinite value in himself and in life as such.[4] The humanist, it may be noted, thinks and lives by just such indefinite values, which become more elusive the more they are defined, but which, when viewed obliquely, assert themselves as potent verities, obscured but not destroyed by logic. After the merciless and inescapable logic with which Sophocles faced life in *Oedipus Rex*, it is consistent with the unreasoned resilience of the human spirit that an indefinite but positive value again begins to affix itself to his estimate of man. His heroism is becoming more humane. The irrational evil of the gods is met by an equally irrational but entirely religious assertion from the human side — an assertion of life, instead of death, as the means of revealing the divine in man. Such an assertion, while it fails to exalt such monolithic and unmistakable figures as Achilles or Ajax, yet raises a greater mystery perhaps, and presents shapes which like the others achieve an equal, though less spectacular, grandeur.

In Sophocles, the two great virtues of Odysseus are no longer characteristic fixities, but develop into a moral process. "Tragic knowledge," in these late plays, means something different from what it did to earlier heroes. Antigone died for what she knew; her knowledge was true, but static. Deianeira died because of what she found out. Now the finding out process itself becomes the essence, and knowledge is not too late, because the hero can endure. Time enters into the fate of man as a mysterious and healing element; suffering is still intense, but time and the faithful act of living bring salvation.

But the mere ability to stay alive is not heroism. Odysseus himself often seems a little marred by it. It is the standard of moral living which counts, and Attic tragedy is a more fitting vehicle for moral standards than the old romantic epic. Odysseus surmounts physical difficulties; Electra, Philoctetes, and Oedipus surmount physical and moral ones, for each has a moral reason to stay alive — for Electra, it is vengeance; for Philoctetes, his own unknown potentiality; for Oedipus, the vindication of his arete. Arete is still the basic motivation, though it takes numerous forms. And to fit this view of life, Sophocles, with his characteristic sensitivity to the demands of inner and outer form, drifts more and more into the molded and supple shape of the later drama, with its broken lines, enjambement, three-way dialogue, and lyric that melts easily in and out of the spoken parts.

As early as in the *Ajax* Sophocles played on the theme of truth and seeming, shadow and substance;[5] in *Oedipus Rex* the deceptive aspects of the world assist in bringing about the catastrophe. Where the revelation of truth brought death with glory in the early plays and unmitigated destruction in the middle ones, now, instead of the fearful suspicion that all life may be deceptive, comes a change of spirit: the world is indeed a dream, but it may unfold a greater truth; man's life is deceptive, and he a shadow; but behind the shadow may be substance, and behind the deception, truth.

In these later works come the first notes of that serenity for which Sophocles was famous.[6] They do not come all at once; there are developments within the last period as there were in the other two. The first play, the *Electra*, is by no means an adequate expression of all that Sophocles was working toward. The *Electra* involves only a very small degree of either serenity or tragic knowledge, and its significance is far slighter than in the other two plays. Nevertheless, the element of tlemosyne is strong, and points the way to the *Philoctetes*.

Sophocles' drama of *Electra* has always been the great enigma. Critics like Jebb, and others who accredit Sophocles with various forms of religious orthodoxy, have been seriously embarrassed in their attempts to explain the moral attitude of this amazing piece. The story of how Electra and Orestes avenged the murder of their father by slaying their mother was followed, as everyone knew, by the story of Orestes' consequent madness and pursuit by the Furies, until he was finally purified of his guilt in the court of the Areopagus at Athens. What did Sophocles mean by allowing his Orestes to do the dreadful deed scot-free, as if it were something admirable? The characters are drawn in such a way that the hero, or at least the heroine, could be treated as guilty of all manner of breaches of sophrosyne; all the usual "faults" appear. But even the closest adherents of the hamartia theory are peculiarly lacking in suggestions about a play whose heroine, however stubborn or extreme she may be, gets everything she wants, murders her mother, and goes off in triumph. There is not the sign or hint of a Fury; Orestes is a stainless hero, and the play has been scornfully called a "mixture of matricide and good spirits."

Nothing could be further from the truth. The classic assumptions about Sophocles nowhere reveal their fallacy and sterility so completely as they do in the case of the *Electra*. Some have tried to read the Furies into the play, or claim that Sophocles thought any crime was justified if it was commanded by a god.[7] Others, in a reckless confusion as to what Sophocles was pious about, maintain that he was too religious to change a sacred myth. Anthropologists speculate on the relative importance of mothers and fathers in early Greece, and arrive at different answers. Some call the play art for art's sake and drop the moral issue. Finally, there are those who, feeling the need for sin and punishment in a tragedy, deflect the tragic essence from Electra to Clytaemnestra, as Creon in the *Antigone* is sometimes regarded as the tragic hero, because it is he who has been wrong and comes to final grief. But whereas Creon can perhaps claim a little sympathy at the end, the characters of Clytaemnestra and Aegisthus are of such manifest and unrelieved blackness that one must recall the truism of Aristotle, that there is nothing tragic in seeing a thorough villain get his just deserts.[8] Indeed, Aristotle'e observation is especially *à propos*. For if the *Electra* is rightly to be called a tragedy — and no other name suits its strained and weary atmosphere so aptly — its tragic core must not be sought in the matricide, which for Sophocles was not the climax but merely the denouement.

When this play was produced, Aeschylus had been dead perhaps forty years, and his *Oresteia* was already a classic monument in the religious and cultural history of Athens. For in that trilogy, Athens had, perhaps for the first time, stepped in her own person, as it were, upon the tragic stage, and in her favorite role of defender and dispenser of justice. Whoever should write again the story of Orestes would have to remember that the intense scenes of the *Choephori* were unforgettably imbedded in the minds of his audience. No one could have known better than Sophocles did that Aeschylus, though a little stiff at times, a little archaic and ritualistic in his approach to the drama, was possessed of an incomparable dramatic genius; the archaic style was not merely a prelude to the achievement of the Periclean times, but complete in itself, an early efflorescence, but as Aeschylus left it, perfect. So far as the tragedy of Orestes went, the *Choephori* could hardly be improved. There was the prologue, with the sorrowful prayer of Orestes at the neglected tomb of Agamemnon, the meeting between Electra and Orestes, and the great moment when mother and son face each other, when Orestes wavers a moment and Pylades, recalling the god's injunction, pronounces his one utterance and decides the issue. Finally, there is the last speech of Orestes, when the Furies are coming and the web of bloodshed and misery seems to stretch interminably into the future. It is all complete; the rest is lyric and invocation of the thirsty spirit of the murdered king, where the roots of the poetry go deeply into the ancient chthonian substratum of Greek religion, seeking the moral impetus by which Clytaemnestra and her paramour shall die.

Sophocles never intended to supplant this masterpiece, or "correct" it with a more civilized version, such as Euripides wrote. Why, then, did he write a play about Orestes at all, when the perfect one was already written? The answer is, he did not; he wrote a play about Electra, who does little more than appear in Aeschylus. He begins indeed with Orestes, but in what a different spirit! Instead of the lonely exile, returning with his only friend to the tomb of his slain father, the Orestes of Sophocles enters before the palace in a bright, clear atmosphere, accompanied not only by Pylades, but also by his old Pedagogue who introduces him to the landmarks of his homeland, whence he had been sent in infancy by Electra, to escape the hands of Aegisthus and Clytaemnestra. It is early morning, the birds are singing, and Orestes is full of confidence and hope, anxious to do the deed of deliverance; only after planning his vengeance in detail does he mention the tomb of Agamemnon. Orestes has come not to suffer, but to triumph. He is singularly free of any emotional involvement with the situation and views it like a stranger or a god. The Pedagogue too is significant, for he is a visible symbol of the young hero's *paideia*, his training for greatness. In a few lines Orestes is depicted, chivalrous and noble, with no problem and no special dramatic interest; he retires shortly and remains away until he is needed. He is so unlike the rest of the play in tone and character that it seems almost as if Sophocles conceived him as a sort of frame for Electra, who is the real tragic picture; the frame is formal and chaste and does not partake of the colors of the picture, but only emphasizes them, as a frame should do. Orestes hears Electra's voice briefly in the beginning, and in the end he meets and consoles her. But he is scatheless and outside all the evil, and obviously more a symbol than a character.

The contrast of Electra's entrance is a carefully designed shock. After the calm air of Orestes and his friends, there suddenly appears the tortured and lonely figure, who chants a long monody in restless meter, and calls the "holy light" to witness her agony. Electra and Orestes are ill-matched by the standards set by Aeschylus, who unites sister and brother in grief and vengeance. Sophocles' Electra is alone, and when she is finally allowed to meet her brother, Sophocles devises the scene with characteristic subtlety, so that it resembles less the meeting of two people with a common cause than the meeting of a person with an image of an unexpected inner self. In any case, what here in the prologue is intense contrast becomes later in the recognition scene a mysterious revelation. Orestes does not join Electra in her suffering, but she rather is able to join him in his strength and victory.

The lyric dirge, which, consistently with the plastic style of the later drama, supplants the more formal parodos of the chorus, allows us to gain direct insight into the soul of Electra before her scene with her sister, Chrysothemis, in which she appears in a harsher and less sympathetic light. In these lyric portions we see her from within, as she seems to herself, pouring out her faithfulness to her father's memory, her hatred of Aegisthus and Clytaemnestra, her passionate adherence to her own anguish — while the chorus gently dissuades her, in well-worn terms, from increasing her own misery by a stubborn resistance to those in power. But Electra defends her position. The sight of Aegisthus in power compels her not to yield, but to resist the more. "In the midst of evils," she says, "there is every need to make evil one's daily bread." [9] She cannot be gentle and polite. She does not say exactly why that which compels others to obedience compels her to rebellion, but the reason becomes clear through the action of the play.

The scene with Chrysothemis, on the other hand, shows us how Electra looks to others — stubborn, sullen, insanely rebellious, even masochistic. Chrysothemis has done the sensible thing, accepted the fact that Agamemnon is dead and Aegisthus is her master. Therefore, she lives in the palace, dressed finely and well fed, while Electra starves in rags. Out of friendliness, Chrysothemis has come to warn her sister that Aegisthus is planning to thrust her into the dungeon to be rid of her.[10] Chrysothemis would gladly do anything she could against Aegisthus, but what could she do? Let Electra be wise and yield, and cease to oppose those stronger than herself. It is wonderful indeed how completely the weak and shallow Chrysothemis has won generations of readers to her side. Electra, they feel, is self-willed and wearisome, and indeed she should learn the lesson of sophrosyne. For some reason, Sophoclean scholars have, almost to a man, concluded that Chrysothemis, though weak, is fundamentally right, and that Sophocles spoke personally through this, almost the least attractive of his characters. Heroism is always ill-timed; but a plea for common sense, whenever it is made, invariably finds sympathizers.

Electra, however, scorns the advice and with her bitter replies drives Chrysothemis back into the palace. As in the case of other Sophoclean protagonists, her violent impatience with advice-givers who understand nothing has been conceived as brutality, blindness, or irreligion. But it is none of these; it rises from an imperative moral conviction, upon which Sophocles must have set the seal of his approval; for Electra is victorious in the end, and there is no trace of her harshness' being punished.

The exit of Chrysothemis brings the first third of the play to a close, and as yet there has been no real action or major conflict. Sophocles seems to have been anxious to let Electra's position be well defined and rounded off before plunging her into the actual events of the play. There is none of the quick deftness of the *Antigone*, where a similar picture of two sisters with equally sharp contrasts is drawn in ninety-nine lines. Instead there is a detailed molding, with infinite chiaroscuro and echoes of varying speech-tone in the verse, so that, as with a living person, one feels one knows Electra, but not what she signifies. It is easier to see Antigone's significance than to understand how she could be flesh and blood.

The portrait complete, Sophocles begins the principal action with a verbal duel between Electra and Clytaemnestra — her "mother no-mother." Of the three dramatists, Sophocles makes the most definite use of the political implications of the murder of Agamemnon. To Aeschylus, Aegisthus is a usurper and Clytaemnestra a murderess, but they are woven into a gigantic nexus of crime already generations old; Agamemnon himself was not guiltless, though his murderers are worse; the problem is one of crime. Euripides, on the other hand, made less of the criminality of the royal pair and showed Clytaemnestra as a mild, weary woman, mellowing with time and full of human sympathies, while his Aegisthus is by no means unappealing. But Sophocles drew them as tyrants who, having slain the good, lawful king, now ruled by terror alone, fearful themselves of the return of Orestes, and fearful even of the helpless Electra who daily reminds them of their crime. The debate between mother and daughter about Clytaemnestra's justification for killing Agamemnon has been taken too much at face value. Herein the critics have tried to find the answer to the moral problem of the play, but their search is made difficult by the fact that Electra seems to condemn the law of blood for blood while her actions confirm it.

Clytaemnestra urges that her destruction of Agamemnon was justified because he had sacrificed Iphigenia in order to obtain a wind to Troy and thus "gratify his brother." [11] Electra answers:

> But if he did so — for I'll even grant
> Your tale, that he did that to please his brother,
> Should he have died at your hands? By what law?
> Beware of making this a law for men,

Lest it bring grief and penitence to you.
For if we are to slay each other, you
Should die first, if you get what you deserve.
Take care, then, lest you urge a hollow plea.[12]

Such are Electra's words, but the point of that debate lies not in the arguments — all of them old and stale as both characters know — but in the fact that Clytaemnestra is forced constantly to take refuge in these rationalizations, failing which she has only force left; while Electra, who is honest and does not fear force, is free to say what she will, to mock, taunt, and even to threaten. Once more we see the bewildering irony of Sophocles: Clytaemnestra protests her innocence with labored consistency and reveals her corruption in every line. Electra makes no attempt to formulate a real answer; she replies almost flippantly in her supreme scorn, but with the voice of the free and heroic individual. Essentially, it is the freedom of the enslaved Electra in contrast to the suppressed terror of the queen, trapped in her own bestiality, which makes this strange scene true. Clytaemnestra's fear is paramount. She originally entered because a terrifying dream had driven her to make a propitiatory sacrifice to the shade of Agamemnon; [13] now, as the scene with her daughter reaches an impasse, she turns to the altar of Apollo where, like Macbeth, she cannot say "amen," but utters dark prayers hinting the death of both her children.

The remaining scenes of the play rise steadily in tension almost to the end. The long *rhesis*, or set speech, of the Pedagogue, relating the fictitious death of Orestes, is followed by a second scene with Chrysothemis where once more the famous Sophoclean irony is used to its fullest effect. Chrysothemis has found a lock of hair on Agamemnon's grave and has guessed it to be Orestes'. She is right, of course, but Electra, who has heard the Pedagogue's tale, convinces her that her brother is dead. Such passion and authority are in her words that she almost makes the audience feel that Chrysothemis was a fool to have thought Orestes had returned, as well as utterly gauche and irresponsible to have come bringing optimistic news at such a time. Even in her right moments Chrysothemis is made to bear out her morally unrealistic character. To the audience, as to Electra, Orestes is dead; Sophocles has so far prevailed that Chrysothemis seems the deluded one. That is because a new and greater truth is arising in Electra:

now that there is no further hope of salvation from without, she is ready to seek the means to salvation within; she will kill Aegisthus herself. Chrysothemis is shocked and retires from any participation in the deed, but Electra persists, and prepares herself.

Then follows the recognition scene, where Orestes in disguise presents the supposed urn of his own ashes to his sister, and finally is so moved by her convulsive lament that he reveals himself. The marvels of this episode are well known. With the coming of Orestes, the play is virtually complete and the frame has met all around. Orestes, without even a shudder, slays first Clytaemnestra and then Aegisthus, and the play ends with a triumphant cry of deliverance from the chorus.

Euripides objected violently to this play and wrote his own *Electra* in answer to it.[14] Presumably Sophocles, in this work at least, was not fully comprehended even by his contemporaries. Euripides, no less than modern scholars, was blinded by the tremendous authority of Aeschylus, who seemed to have fixed the myth's outlines permanently; and morally his own play differs from that of Aeschylus only in that he can find in the matricide no justice at all. For him as for Aeschylus, the murder of Clytaemnestra constitutes the major problem, and the belief that it did so for Sophocles is what has led scholars astray. They feel that Electra and Orestes must be wrong, and either conclude that the play is a failure because Sophocles apparently does not agree,[15] or else hunt diligently through the text for minute relics of the Aeschylean moral, and failing to find them, make them up.[16]

Some indeed have recognized that the vengeance of Orestes is treated by Sophocles as a perfectly justifiable deed, but are still so far influenced by Aeschylus as to feel that this vengeance is the main point of the drama, and that Sophocles' purpose was to justify either the "sacred story," [17] or else a kind of hard world-order, in which occasional matricide may be a means to a moral society, sanctified by an unmerciful Divine Justice.[18] But Greek myths were not holy writ. They were the values and thoughts of the early Greeks in dramatic form, and they were always subject to reinterpretation, and even, in the course of time, revision. Thus Euripides' attack on the story of Electra was a confession of his inability to understand it as it stood; for Sophocles, however, it had a meaning, which he extracted. He did not defend it, as a fundamentalist defends the Bible. Neither did he defend any merciless divine world order, for when the world seemed too cruel to him, he said so, as he did in the *Trachiniae* and the *Oedipus Rex*. Sophocles championed neither myth nor matricide; his eyes were fixed elsewhere.

That this is true is proven by the focus of the tragic conflict. In the *Choephori*, there is conflict between Orestes' conscience and the command of Apollo. But in Sophocles' play, there is nothing of the sort.[19] It is, in fact, just this lack of conflict which has occasioned all the embarrassment. Vengeance runs a straight course; its justice is never questioned, but assumed for a purpose. The case is similar to that of the *Oedipus Rex*, which must not be approached as if the main problem were the guilt or innocence of Oedipus; his innocence is assumed as the first premise of the play. So here, Sophocles wrote a play in which matricide was incidentally treated as just, in order to make clear a different and more interesting point. That point lies where the moral conflict lies.

Oddly enough, the belief that Sophocles was a poet who wrote only for art's sake and cared little for the moral problems of his plays pointed to the discovery of the real moral conflict in the *Electra*.[20] Tycho von Wilamowitz, whose limited approach permitted him to pass by the religious question, recognized that the *raison d'être* of the play must lie in its most intense moment — the great scene of recognition — and that the murder was merely an unavoidable part of the story.[21] To Wilamowitz, everything said in the play about the murder, including the long debate on blood vengeance, seemed irrelevant and inconclusive, while the recognition scene, the climax of the portrait of Electra, showed Sophocles' real purpose. This scene, he concluded, was the chief "work of art" for which the larger one, the play, existed.[22] The *Electra* is indeed a work of art, and, as is not generally the case with Sophocles, the art shows. For this reason, presumably, it remains a favorite virtuoso piece for eminent actresses to the present day. But it is more than a cadenza: it was not written merely as a setting for a superb recognition scene. And yet the fact that this scene is the most highly developed one in the work is important, not for Wilamowitz' reasons, but because it brings to pass the long-desired coming of Orestes. The dramatic conflict which culminates in this scene is the problem of Electra's salvation, and herein lies the secret of the drama. How was Electra, powerless before tyrants, to activate the moral integrity for which she stood? The recognition scene tells how Electra was saved, and how Orestes came back to her; the moral has to do with Electra's endurance, not with Orestes' vengeance.

If such an emphasis seems new and surprising after the *Choephori*, it should be noted that up until the time of Aeschylus, probably, Orestes was a stainless hero, whose act was looked upon as the deliverance of his country. Homer, though he seems to veil the murder of Clytaemnestra, presents Orestes without Furies, and with the gods' approval.[23] So also does Pindar.[24] The one reference to him in the Epic Cycle[25] and the few fragments of Stesichorus[26] show nothing very definite, though the latter probably treated the story as Homer had done.[27] It would seem therefore that Sophocles, though he differed from Aeschylus, stood in the main stream of tradition when he omitted the Furies and treated the murders as simple justice.

The *Choephori*, however, existed; if Sophocles was to write a play about Electra's suffering and triumph, he had to make the matricide seem sufficiently justified so that the play could free itself from the prejudices created by Aeschylus. Electra, it is true, was never punished in any case, even in Aeschylus, but Orestes himself must appear purely as a deliverer and the play must end on a note of victory and peace. Such a task seems to have been almost beyond even Sophocles' surpassing powers. The *Oresteia* of Aeschylus remained an unforgettable landmark, and even today the mind inevitably drifts back to the scene of Clytaemnestra's ghost.[28] And yet, taken by itself, the *Electra* lacks nothing to make it a sympathetic play. Every artistic device is deployed with almost indescribable skill and tact; if the play fails, it is only because Sophocles chose to illustrate tragic endurance by a myth which had already been used by an equally great artist to illustrate something else. The fact that the matricide actually was justified in the end of the *Oresteia* does not make it any easier to accept its immediate justification here. Sophocles must have foreseen fully the prejudice which the superb Clytaemnestra of Aeschylus would create in the minds of his audience.

One means of obviating this prejudice was to avoid any scene in which Clytaemnestra faces her son. There is no such terrible dialogue as occurs in the *Choephori*, with Pylades the silent suddenly speaking like the Delphic Oracle itself; there is no such sickening enticement scene as Euripides used to his purpose. Orestes goes calmly into the palace, we hear some brief commotion, a cry for mercy, and then the two grim echoes of the dying words of Aeschylus' Agamemnon, which, of course, bring the queen's original crime strongly to mind.[29] Electra calls to her brother to strike again; then, as he comes out, the chorus murmurs approval. Electra asks if the deed is done, and Orestes answers, "Fear no more that your mother's arrogance will dishonor you." [30]

The subject then changes to Aegisthus, who is approaching, and the brief remainder of the play is devoted to a somewhat more developed treatment of his destruction. In contrast to the brief scene of Clytaemnestra's death, the children here play triumphantly with their victim, who appears in an odious enough light as he gloats over what he supposes to be Electra's grief [31] and happily announces to all the Mycenaeans that their last hope is gone, and they must now submit to his "bridle." [32] He is presently allowed to discover his mistake, while Orestes, with a dreadful leisureliness, looks on. Strangely enough, it is impossible to feel any sympathy with Aegisthus. In sixty-odd lines Sophocles has created an astonishingly repulsive figure, a veritable model of pettiness, effeminacy, and tyranny. The quiet scorn of Orestes and Electra's weary disgust are limned suddenly in the light of a universal judgment. Instead of warped outcasts, they emerge as a human norm asserting itself over something indescribably contemptible. "Slay him quickly," says Electra, "and throw him out of our sight." [33] Orestes does so, but very calmly. His commands are spoken ironically, in a strangely low, almost courteous tone, in marked contrast to the martinet manner of Aegisthus: "You might go inside quickly," he says, using the mildest form of the Greek imperative.[34] As he edges his victim slowly inside the doors, though it is clear what is about to happen, there is no savagery, no violence, but only a calm invincible determination, capped with a claim of justice and order.

Thus, the death of Clytaemnestra is only an introduction to the death of Aegisthus; [35] and Sophocles, so far as we know, is alone in placing the murders in this order. He could have done this for no other purpose than to let Orestes emerge as the hero which he is in the *Odyssey*, instead of as the half-guilty fate-driven sufferer of Aeschylus.[36] Homer similarly endeavored to veil the horror of matricide, by saying merely that Orestes killed Aegisthus and then made a tomb for him and also for his "hateful mother." [37] Within the framework of the tribal custom of vendetta, the Homeric Orestes is held up as an example of heroic behavior, while Clytaemnestra, of course, can be mentioned only with reserve, and at that, branded with the epithet of "hateful." [38] The Homeric account seems therefore to be the true background for Sophocles, which should not be surprising, since Sophocles was frequently far more directly dependent upon Homer for his ideas of heroism and arete than on his older contemporary, Aeschylus.

But it was not enough simply to pass quickly over the matricide. It had to be made to seem just. In order to present Electra as an example of heroic fortitude, Sophocles set out to recreate the situation in the light of the old epic, in which Clytaemnestra deserved her fate. He took his cue from Homer therefore, and made her completely loathsome.[39] The fact that she is more credible perhaps in either Aeschylus or Euripides only proves that here she is made for an occasion. Sophocles would hardly have taken all this trouble merely to show his contemporaries that Clytaemnestra really was an evil woman, and his artistic integrity would have prevented him from stacking the cards so heavily against the queen, if he really were treating the problem of her deserts. In short, he is too honest to say, "Clytaemnestra must have been wicked, for a god commanded her death"; instead he says, "Clytaemnestra was admittedly a murderess; supposing she and Aegisthus were, as Homer says, a pair of weak and heartless tyrants, what a soul Electra must have had!"

The evil of Clytaemnestra's character needs no demonstration. The last word which the chorus leaves rankling in the mind just before her entrance — "torture" [40] — symbolizes the spirit of the great second episode and of the whole relationship between Electra and the rulers. The queen's opening words, "You are behaving impudently again, it seems, for Aegisthus is away," [41] are a refined sort of cruelty, and the motive of torture and shame grows constantly more threatening. To her brother, Electra later confesses in one line the whole shameful treatment she has received.[42] This scene between mother and daughter, or better, mistress and slave, reveals the central moral interest. Clytaemnestra can torture, but not frighten Electra. With all her power and position, the queen is in constant terror, as her dream shows, and as she later admits.[43] Electra keeps her constantly reminded of her danger, of her own evil gain, of the fact that Orestes is still alive — and Electra is only too anxious to speak of these things. Electra's famous and much disputed reference to the law of tooth and nail, quoted earlier, should be received in this light. It is not a refutation of the validity of blood vengeance, but a threat. We know that Electra thinks that Clytaemnestra deserves death, both from the action of the play and from a specific statement.[44] It is not surprising, therefore, to hear that Aegisthus is planning the rather escapist device of shutting her up out of sight and hearing.[45] It is possible that his intention is to bury her alive, but that is doubtful. Apparently even Clytaemnestra hesitates to go so far. Her feelings are definitely mixed at the news of Orestes' death,[46] and besides, Electra herself, though obnoxious, offers no physical danger.

Electra is not a very engaging character, in the sense that Deianeira is, nor has she the splendor of Antigone. Antigone is illuminated from within, and though a flame burns in Electra too, it is dark and lurid. Both women are of the heroic stock, but Electra's heroism lies in the long years of suffering she is able to endure out of faithfulness to her dead father. The nature of her endurance, the moral strength which she possesses, the degree of her suffering, and the final release from it constitute the real purpose of Sophocles in this play. Electra's devotion to grief seems to her the one thing worth living for; she regards it as divinely sanctioned.[47] The chorus, plying its usual task of mitigating all emotion, good or bad, remonstrates with her, and bids her cease breeding woe on woe for herself. But Electra answers:

> And what is the measure of wretchedness? Come,
> How is it fair to forget the dead? [48]

This passage directly counters all the habitual Greek admonitions to moderation. For Electra, moderation in some things cannot be noble. Grief for her is virtue, and she would rather have her virtue in excess.

Hers is a noble excess, as Antigone's was.[49] And like Antigone, she compares herself to Niobe:

> Ah, all-suffering Niobe, I count you a goddess,
> For that within your rocky tomb
> You weep forever.[50]

In Antigone's case we saw that the symbol of Niobe implied the mantle of divinity falling on Antigone herself; what can it mean here except that for Electra too, Niobe is a divine type of herself, the image of her own faithfulness to sorrow projected large on the enormous world of myth? Niobe is even more appropriate to Electra than to Antigone. Both displayed in their unyielding insistence on grief their bitter refusal to acknowledge the lordship of the powers which were destroying them. For both, suffering was evidence of an unconquered will against the overwhelming tyranny of time and circumstances. Thus in those first lyric outcries, Electra wears her torment as a badge of her nobility, the one proof that she is still a princess. There her grief, like love, is an end in itself; only later, in the speech that follows, does she finally offer a more factual and rational defense of her state of soul. But the inner side which we see first is characterized by its peculiar single-mindedness, its endurance and faithfulness to a moral idea supported in pathetic isolation only by a bare thread of hope.[51] The will and ability to suffer are Electra's arete.

She is deeply self-conscious. She knows well the forbidding and intractable impression she creates, and that she transgresses all the social norms by her steadfastness of temper.[52] But her very self-consciousness tends to mitigate harsh judgment of her. She even apologizes for her attitude [53] — a rare thing for a Sophoclean protagonist. But that is only before the sympathetic chorus. Before Chrysothemis she is the picture of haughty contumely. "What would I gain," she cries, "if I should leave this wailing? Don't I live? Wretchedly, of course, but well enough for me. I cause them grief, and so pay honor to the dead." [54] Chrysothemis is willing enough to admit her own weakness,[55] but Electra despises her anyway, as an example of the moral worthlessness which can be the result of the attachment to an undefined sophrosyne. Yielding to necessity may be nothing more than spinelessness.

The essential difference between the two sisters lies in what each calls necessity. To Chrysothemis, it is the right of the stronger, which, if she had strength, she would resist.[56] She trusts that her father's ghost will forgive her compromise.[57] Electra does not know whether her father has any consciousness of her faith or not,[58] but she too feels a necessity, a strong inner necessity for revenge, wherein alone lies honor. The effect of the evil which she has suffered has driven her to the moral strength she possesses.[59] But the point of this contrast is that evil breaks the common soul, but confirms the noble one; therein we begin to see what tragic tlemosyne means. For to fulfill the function of the noble soul in adversity means to choose that adversity in preference to a less creditable ease. In her long speech to the chorus, Electra explains all the dishonorable circumstances of the new regime, which compel her to feel as she does: her murderous mother in triumph, the weak Aegisthus playing king — and "Therefore, friends," she concludes, "in such conditions it is impossible to practise sophrosyne" — that is, keep still.[60]

At this line Electra reveals for the first time an extremely central, though badly neglected, facet of her nature. Although she seems to be merely a sufferer, her chosen attitude is really quite positive and deliberately consistent. She is therefore the more fearful to her mother. In the face of the king's and queen's abuses, she feels that she must act, and it is important to recognize that she considers her free-spoken display of hatred to be action.[61] Her very suffering is action, and like every tragic protagonist she chooses action above safety. She had chosen it without hesitation when she saved Orestes, and she is always ready to choose it, at whatever price.[62]

Perhaps the essential difference between Sophocles' Electra and the Electra of Euripides is that the latter represents herself constantly as a victim of circumstances alone, an outcast, mistreated out of personal dislike, without proper clothes, and in general an object of pity; but Sophocles' heroine asks no pity and makes it clear that she has willfully preferred her lot to that of Chrysothemis.[63] The element of free and continued choice, therefore, keeps her in a moral, active position and has brought on much of her distress. As Weinstock rightly says, Electra rises "above everything bourgeois into the heroic."[64] She has indeed the heroic characteristic of self-destruction, and acts upon herself.

The choice of adversity and suffering for a moral reason is only a slight variant of Achilles' heroic choice of early death and eternal kleos. It is merely a slower kind of self-destruction entailing sorrow, with death if necessary, but clinging desperately to life for the accomplishment of an end. Tragic tlemosyne is the moral activity of the will divorced from outer action — the vital necessity of the soul to function, even if it be violently detached from every instrument of external effect, even if it must function only upon itself and to its own ever-increasing pain.

The *Philoctetes* and *Oedipus at Colonus* remain the fullest studies of this tragic pattern, but in the *Electra* the idea is already clear. Electra's endurance, however, reaches its climax in a resolution to act externally, and thus for a moment she reverts nearly to the pattern of Antigone. In the hour when she believes Orestes to be dead, her tlemosyne suddenly shifts, and something more like the arete of earlier protagonists begins to show through. She resolves to slay Aegisthus herself.[65] Tragic tlemosyne in reality is only arete hindered and made impotent by circumstance, but surviving in time. At this point in the play, circumstance has done its worst, and time has grown irrelevant, since there is nothing more to wait for. Now the moral essence which had taken the form of tlemosyne so long flashes out in the old form of almost warlike arete. In a passage which oddly recalls the Spartan poet Tyrtaeus, she pictures herself and Chrysothemis, when the deed is done, being praised by the populace for their stout courage, and for being unsparing of their lives:

> Of citizens or strangers, who, seeing us,
> Will fail to greet us with such praise as this:
> Behold, friends, these two sisters, who on a time
> Were the redeemers of their father's house,
> And when their enemies stood high in fortune,
> Unsparing of their lives, devised their doom.
> All men must love them, all must reverence them;
> In festival and populace at large,
> From all the meed of valor must be theirs.[66]

It was with such words that Tyrtaeus called upon the Spartan soldiers to look upon themselves in the historical light of glory (kleos) and drew within the scheme of the polis the ancient heroic individualism. Electra too sees herself in the framework of the polis; she is striking for justice, not power; her rewards are to be only honor at the public festivals and general acknowledgment among the people. Her vision is, of course, anachronistic, for ancient Mycenae was not a polis, in the classical sense. Nevertheless, this was one way for Sophocles to show Electra's character as reflecting a universal; it shows once more his ability to employ freely a political analogy for a spiritual end and to evoke the moral sources which lay beneath all Greek political theory.

This passage should make it clear why Sophocles had recourse to the device of Orestes' reported death, and why above all he described it at such great length. Verisimilitude is one answer: a detailed lie works better than a sketchy one. But most of all Sophocles wanted these details to sink into Electra's soul in order that he might show to what lengths she could endure and with what courage she could act in the face of the uttermost despair.[67] We must take her resolution seriously both at first and when, after her sister's defection, she chooses the ultimate resort, to do the deed entirely alone.[68] As is usual, her decision incurs the accusation of folly.[69] But it is the natural consequence of her choice of resistance and suffering. Throughout she has seen herself as the avenger of her father, waiting only for the arm and the weapon of Orestes. At the beginning of the play, she felt that unless he came soon she could not hold out any longer.[70] Now that she has heard that he will not ever come, she finds a fund of unexpected strength. She alone with her own hands can ratify her will, though it will probably mean her death. She turns toward the palace, while the chorus sings an ode in celebration of her valor and nobility. And Orestes enters.

His entrance at just this moment shows that, so far as the action is concerned, he is no longer of importance. As we noted earlier, he is outside the suffering which is the major action of the play, detached and serene as Apollo who sent him. In every moral sense the deed of vengeance is done, and Electra is victorious. Her will is complete, and she is at once emotionally spent and infinitely strong; the lamentations which she can still call forth over the urn of Orestes seem only like another and even more appalling extension of her devotion to tears, another reassertion of her fidelity.

Orestes is, in reality, a *deus ex machina*, but one of the Sophoclean type.[71] When Euripides used this device, he did so to solve a plot-situation or to clarify a moral issue. Sophocles does just the opposite. His gods enter, like Athena in the *Ajax*, to symbolize a situation already solved or a moral value already illustrated by the tragic action. The gods therefore enter not from without, but from within. The great recognition scene pictures the conscious dawning of godhead in Electra's soul, out of the final and blackest depths of human anguish. The lament over the urn corresponds psychologically to Antigone's fine passage of lyric as she is led away. Such scenes are the testimonials of the protagonist's full recognition of evil and of the personal tragic fate which has befallen. In the midst of her great outcry, Antigone saw her own likeness to Niobe. To Electra, as she weeps over the urn, Orestes the savior reveals himself, dispassionate, strong, and calm. On anything but a symbolic level, Orestes' appearance would seem anti-climactic and flat. As it is, his presence embodies the triumph of Electra's soul, as the urn she holds symbolizes the anguish she has passed through in order to achieve that triumph. For a moment, light and dark are almost one, good and evil almost concentric and co-extensive.

If Orestes' death had meant that Electra could give up her cause, there could have been no triumph for her, no vision. She would have abandoned her claim to the divine in man. But Orestes' death meant only a greater self-mastery, a greater adherence to her cause, and a greater sacrifice. She is the active one, and her violent extremes are the necessary symptoms of her fortitude in unendurable torment. It is her strength and her suffering which achieve the purpose. It may seem strange therefore that Orestes is in the play at all, that he can symbolize anything of Electra. But his very antithesis is what makes him so apt and accurate a symbol. Orestes is effective according to the same law of "double motivation" by which the tempest-driven Odysseus endures all the trials while Athena calmly guides and protects him. On the one hand it is a typically Greek system of inner and outer, but it is also a system of the immediate and the eternal, or historical. Adherence to a moral fact carries one through time and out of time into the "artifice of eternity." [72] The invincible tlemosyne of Electra had gained a point over time, and had won itself a kind of timeless ratification.

In noting the importance of this meeting, Tycho von Wilamowitz also points out that the prologue prepares us for it.[73] The prologue falls into two halves, with the stage empty between, introducing thus the two figures whose separation creates the rising action, and whose meeting the falling action, of the drama. So from the beginning, the play is subtly devised to show the drawing together of two aspects of human supremacy, of which the dramatically interesting one is the one which is most completely human. And that is Electra. Her moral salvation consists of turning the oppressive length of time to the inner uses of tragic knowledge. Those values which in the dramas of the middle period seem doomed and driven to vitiation without reward, have found a new medium in which to achieve dignity once more. The universe is fed by time, and so may the human spirit be, if it has the strength to endure the burden of its own moral will.

In the *Electra*, as also in the *Oedipus at Colonus*, there is a distinct contrast between what the protagonist learns from time, and what the other characters expect time to teach. Electra is expected by all to let her grief be soothed and to yield at length to her betters.[74] But as it turns out, her spirit is not quelled. The longer she resists, the more she learns how to resist, until, when her knowledge is complete and Orestes stands before her, she can refer to her past sufferings saying, "Every moment of time, as it comes, fittingly and justly reminds me of them." [75] Time had soothed nothing, but had strengthened much. And the end of it was her brother's coming; she had forced the years to bear fruit for her by her ability to live morally through them.[76]

> Ah, you, who after a long time
> Have granted your dear return,
> Do not . . . leave me.[77]

The contrast with the *Trachiniae*, where time and long waiting in faithfulness brought knowledge indeed, but only too late, is sharp enough. Time as a tragic factor in Sophocles goes through three successive aspects, from the general force which breeds and withers the obscure lives of this world, through the all-destructive enemy by which we are discovered and rudely awakened, to the almost benign medium through which man may substantiate his morality and his claim to dignity.[78]

To interpret Electra's victory as an achievement of the divine within her own life may seem like mysticism, and perhaps it is. But such a mysticism overlooks no moral consideration, and asks no greater act of faith than the moral act within the range of the human spirit. The real morality of Sophocles lies in what actually happens, not, on the whole, in what is said about it. Character, choice, and will are the action, in the light of which the factual deed is of lesser significance. There was no need to make Electra herself participate in the murder, as Euripides does; her presence on the stage while it is accomplished, and her fierce and urgent reminders are action enough. The divinity she had just discovered in herself is at work in all its superior calm, while her impassioned will continues its outcries. Once more, allegory and symbolism must be carefully distinguished. Sophocles imposes no arbitrary meaning on the myth; Electra and Orestes play their own familiar roles. Sophocles means only that the moral deed was Electra's and that her moral faith and suffering were tantamount to its accomplishment, while Orestes arrived only as a dispassionate and divinely sent adjutant.

But this very arrival corresponds in time exactly with the moment when Electra found, beyond hope, in herself the ultimate extension of that arete [79] which Sophocles considered to be the divine in man and the standard by which he measured the universe. Hence, how naturally the divinely and humanly motivated elements shade into each other, when Orestes says that Apollo has sent him. In her answer, Electra all but calls Orestes a *deus ex machina*, and later she speaks of her willingness to serve the "present deity." [80] That is precisely who he is, and he typifies in its most real form the effectiveness and triumph of Electra's moral being. The god is brought within the human scheme.

IX

THE PARADOX OF WILL: PHILOCTETES

T HE *Electra* reveals its art. As an example of stage technique it is almost too perfect, and therefore it has been regarded as a virtuoso piece by an aging master of dramaturgy. But Sophocles never intended art for art's sake. If the *Electra* fails to conceal at all times its technical mastery under the meaning of the whole, that is because the outlines of the myth demanded it; the story of Electra's long-suffering was such that Sophocles could reveal his dramatic intention only by devious ways and many a tour de force in order to counterbalance the inevitable tendency toward a neo-Aeschylean interpretation. The story of Electra was not the perfect medium for the full expression of Sophocles' newest beliefs about the human soul, and the right myth had not yet presented itself. The *Electra* remains, therefore, a study. Its intricate perfection fills every corner of the tragic page, but there is lacking that margin of conviction, that sense of at-homeness in the myth which can free the poet from overprecaution and let him move naturally. Every line of the *Electra* aims closely and subtly at the poet's design. Almost every word strives carefully for a picture which must be correct, lest it be misunderstood. There is a kind of *horror vacui* in the writing which at once partly accounts for the play's sheer intensity, and at the same time makes it hard to find focal points. With its paucity of external action and its indestructible finesse of detail, it is a classic play par excellence; and by contrast with it, the *Philoctetes* seems a romantic holiday. Yet the *Philoctetes* is the truer piece and says more honestly, albeit more easily, what Sophocles meant to say; for in this play he found the myth to his hand.

The similarities in conception go deep,[1] however the two plays may differ on the surface. Electra and Philoctetes are both outcasts, and both have reason to detest the society which cast them out. Electra was driven by the evils she witnessed under Aegisthus to embrace her own reactions as a kind of law, or Necessity (*ananke*), whereby her passive condition of suffering became active resistance in the fullest sense of the phrase. So too, Philoctetes was at first compelled by the cruelty of his generals to live in isolation, and thereafter made suffering his choice, rather than yield to what he felt to be the injustice of the world. In both plays, the protagonist utterly rejects the popular morality of yielding to unavoidable evil because one is only human, asserting instead a superhuman resistance, which he carries to an almost incredible extreme: Electra will slay Aegisthus herself; Philoctetes will remain helpless on Lemnos, die of starvation, and be eaten by the sea-birds.[2] In both dramas the motif of time is prevalent.[3] Each of the protagonists is overshadowed by a divine archetype of his kind of endurance — Electra by Niobe, Philoctetes by Heracles. Both archetypes are in some sense deified mortals. Both plays begin with the hero in wretchedness and isolation, and end with unexpected triumph — the reverse, in short, of the earlier tragic plan. And both plays end with a *deus ex machina* so organically fitted to the action that it becomes very difficult to say where humanity ends and divinity begins — which is deeply appropriate, since these "gods" appear primarily as symbols of those merging boundaries.

Yet, in the kind of action, as well as in the kind of knowledge involved, the two plays differ greatly. When Electra found that she had the courage to attempt the murder herself, the discovery involved no reversal of will, but only a further extension of it. Hence the action of the play seems unilinear, almost bland, and the recognition corresponds with an external but not an internal change of fortune. The climax of the *Philoctetes* is much subtler: here, any change in the fortune of the hero presupposes a change of will, and it is the hero's desire to change his fortune but not his will which bifurcates the action, and makes the self-understanding which he achieves of greater significance and mystery than that of Electra. The conflict therefore is sharper, and the recognition, for all the splendor of the great recognition scene of the *Electra*, is more dramatic.

Sophocles was not the first to treat the story of Philoctetes. Aeschylus and Euripides, and possibly others also, had done it before him. But in composing this play, he was probably more helped than hindered by his predecessors. For unlike Orestes, Philoctetes represented no *idée fixe* in the minds of the Athenians; his story was not charged with vital and tormented moral issues, but rather, after the manner of the *Odyssey*, it was the story of an adventure, which originally figured as one of the exploits of Odysseus, on a desert island in a later phase of the Trojan War — romantic territory, always beguiling, always accessible to new insights and finer embellishments. The point which kept the story everlastingly interesting — especially to the men of Athens who never tired of good arguments and clever tricks — was how Odysseus managed to bring back Philoctetes, his own bitterest enemy and the enemy of all the Greeks, to fight with them against Troy.

Philoctetes, bitten in the foot by the serpent which guarded a shrine at Chrysa, had been marooned by the Greeks, notably Odysseus and the Atreidae, on the island of Lemnos in the first year of the war, because when his wound festered and failed to heal, he allowed them to make "neither libation nor sacrifice in peace, but always filled the camp with wild blasphemies, shrieking and groaning." [4] In the tenth year of the war, the Trojan seer Helenus fell captive to the Greeks, and told them that Troy could not be taken without Philoctetes and the miraculous arrows which he had inherited from Heracles, his old companion, now deified. Odysseus at once boasted that he would bring Philoctetes back, and staked his head on the event. After ten years of loneliness, illness, and partial starvation, during which time his bow and unerring arrows have been his only means to survival, Philoctetes was not likely to be in a mood to trust the Greeks or give them much assistance, and it would take no little tact on the part of the person who brought the embittered exile once more into the bosom of society.

We have scarcely a hint as to how Aeschylus handled the story; but to Euripides [5] it must undoubtedly have presented a problem in political oratory, in which Odysseus was confronted with the question: How can I, who have certainly wronged this man, persuade him that I am acting for his own best interest by taking him back to Troy? Sophocles does not see it as Odysseus' problem at all, but as Philoctetes'. Odysseus arrives, to be sure, with Achilles' young son, Neoptolemus, determined to make good his boast and indifferent to everything else. But Sophocles has taken the prophecy of Helenus to mean that Philoctetes must come to Troy willingly, and thereby he raises a question that leads legitimately into inner moral conflict and hence to a tragic scheme. Odysseus' efforts are misguided, for he ignores the whole problem of Philoctetes' will:

> He [Helenus] prophesied to them, amid much else,
> How never they would sack Troy's citadel
> Unless they could persuade this man by speech
> And bring him from the isle where now he dwells.
> And when he heard the seer speak thus, the son
> Of Laertes upon the instant pledged
> To bring this man and show him to the Greeks;
> He thought that he might fetch him with good will,
> But failing that, unwilling. And he bade
> Whoever wished behead him if he failed.[6]

It is a point that has never been sufficiently emphasized by critics of this play that Philoctetes must — and finally does — come of his own free will. In fact, it could be said that the principal theme of the *Philoctetes* is the problem of the volitional freedom of the individual in society. It is characteristic of Odysseus, however, that he ignores that part of the prophecy which says that the Greeks must persuade Philoctetes, and aims solely at getting him back.

Far more interesting than Odysseus is Neoptolemus, his antitype. As the play opens, the two are standing on the beach at Lemnos, and Odysseus, as leader of the expedition, is giving his instructions — a task requiring some diplomacy, for the son of Achilles, though un-fledged and anxious to distinguish himself, nevertheless produces some moral scruples about Odysseus' methods. The latter cannot, of course, let himself be seen by Philoctetes; the boy therefore must be a "front" and win the exile's confidence by making him think that he will take him back to his home in Greece. Neoptolemus would much prefer to tell Philoctetes the truth and persuade him to come to Troy; he would even be willing to capture him in open fight. But Odysseus reminds him that Philoctetes is not amenable to persuasion and that the magic arrows of Heracles make force out of the question; the boy had better do the sensible thing if he wishes to succeed. Neoptolemus is con-vinced for the time being, and as Philoctetes is seen approaching, he prepares to tell him the story Odysseus has prompted: how the Greeks

denied him the inheritance of his own father's armor, giving it instead
to Odysseus, and how he therefore has left them and is sailing home
in anger, their sworn enemy and a friend to all who hate the Atreidae.

Philoctetes comes in, limping, hails the stranger, and asks who he
is. Neoptolemus proceeds to tell the tale, which Philoctetes believes
without question; of course the son of the noble Achilles would be by
nature the enemy of Odysseus. Overjoyed to have found an ally in
his feelings, Philoctetes questions Neoptolemus about the state of the
Trojan War and finally begs him to take him back to Greece in his
ship. Neoptolemus agrees, but as they prepare to start, one of Odysseus'
men enters in the guise of a merchant; in reality, he comes only to find
out how Neoptolemus is faring, but he pretends that he has landed at
Lemnos by chance, and learning that Neoptolemus is there too, wishes
to give him the friendly warning that the Greeks have sent a ship to
bring him back to Troy. This information leads by devious paths to
a further report from the supposed merchant: Odysseus has also set
out with Diomede to bring back Philoctetes from Lemnos, because
of a certain prophecy of Helenus.

This little scene, with its redoubling of falsehoods, does not advance the plot in the least, but it greatly increases the irony and the
tension of the relationship between Neoptolemus and Philoctetes.
The latter now begs the boy, as his only friend, to hurry, set sail at
once, and put miles of water between him and his enemies. Neoptolemus' position begins to grow unbearably false, but he still keeps
up the subterfuge. He gives orders for sailing, and Philoctetes gathers
his few belongings, including the great bow, which he gives Neoptolemus to carry. At this moment, his disease overcomes him, and
he sinks into a feverish sleep. The chorus of sailors suggest that now
is a good time to make off with the bow, but Neoptolemus refuses.
It is his first moment of conscious moral action. When Philoctetes
wakes and offers to go aboard ship, Neoptolemus can stand it no
longer; he tells him the whole truth. Philoctetes bursts out in a blaze
of wrath, alternately denouncing Neoptolemus and begging for the
return of his bow. But Odysseus, entering suddenly, prevents this;
he has his men bind Philoctetes and drags Neoptolemus away, saying
the bow is all they need. Philoctetes is left alone in chains, to face
starvation. The sailors, now grown sympathetic, try to persuade him

to come willingly, but he will have nothing to do with their entreaties. He will die first.

Neoptolemus is now in open revolt. He comes storming back, threatening Odysseus with death if he interferes, releases Philoctetes, and restores the bow. Neoptolemus himself tries to persuade Philoctetes honestly to come, but in vain. Philoctetes still resists, though he is tempted by his young friend's clear sincerity and friendship. In the end, instead of persuading him, Neoptolemus gives up the war himself and throws in his lot with the outcast; in sworn friendship the two heroes prepare to return to Greece. Then Heracles appears in the sky, and reminding them of "immortal arete," sends them off to victory before Troy, and the play closes.

The irony of the scenes between Philoctetes and Neoptolemus lies in the fact that Neoptolemus' story, though untrue at the moment and in certain details, is basically a true statement of an irreconcilable difference between himself and Odysseus, which is to show itself before the play is out. To gain Odysseus' end, the boy feigns hatred of Odysseus, and finishes by hating him in truth; he promises falsely to take Philoctetes home, and ends by promising it truly. And this true promise is actually of far greater importance to the solution of the plot than is the brilliant but completely symbolic appearance of the divine Heracles, whose presence motivates nothing, though it sets the seal of reality and truth upon an end already achieved.

The whole design is characteristically Sophoclean: everything comes to life through its opposite. So too, it is neither force, nor persuasion, nor guile which succeeds in bringing Philoctetes to Troy, but rather the admission that all these have failed. On a still broader level, the law of opposites holds in regard to the question of the individual versus society: for society has rejected a great man and then has tried to recover him for its own ends when he has become a helpless beggar; but the beggar now rejects society and is brought back into it only by his own resistance to it. The problem is just such a paradox as Sophocles loved and could manipulate with consummate skill; one may see at a glance that his discovery of truth in the utterly paradoxical — the unexpected and unexpectable — is an extension of his concern with the lateness of knowledge. But he is concerned now with a further ridge of knowledge, the knowledge of those who are already plunged in misery and yet endure. For them the paradox is benign, time itself fights for their dignity, and the knowledge they gain is the knowledge of a victory implicit in a standard higher, or at least more remote, than the norm.

Current interpretations of the *Philoctetes* insist that up until the moment of the epiphany of Heracles, Philoctetes is confused, stubborn, and in general wrong. The supposed gap between mortality and divinity, which all scholars assume to be basic to Sophocles' religious belief, leads them to take Heracles literally as an expositor of the "gods' will." [7] But herein they fail to see that in Sophocles the gods do not really plan for man and that when he asserts that they do, it is only a manner of speaking, the "tragic cliché," derived essentially from the "double motivation" method of heroic characterization, habitual since Homer. Heroic man is not so separate from the gods, nor did Sophocles write his plays to illustrate the confusion and chaos of the human spirit.[8] Philoctetes is not confused. He is right in his judgment of the Atreidae and Odysseus, and he is right to refuse to help them; even Neoptolemus, in his most persuasive moment, cannot deny that.[9] But the factor which obscures the hero's rightness and complicates the play is that very element of self-destructiveness which is necessary to the heroic nature and which forces it to injure itself and sometimes others also. Philoctetes' position is just and courageous. His refusal represents firm integrity. On the other hand, however, apart from its moral aspect, it achieves nothing but harm — the hero's own inglorious isolation and suffering, the failure of the Trojan expedition, and the ruin of his young friend's expectations. To persevere in such a moral stand would destroy all; to give way would mean dishonor.

No such ambivalence existed in Electra, who simply willed vengeance, and at length achieved it. In the *Philoctetes*, as in the Oedipus plays, the problem is once more that of the irrational old goddess Ate, the evil that comes of trying to act justly, the unwilled evil arising from willed good, which Solon was the first to formulate.[10] Here, however, the picture is not one of man alone against the gods. The problem is presented in terms of society versus man, a heroic contest between the great individual who, rejected by society, rejects it in turn, and society itself — with its many-sided selfishness, deception, and rewards — which demands the use of the great man's talents. The question of how the great man should answer this demand raises a personal and sociological crux which is the chief motivation of the *Philoctetes*. For the most part, however, this problem has been ignored by scholars, while much attention has been lavished on the fine and understandable Neoptolemus.[11] But it is Philoctetes who suffers in the cause of the individual and who in the end beats society to its knees.

This interpretation perhaps appears abstract and cold. But it should be remembered that in antiquity social problems were regarded as fundamentally moral problems, and even in some sense, religious. The availability of myth enabled the Greeks to be abstract without coldness, symbolic without allegory, and enlightening without dogma or propaganda. If Sophocles approached a social problem in the *Philoctetes*, it was not because he held any sociological doctrine, in demonstration of which he composed his play. To the last, Sophocles viewed life through the eyes of the individual, in whom, in the very largest sense, he saw the eternal hero. The triumph of Philoctetes is that he finds a way to return to the world, without compromising his heroic integrity.

The other characters in the play are, of course, emissaries from the world at large to the great man in his isolation. Again, they are social, or as the Greeks would say, political types; but it is their moral essence which is relevant. Odysseus is, as has been observed, the embodiment of certain practical political theories prevalent among the later and lesser Sophists, during the Decelean War.[12] He does not hesitate to say that the end justifies the means,[13] and he well knows the power of persuasive eloquence.[14] The reputation for both ability and uprightness, which he promises Neoptolemus,[15] if the latter will only assist his plan, is the politician's dream. Just before he departs, he mentions "expediency,"[16] a word of peculiarly sophistic overtones, and then with a brief invocation to "tricky Hermes," leaves us with a distinctly unpleasant flavor of bribed juries and rigged elections. The current years of the war had produced many examples of this sort of character; for instance, the reigning demagogue, Cleophon. But there is nothing specifically to identify Odysseus here; it seems probable that he follows to some degree the model in Euripides' *Philoctetes* of

431. The rhetorician Dio Chrysostom has left us a brief comparison of the three plays on the subject, in which he says that Sophocles struck a mean between Aeschylus, whose play was bold and simple in design, and Euripides, whose manner he calls "keen, precise, and political." [17] This, of course, tells us little we could not have guessed, and it is a commonplace to put Sophocles in the golden mean. Yet perhaps in the character of Odysseus we can see what is meant. Euripides' Odysseus was unquestionably a regular demagogue of the day, beside whom Sophocles' character retains a certain dignity from the world of myth. For all his ends-and-means morality, Odysseus is no mere caricature; his wisdom is worldly and unscrupulous, no doubt, but it represents a broader kind of second-rate wisdom than is to be summed in the mere politician. Sophocles' character may stand on a familiar political platform, but it is not so detailed but that he can also embrace the world's demands on the individual in general, and the world's ways of satisfying them. In this way, perhaps, he stands between his predecessors as a mean, and what is more important, he can reveal social evil in a universal as well as a particular light.[18] Whatever he does, good or bad, he has the full sanction of the Greek host and their leaders; he is their representative, and to them he is responsible.[19]

Neoptolemus, however, although he begins with a similar allegiance, shows finally that he holds no such responsibility supreme. The inner law of "honor," as opposed to the socially explicable "expediency," asserts itself in him, and stands alone.[20] Even as Odysseus goes beneath the demotic exterior and reveals its most grasping and unscrupulous side, so Neoptolemus goes beneath the aristocratic exterior, mere social *kalokagathia*, and shows once more the old Apollonian picture of arete and spiritual law. Philoctetes is drawn by his innate excellence,[21] but that which gives them most in common is their mutual disgust with Odysseus.[22] For both it is a hallmark of conscience, a token of heroic understanding similar to that which is to appear again between Oedipus and Theseus in *Oedipus at Colonus*. In the character of Neoptolemus, Sophocles is still exploring and molding what seems to have been an almost personal love for the aristocratic side of Greek culture.

But these aristocrats, these heroic men of standards, have a complaint, not merely against Odysseus, but against the world in general —

in fact, against the gods. After the boy has told his original story,[23] the questions which Philoctetes asks about the Trojan expedition and how it has fared seem a natural enough piece of simple curiosity. Actually sixty-five lines of simple curiosity would be a little otiose. The scene is very pointed, and gives Philoctetes a chance to burst out twice against the prevalent injustice of the world.[24] There can be no mistake as to what the play is about. The whole world is out of joint. Not only Achilles is dead, but also the chivalrous Ajax and Antilochus, while Diomede and Odysseus, tricky villains, live on. One is forced to accept here, of course, the evaluation, partly derived from Homer, which Philoctetes puts upon these worthies. Neoptolemus agrees with him: war takes the noble and leaves the slick and clever talkers.[25] But the matter is not dropped here. The news that Patroclus is dead, while the vulgar talker Thersites is not, elicits a second diatribe, now in more general terms: the gods contrive to keep plenty of wretches on earth, while the good man is irreplaceable; the gods are evil. The complaint is familiar. When society grows so corrupt, why should we reverence the gods? Neoptolemus agrees again and asserts that he is ready to abandon the company of all save those few whom he loves [26] and leave the wickedness and injustice of the world to its own disreputable way; and these remarks bring us back to the main thread, the immediate fate of Philoctetes.

But now through the pretense of Neoptolemus the whole moral issue is clear. In deserting the Trojan expedition, Neoptolemus is defending his self-respect; he is seemingly putting himself exactly in line with Philoctetes, who has rejected the world in defense of his own honor. Yet both are also rendering honor pointless; no one can regard a "fugitive and cloistered virtue." Achilles had once found himself in this situation, and had similarly threatened to go home from Troy, even at the expense of his fame.[27] The tragedy of Ajax was scarcely different, though his answer was just the opposite. But there is no real answer. Achilles, of course, since he did not actually carry out his threat, finally forced society to admit his claims. But Ajax could no longer live, and Neoptolemus, if he left Troy, would be as good as dead, or as good as Philoctetes, the isolated invalid. Both would be worse than Ajax, for Ajax kept his glory. In one way or another, the heroic character inevitably becomes inappropriate to the world he lives in, and generally there is no way for him to preserve both his honor and his living usefulness. In the *Iliad*, Achilles was doubtless right to be offended at first and retire when Agamemnon slighted him; if he seems wrong, in the later scene of the Embassy, to refuse the king's amends, that is because Achilles made no moral generalities but apparently stood on pride alone. The point of the scene where Philoctetes asks about the state of the Trojan War is that it gives the hero a chance to express his full moral dissatisfaction as a justifiable ground for refusing to forgive his enemies. Philoctetes therefore is not in the position of Achilles, exactly, but in a far more defensible one. Besides, no one has offered him any amends; the Atreidae have simply found out that they need him and have sent his worst enemy to beguile him into coming — or at least to bring the indispensable bow and arrows. Sophocles has looked to the ninth *Iliad* for the general situation and has filled in the moral implications, making them more sharply in favor of Philoctetes, and yet has managed to keep the whole question insoluble by argument, and therefore tragic. For the hero, to remain a hero, must observe and defend his standards; but he must also seek kleos, and all that that means. Philoctetes, in refusing the world and the war, is defending his standards of honor, but he is throwing away the real and eternal thing for which he, and every hero, lives.

In order to point the problem more keenly, Sophocles transforms the bow of Heracles into a simple and natural symbol. Odysseus, the advocate of society, places all his emphasis upon getting this useful weapon into his hands.[28] Far from remembering that Philoctetes must come of his own free will, he even thinks the man himself is unnecessary, if only the bow be secured:

> We have no need of you,
> Having these weapons; for there is among us
> Teucer, who knows this skill, and I myself,
> Who, as I fancy, am no worse than you
> In mastery of these arms and skillful aim.
> What need of you? Trudge Lemnos and farewell!
> But let us go; and likely this your office
> Will bring me honor which you might have had.[29]

His brutal "What need of you?" contains the simple truth of his attitude. He and the Atreidae do not need the man; they want only what is useful about him. But when Philoctetes lies asleep and Neoptolemus has the weapon in his hands, and the chorus whisperingly suggests that now they might as well go and leave the man helpless,[30] suddenly their song is interrupted by the first piece of divine insight. We know it is divine, because it is in the meter of the oracle, which Neoptolemus suddenly remembers.[31] Unfortunately the hexameters cannot be reproduced in English:

> Yes, he hears nothing. But I see that we have won
> But an empty prize in the bow, if we sail without him.
> For the crown is his, and the god's behest was to bring
> Him, and it were a shameful blot to boast falsely
> of what we cannot do.[32]

These two passages contrast the characters of Odysseus and Neoptolemus in the sharpest possible way. Neoptolemus is not simply remembering that the oracle is to be fulfilled to the letter, because it is an oracle.[33] It is part of his character, with its heroic potentialities, that he suddenly sees why the oracle must be fulfilled to the letter. The oracle symbolizes the unity of goodness and expediency, a unity which later became fundamental to the moral philosophy of Plato.[34] Here, of course, it appears in only a rudimentary form, but its emphatic position, and the sudden incursion of the oracular, heroic meter, give it the tremendous solemnity of revelation. The mere use of a man, which Odysseus wants, is not enough. The man himself is necessary. Society consists not of functions but of individuals. Neoptolemus acquires full moral self-consciousness in this moment. The world can wait; success can wait. "The crown is his."

The prophecy of Helenus had stated that Philoctetes must come willingly; Neoptolemus' sudden wave of moral insight makes the boy, for the moment, prophetic. Philoctetes must realize his own worth as he, Neoptolemus, has just realized it, and he must will its use; otherwise he can do nothing. It is arete that wins the battle; the magic bow is only a picture of the mysterious divine side of the hero himself, the superhuman result that emanates from greatness. Such results are impossible without the greatness, and Odysseus is sadly mistaken in his doctrine of expediency. But the son of Achilles is wiser, or he suddenly becomes wiser, and in the following scenes this ambassador of society puts himself more and more into the position of Philoctetes, until he too is ready to give up (in reality, this time) both society and his own glory for the sake of the man himself, whose friendship he has begun to value above everything.[35]

And thus the paradox drives on, becoming deeper and deeper, more and more intricate and hopeless. Philoctetes must decide freely to come to Troy, if he is to come. Force, guile, persuasion, all are useless; his knowledge and vision of his own heroic self must lead him to a decision to save his kleos. But Philoctetes has no moral ground for making that decision. He has every moral right to refuse, and refuse he does, resolutely. The same quality of resistance with which he had met his long trials and agony on Lemnos [36] he now turns to the defense of his freedom of will, against the tricks, threats, and entreaties of the men who want him back. Philoctetes conceives his endurance as a kind of virtue, a special characteristic which he alone has. The consciousness of his strength shows itself in such remarks as:

> Let us go, son, but first, greet this my dwelling,
> No-dwelling, that by seeing how I lived
> You may behold how hardy is my nature.
> Anyone but myself, seeing no more
> Than the sight of it, I think, would scarce endure,
> But I perforce, have learned to be content.[37]

Like Electra, or the old Oedipus, he has found the outcast's one claim to dignity is to endure. His training in endurance makes it impossible for his enemies to break his will. Philoctetes defends his soul with a stubbornness which, though it is duly censured by the chorus,[38] is no less a virtue than Antigone's.

He carries it to the full heroic extreme in the scene where Odysseus, perceiving that his trick has failed, has recourse to violence. Already in possession of the bow, he binds his victim to prevent his making an end of his misery, and leaves him the choice of yielding or starving. And now, in the lyric scene which follows, Philoctetes shows how far he can resist and the nobility of his resistance. All he thought was true. Manacled, robbed of his one means of livelihood, he faces the full bitterness of the hero's position. He must either submit to the world's shabby and dishonorable treatment, or die on the island while Odysseus sports his bow.[39] Even Neoptolemus deserts him, in the hope that he will come to his senses.[40] But Philoctetes has his senses. To yield at this moment would mean that he would have to manage somehow in time to come to forgive himself for the weakness of preferring to live. Therefore he pours out his great farewell to life, invoking the rocks and the sea, the sea-birds and his own hopeless fate, in which he recognizes the operation of some divinity.[41] To all entreaties he returns the same bitter but heroic answer, finally in rolling dactyls that rise to a climax in a single hexameter.[42] Then he prays for a sword to slay himself, and the dirge closes with a theme suggesting the unreality of life: "Now am I nothing." [43]

As long as he struggles with Odysseus, there can be no question that Philoctetes wins sympathy. When, however, it comes to the contest with Neoptolemus, he may appear less right. To resist one's archenemy is one thing, but to refuse the earnest and well-meant entreaty of a friend may seem a little less than magnanimous. Nevertheless, the last scene with Neoptolemus is the most mysterious and significant of all, the very core and center of the paradox. Guile has failed and force has failed, and the son of Achilles has repented his part in both. He now makes the *amende honorable*, returns the bow to Philoctetes, and gives himself wholeheartedly to the task of persuading the hero with words, as the prophecy had directed. Odysseus is now out of the action, defeated. It is left to these two who fundamentally understand each other to reach a decision. The full excellence of each is now displayed in rounded terms. The boy will do nothing more against his nature; he has promised to take Philoctetes home, and he will keep that promise, if necessary, even at the price of forfeiting his own hopes of glory. Even as he pleads, Neoptolemus never doubts Philoctetes' right to refuse, nor tries to convince him that he has any reason to regard the Atreidae or their needs. He only begs him to come, to "yield to his fate," and not to incur worse troubles; he urges that Philoctetes' disease will not be cured unless he comes to Troy; he urges the promised glory, and begs him in the name of friendship.[44] He rouses a definite conflict in Philoctetes, who, unable to refuse this plea easily, curses his own life and wavers a moment.[45]

But the next lines show it is a matter of conscience:

> Oh, how can I, poor wretch,
> Do this and look upon the light? At whose
> Persuasion should I? How, ye all-seeing stars,
> Could you bear this, that I should join the sons
> Of Atreus, who destroyed me? [46]

Philoctetes cannot coöperate with what he feels to be evil; he will only suffer for it again.[47] And so persuasion also fails. Philoctetes' reasons are still perfectly sound, and Neoptolemus at last is compelled to submit to them. Just before he does, however, Sophocles keeps us aware of the problem of free will, when Philoctetes says he will never *willingly* see Troy again.[48] He does see Troy again, of course, and quite willingly; but he cannot as yet see how that will be possible. In order for the will to formulate itself in freedom, all coercion must be broken down. A free will is not, after all, one which is shaped by the mere importunacy of friends. Philoctetes must, therefore, resist even persuasion in order to come freely, and in doing so he acts upon himself in the way characteristic of the Sophoclean hero. The situation, as the characters make it, and as the oracle has expressed it, is that Philoctetes alone can make Philoctetes come to Troy, because his will is his own. Hence it is that he conquers Neoptolemus, charges him to keep his promise, and the boy agrees.[49]

But there the paradox has come full circle; the situation changes. Sophocles changes the meter as well, with electrifying effect, into the allegro of tetrameters. The boy and the hero have agreed, and by virtue of that agreement Philoctetes is no longer an isolated and forsaken being. He has driven society to respect his rightness and to keep its promise. There are now two heroes, between whom there is a social agreement on the basis of arete. In refusing the world, Philoctetes has maintained his freedom with the uttermost fortitude, and is now free to change, if he desires, and accept the world.[50] And, as it happens, he does desire to. He does not, indeed, agree instantly to go to Troy; there is an intermediate step. Neoptolemus momentarily fears the vengeance of the Greeks, if he espouses Philoctetes' cause against them. When the latter assures Neoptolemus that he will defend him, he shows a will to use his mighty arrows in a friendly effort.[51]

Of his own accord he offers his hand to the world. His arete is now with him, in an active sense. It is released for action because he has not yielded. He is victorious.

And suddenly his victory appears to him. There are few moments in drama more breath-taking than this one. Heracles is divine, but his divinity comes from within Philoctetes. He explains this at once, by comparing his own hard toils, and the "immortal arete" which rewarded them, with Philoctetes' sufferings and his glory to come.[52] Heracles is Philoctetes' own special god, who gave him his bow when he ascended to heaven, as Elijah passed on the divine mantle to Elisha. He is the archetype of Philoctetes' greater self, the pattern of his glory. And what is this "immortal arete"? Arete is a specifically mortal attribute.[53] If it is immortal, it is because it is a god in man, the yardstick by which he measures himself against fate and circumstance, and even the gods themselves. The whole burden of Heracles' revelation is arete. The word keeps flashing out,[54] as the idea of it shone through Electra's "Tyrtaeus" passage. He sends forth the two heroes, "like lions," to guard each other and conquer; he will send Asclepius to cure Philoctetes' disease.[55] Finally he enjoins "piety" on them both.[56]

Heracles brings no new information at all. Everything he said was said before by Neoptolemus in his long appeal — the promised victory, the curing of the wound, even the reverence of the gods. But now Philoctetes himself has resolved on these things, and the resolution is like a god awakening in him. It is a vision of sudden spiritual liberation which can scarcely be paralleled elsewhere. To regard Heracles as an external emissary from Olympus who enters and arbitrarily overrides the hero's hard-won victory of endurance is to obliterate the whole paradox, the whole meaning of the play, and reduce it to a platitude. It is even illogical from the simply literal point of view: would the gods first declare that Philoctetes must come of his own free will and then send a god to make up his mind for him? It is not the "will of the gods" which operates. It is the will of Philoctetes which suddenly operates divinely. His endurance, like that of Heracles, has won for him a higher self to which he cannot choose but yield. The crown indeed is his, as Neoptolemus said, and it would be idle for Neoptolemus or any other to boast of what none but Philoctetes could do.

Heracles is no ordinary *deus ex machina*; he does not solve a diffi-

culty otherwise insoluble,[57] nor does he enter simply to bring the story
to its "proper conclusion." [58] The story's inevitable ending lay implicit
in its action, and it was the poet's business to find the implications.
Perhaps the meaning Sophocles found accounts for Dio Chrysostom's
judgment that this was the best treatment of the story, full of "delight,
together with a lofty sublimity." [59] The special appropriateness of
Heracles to Philoctetes has been recognized, but he is still sometimes
taken as an external god, who corrects Philoctetes, consoles him, and
teaches piety.[60] But Philoctetes was right, and needed no correction;
he was victorious, and therefore needed no consolation; and he was
pious as only a tragic hero can be — therefore a god appeared to him.
It would be unfortunate, to say the least, to see in Heracles a Christian
act of grace, vouchsafed to the stubborn mortal because grace is for
the unworthy. All in all, Weinstock has seen most clearly the meaning
of the epiphany. He interprets it as the divine impulse of Philoctetes
himself, and adds: "The epiphany of Greek gods is nothing other than
the strongest sensible expression of the belief in the divinity of all
being and all happening." [61]

True as this is, one must go still further. Even a divine impulse
may be as irrelevant as a divinity from Olympus unless it has been
necessitated by the play. But this divine impulse was necessitated by
the play. The hero's free will implied the hero's resistance; when
Neoptolemus yielded, that will was complete, and ready to choose.
Furthermore, society had made just and sufficient amends, was ready
to repair its wrong and to do the hero's bidding, by virtue of a promise. Then suddenly the world became appropriate to Philoctetes again.
The appearance of Heracles symbolizes the heroic essence at liberty
to act in the service of itself and its friend; it is the epiphany of arete.

Characteristically, the play ends on a quasi-romantic note. As he
sets forth in quest of his "immortal arete," Philoctetes utters a passionate farewell to Lemnos, the scene of his long endurance. The
passage is one of those rare moments when Sophocles invests the
mise-en-scène with lyric, momentarily transfiguring the inanimate
landscape with flashes of the hero's own exaltation. Poetry of this
kind, bordering upon the pathetic fallacy, is extremely scarce in Greek,
yet similar instances may be found in the Odyssey, such as the description of Calypso's isle, where the scenery partakes a little of the lady's

own charm. But there the description precedes, in order to set an
appropriate scene in which to discover a piquant and wayward nymph;
here in the *Philoctetes*, it comes at the end of the action, in token of
a scene which has grown to be appropriate to a character we already
know. And this is no mere sentimentalism, but again symbolism, one
last touch of meaning, a final variation on the central theme of long-
suffering and triumph. As a battlefield becomes the victory or defeat
which took place there, Lemnos is now for Philoctetes the symbol of
tlemosyne, his moral being:

> To thee, my cave,
> Where I so long have dwelt, I bid farewell!
> And you, ye nymphs, who on the watery plains
> Deign to reside, farewell! Farewell the noise
> Of beating waves, which I so oft have heard
> From the rough sea, which by the black winds driven
> O'erwhelmed me, shivering. Oft the Hermaean mount
> Echoed my plaintive voice, by wintry storms
> Afflicted, and returned me groan for groan.
> Now, ye fresh fountains, each Lycaean spring,
> I leave you now. Alas, I little thought
> To leave you ever. And thou sea-girt isle,
> Lemnos, farewell! Permit me to depart
> By thee unblamed, and with a prosperous gale
> To go where fate demands, where kindest friends
> By counsel urge me, where all-powerful Zeus
> In his unerring wisdom hath decreed.[62]

X

APOCALYPSE: OEDIPUS AT COLONUS

THE *Philoctetes* contains the key to Sophocles' late period and throws light backward to the *Electra* and forward to the *Oedipus at Colonus*. It is often said that Sophocles in his later years showed the influence of Euripides in that he began to stage beggared kings and heroes in rags as his protagonists. But the merely theatrical aspects explain little. What Sophocles saw in these crownless and shattered figures was the everlasting contradiction of inner and outer value. It is hard to see how the supremacy of man's inner divinity could have achieved fuller expression than in the shimmering vision of Heracles. And yet, even there the poet had been forced to introduce a divine character who was, technically at least, outside the plot. He was still to some extent bound by the old form of bringing the gods to man, though his real meaning was to raise the god within man to the dignity of a legitimate and recognized universal.

In the *Oedipus at Colonus*, there is no *deus ex machina* in any sense. Everything appears through the man himself, and from the messenger who relates his last hour. The understanding of a certain heroic, albeit paradoxical, supremacy attainable within the scheme of time, and itself constituting a kind of victory over time, grew steadily in the *Philoctetes* from a dim intuitive force into clear religious knowledge. Oedipus, beginning with that knowledge, now becomes a god — in the specifically fifth-century sense of a god such as man can become. His anguished burden of tragic courage has by its very weight prevented him from turning into the shadow the gods would make of him; for his tragic courage is as divine and inviolable as they. The gods are shattering truth, but they are also moral perception and inner law. Herein, therefore, in the transfiguration of Oedipus, "deep calleth unto deep," and the gods meet. It is with a strange ambivalence, in his enormous strength and utter helplessness, guided at once by his oracular soul and by a frail girl, that Oedipus comes once more upon the stage.

The *Oedipus at Colonus*, it has often been observed, lacks the daemonic *élan* of the other two Theban plays; it contains less obvious conflict, save what is concentrated in the scenes with Creon and Polyneices. But in Sophoclean tragedy, action may be defined as the functioning of the hero's will, in whatever form. Since all his heroes exercise will, it follows that there are no so-called "passive" protagonists. The *Oedipus at Colonus* does not lack action, for the will of Oedipus functions steadily with great power and effect; but there is one element of heroic action which is absent for the first time in the extant works of Sophocles. That is the element of self-destructiveness which hitherto inevitably accompanied the operation of the hero's will. Even in the late works, where self-preservation plays so important a part, the conditions of self-preservation are sufficiently rigorous so that, in order to preserve integrity, the hero may choose rather to destroy himself, as Philoctetes does at first, or risk almost inevitable death, as Electra does when she elects to slay the tyrants herself. But Oedipus is beyond all such choices and risks. He would not be what he is, the most exalted of Sophocles' heroes, if he still had to achieve his height by self-destruction; he has been destroyed enough, and his tlemosyne is complete. If victory costs him little, that is because life has already cost him so much. Action, insofar as it means simply the functioning of the heroic will, is present in dynamic abundance. But the struggles which had been deadly in earlier works appear now in a diminutive and fine focus; their issues are settled before they take place. All is still passionately felt, but more through the distilled medium of the intellect than directly through experience — a fact in itself appropriate to Oedipus, who had put faith in the intellect from the first.

The *Oedipus at Colonus* is a folk tale, a mystery play, and a national festival piece, the essential elements of whose plot may have belonged to the mythology attached to the hero-cult, though certainly not to the oldest form of the myth.[1] Aeschylus in the *Seven against Thebes* dramatized the consequences of the curse which caused the sons of Oedipus to "divide their inheritance with the sword," and the poets of the Theban cycle knew of the curse;[2] but in both the

Iliad and the *Odyssey*, Oedipus is supposed to have remained king of Thebes, even after his self-discovery, until he died.[3] Sophocles' account of how he came to the Athenian suburb of Colonus as a wanderer, underwent deification, and subsequently was worshipped, seemed to Pausanias doubtful, since it conflicted with Homer's version. Therefore the great archaeologist made inquiries, and learned still another story, that the bones of Oedipus had been brought to Colonus after his death.[4] Yet Sophocles did not invent his story, for Euripides alludes to it in the *Phoenissae* of 409 in a way that would have been incomprehensible if the tradition were not common knowledge.[5] And two years before, when the Athenians won a slight cavalry skirmish over the Thebans near Acharnae, which is not far from Colonus, the credit for the victory had been accorded to the deified Oedipus.[6] Neither Euripides nor Sophocles therefore can be the source of the tale. What is perhaps likely, though quite hypothetical, is that during the fifth century the tide of Athenian nationalism found religious expression not only in the monuments of the new age which were rising on the Acropolis, but equally in a revival of interest in the chthonian cults of the old Attic heroes, of which the greatest was Theseus. His bones were recovered from the island of Scyros in 473 by Cimon. If, as Pausanias seems to have found out, there actually was a similar "recovery" of the bones of Oedipus, the growth of such a story as Sophocles tells would be an almost indispensable means for explaining Oedipus' otherwise feeble connections with Attica. In any case, there he was, sharing his shrine at Colonus with Theseus, Pirithous, and Adrastus.[7]

The plot which Sophocles presents fits smoothly into the *Oedipus Rex*. Not all the intervening events are told, but it is significant that Oedipus is now in exile, not of his own free will, but because he has been ejected from Thebes by the new ruler Creon, while his two sons, Polyneices and Eteocles, did nothing to help him.[8] When the first of his shock and fury was past, Oedipus had thought better of his wish for death or exile. Even in Thebes his extraordinary resilience had partially restored him to his belief in himself, so that he was content to live his life out among his children. Not until then had his masters decided to drive him out. Much time has passed; Oedipus is now old, and Antigone, who was a little girl in the *Oedipus Rex*, is fully grown and able to accompany her father's wanderings.

The prologue, like all Sophoclean prologues, introduces not only the matter but also the spirit of the play. As Deianeira's monologue suits her peculiar isolation, or the clean-limbed issues of the *Antigone* are first symbolized in the formal, balanced contrasts of the opening scene, so the last two plays, where quiet deliverance after pain and true insights of inner value are the aims, have prologues where people enter searching, either on an unfamiliar island or at the fringes of an unknown city. Oedipus enters searching for a world in which the value that he has set upon himself through years of suffering may be acknowledged as true. Alone at first with Antigone, he enters the outskirts of Athens and asks where he is. Not recognizing the place, Antigone gazes about her and says:

> Straight ahead
> I can perceive towers that crown a city:
> And it is safe to guess, this place is holy,
> Teeming with laurel, olive, and the vine;
> Within the grove itself, the nightingales
> In numbers sing.[9]

Shortly a stranger enters who, shocked to see that the old man has seated himself on a sacred stone, will answer no questions till Oedipus moves. He then tells them that they are in Athens, the realm of Theseus, and more specifically in the sacred grove of the Eumenides in the deme of Colonus. Oedipus wishes to see the king at once; he says he has come to perform a great service. But the stranger begs him to stay where he is until he can fetch some of his fellows to decide whether Oedipus is to be allowed to remain or not. Oedipus waits patiently, and prays meanwhile to the dread goddesses to pity "this wretched shadow of Oedipus." But he has already won a sign of respect. Before he leaves, the stranger remarks that he seems noble, "save for what the gods have done to him." [10]

The people of Colonus now enter as chorus and question the wanderer further. They note his blindness, grow increasingly suspicious, and finally wring from him that he is Oedipus. In horror they order him to leave at once, lest he bring his guilt and pollution on the city. Oedipus defends himself vigorously, and the chorus, pitying him, agrees that Theseus must decide. A woman is now seen approaching on horseback. Antigone recognizes her as her sister Ismene, who has come to warn Oedipus of his danger. The latter manifests no surprise when he hears that a war for the throne of Thebes has broken out between his two sons, Eteocles and Polyneices. The combatants have need of Oedipus, for they have heard a prophecy that whichever side is favored by Oedipus' presence will be victorious, and Eteocles, the present ruler of Thebes, is sending the ex-regent Creon to fetch Oedipus home. The Thebans, however, have no intention of risking the presence of a polluted parricide within their walls; they merely want him near by, where he can be useful; but he is not to be reinstated in his home. Oedipus listens grimly and then with bitter words swears that neither of his sons shall have help from him. He will remain at Athens.

A lyric scene follows, in which Oedipus makes his peace with the Eumenides for having trespassed in their grove, and presently Theseus enters. All action halts as the two great men confront each other. During the whole scene, Antigone is silent, and the chorus makes only one shy interruption. The king's address is notable for its broad humanism:

> I myself was reared in exile
> Like you, and the perils of a foreign land
> I bore in my own person on my head.
> Wherefore I would not turn away, or fail
> To succor any stranger, such as you.
> For being a man, I know I have no share
> Of tomorrow which is greater than your own.[11]

Oedipus comes immediately to the point. He craves burial in Attica and has brought his own body to Theseus as a gift.[12] These lines are only comprehensible, of course, in the context of the heroic cults of the dead. In order to receive any benefit from a hero, one had to possess his bones. The dead man was thus a chthonian divinity whose remains, albeit buried, performed a lively service of protection throughout a relatively small region. Greece was full of such heroic graves. The chthonian religion connected with them was much older than the Olympian hierarchy, and it seems to have suffered no comparable loss of belief in the fifth century, or even much later. Tombs of nameless heroes were carefully tended in Greece long after the Parthenon became a museum. Oedipus was, therefore, offering Theseus

a real blessing in the form of his corpse, for both are perfectly aware
that Oedipus is a heroic personage. The only surprising thing is that
Oedipus can consider himself a hero before he is dead. This fact only
emphasizes Sophocles' concern with the heroic nature, and how it
comes to be. The mere superstition about dead bones is not enough
for him.

Oedipus now leads the conversation around to the approaching
war, and here again Sophocles does a characteristic thing. He deliberately confuses the prophecy. Ismene has reported from Delphi that
Oedipus will be useful in the war threatening between Eteocles and
Polyneices; Oedipus now prophesies that his body will be useful in
the coming war between Thebes and Athens.[13] Theseus in some surprise asks what will cause war to break out with this friendly power,
and Oedipus, in a splendid speech, lays the cause at the door of time:

> O dearest son of Aegeus, for the gods
> Alone it is to feel nor age nor death:
> All other things almighty time confounds.
> The strength of the earth wanes, the body wanes,
> Faith dies and falsehood blossoms in its place,
> And so in men the spirit does not rest
> The same, either in cities or in friends.
> For some today, for others not long after
> Sweet turns to bitter, and again to sweet,
> And if today the weather's fair twixt Thebes
> And you, no less does countless time in passage
> Breed on and on his countless nights and days,
> Wherein your present bonds of harmony
> Shall scatter at the spear's point, for a word:
> And there my sleeping and long-buried corpse
> Cold in the earth shall drink their hot blood down,
> If Zeus be Zeus, and his Apollo true.[14]

Thus in his own person Oedipus prophesies; but his words tell only
what his own action shall bring about. Like the gods, who "feel nor
age nor death," he can already speak from outside time. This prophecy
is, like all the others in Sophocles, symbolic, not causal, and of greater
significance to the character of the hero than to the plot. Theseus is
impressed at once by the authority of the old man's manner and promises him not only burial in Attica, but also full protection and citizen-

ship.[15] He may even come and live in Theseus' own house, so little does the prince fear ritual pollution. But Oedipus declines, saying he is now on the spot where he will conquer those who have exiled him. Theseus then, with a few last words of reassurance, retires, and the chorus brings the first great section of the play to a close with one of the most exquisite lyrics to be found in Greek tragedy, the famous ode on Athens.[16]

From the first moment of his arrival, Oedipus has put down roots in Attica; he has begun to assert a spiritual authority over his environment. Blind and beggarly as he is, he is nevertheless irresistible. The next section, or act, of the play shows Oedipus' struggle to defend his new position. First Creon arrives from Thebes and attempts to win Oedipus' support in the impending contest. He begins with a specious pretense of pity for Oedipus' sufferings and says he has come to take him home. Oedipus denounces him roundly. Creon then resorts to force, abducts both Ismene and Antigone and tries to drag away Oedipus himself. His attempt is balked by Theseus, however, who leads out his soldiers, rescues the girls, and sends Creon off with a lecture on manners. Creon's answer is a declaration of war, and he departs.

Polyneices, the elder son of Oedipus, is now reported near. Oedipus at first refuses to see him, but finally agrees to do so, on the intercession of Antigone. In a long and moving appeal, Polyneices confesses his negligence and begs forgiveness and assistance. He wears the look of a man blasted and going to his doom. Unquestionably sincere both in his need and his remorse, he has come to Oedipus as a last hope to avert the destruction he feels overhanging the seven champions who are to attack Thebes. Oedipus is silent for a long time; then his answer comes in the form of one of the most inspired and daemonic execrations ever pronounced. He curses not only Polyneices, but Eteocles also, and offers not the slightest word of comfort or farewell. Shattered, Polyneices takes a sorrowful leave of Antigone; she begs him to abandon the expedition, but he feels his duty as a leader and returns to his forces.

These two scenes have caused much difficulty. They seem somewhat extraneous and, in the eyes of many, give the work a quality of melodramatic pastiche. Creon's abduction of Antigone and Ismene, for instance, and their rescue by Theseus may seem more at home in a medieval chivalric romance than in an otherwise religious piece. Nevertheless, in the earliest and most austere monument of Attic drama, the *Suppliants* of Aeschylus, not two but possibly as many as fifty girls are barely saved, by the timely arrival of the king, from being herded off into captivity and enforced marriage. Such scenes, in which a Greek prince prevents the incidence of barbarian outrage, or an Athenian ruler thwarts the highhandedness of an oligarchic authoritarian, embodied serious ideational contrasts for the Athenians of the fifth century. They were not mere action and excitement; they were commentaries on what it was felt Greek civilization was and should be, providing important evidence for the self-consciousness and world-outlook of the Athenians.[17]

When Polyneices has departed, a roll of thunder, the sign for which Oedipus had waited, finally comes. It comes like the Sanctus Bell between the Ordinary and the Canon of the Mass, and it introduces a comparable communion between God and man. Oedipus sends hastily for Theseus, to whom he announces the hour of his death and gives final instructions. It is now the blind man's turn to lead. The dramatic effect of this moment is deeply thrilling. Oedipus, whose physical blindness and helplessness have been so carefully established throughout the play, now rises to his feet and without guidance from anyone present, leads the others into the sacred grove of the Eumenides. The rest is told by a messenger, how he prepared himself, tarrying until a mysterious voice called him by name, then bade farewell to his daughters, and unaccompanied save by Theseus, went into the most holy part of the glade and there was translated, while Theseus remained standing, shading his eyes from the unbearable vision of godhead. The play ends with a lyric scene, full of bereavement and yearning, as Antigone and Ismene mourn the loss of their father, and ask safe conduct back to Thebes. Then the chorus moves off singing a mysterious line:

> Weep not; for altogether, these things have authority.

If the *Oedipus at Colonus* fails to exhibit the dramatic alacrity of earlier plays, it is for a good reason. The play presents the long slow reversal of the *Oedipus Rex*. Instead of the abrupt plunge down the precipice, the movement here is laboriously uphill, and endurance is the criterion. The gods who speak from the whirlwind imparted their lightning swiftness to the *Oedipus Rex*. Oedipus himself sets the tempo for the play in which, hated by the gods and abandoned, he finds his answer to them. The gods who destroyed him earlier make no further move, either for or against him, until they finally acknowledge his dignity with the affidavit of their heavenly thunder and bring to pass the moment in which he is complete. The timeless divinities are the lords of time, but Oedipus is the actor, and he looks to them for nothing save the continuation of their dread function. If time continues, endurance continues; but while time remains the same in essence, endurance grows greater, and so does knowledge. Given time, tlemosyne must achieve its victory.

Almost in his first words, Oedipus lists time as one of the three great elements of his moral fibre:

> Who will receive today the wanderer
> Oedipus, with some scanty charities?
> Who begs but little, and of that little still
> Gets less, but finds that it suffices him:
> For sufferings, and length of time, my comrade,
> And third, nobility, teach me content.[18]

Previously, Oedipus had spoken of himself as the "brother of the months." [19] He now has time as his constant companion. Once time had "found him out"; [20] now it stands by him as a medium of greatness and even as a teacher.[21] Again, as in the *Electra*, there is a contrast between what Oedipus is expected to learn from time and what he actually does learn. In the scene with Creon, the latter, staggered by Oedipus' proud replies, says that an old man in such misery ought to have learned to be mild and acknowledge his own weakness.[22] But time teaches every man what he really is, and in Oedipus' case it has rather confirmed his high spirit and strength. It has, in a way, brought the man to pass, as it brings all things to pass, especially the most unexpected.[23] Itself a paradox, time fosters paradox, and turns things into their opposites; it is the inevitable condition of Becoming, yet in the end it reveals Being, even as Oedipus implied to Theseus in the great speech already quoted. The gods are free of time, deathless and ageless. Yet in the world they govern, in the events wherein they

Howard County Library
500 Main
Big Spring, Texas 79720

Gentry Lunsford
Patron Number: 510
Date: 04/05/05   Time: 10:35 AM

Materials being checked out/renewed:

87686 Sophocles, a study of heroic human
   Date due: 04/26/05

432-264-2260
432-264-2263 FAX
Hours: M-F: 9-6; Saturday 9-5
Unless Book is Reserved for Another,
Call & Renew Your Book Before Due Date

manifest themselves, all things are inverted to their opposites, friend becomes enemy and enemy friend, faith dies, and falsehood blossoms. But the helpless and aged Oedipus, the prey of time, will become a timeless blessing, a member of those heroic dead whose power represented to the Greek mind one of the most holy and inviolable forces in the world.

This speech of Oedipus is somewhat reminiscent of Ajax' "yielding" speech, save that when Ajax says that in time things become their opposites, it is clear that he is resolved to be no more a part of the shoddy flux, but to get out of time, seize Being at a blow and be himself forever.[24] The inflexible standard of the old arete compelled Ajax. But Oedipus' virtue was one of the intellect; like the Homeric Odysseus, he could accept time with its contradictions as the framework of man's existence in which through devious ways he comes to fulfillment. His inner law has made survival difficult, but necessary. For the same intellectual honesty and skill which drove him in the earlier play to find out who he was, and to boast that he could bear the knowledge, has given him both the will and the strength to achieve that boast.

Oedipus himself states clearly his moral independence of the gods in the scene with his daughter. Ismene has told him that the victory in the war depends on him, and Oedipus, half-aside, reflects on the strangeness of the news; Ismene tries to give a pious answer:

ISMENE

They say their victory lies in your hands.

OEDIPUS

When I am nothing, then am I a man?

ISMENE

Yes, for the gods who smote now raise you up.

OEDIPUS

Cheap gift, to raise an old man, who fell young![25]

The rejection of Ismene's pietism is unmistakable. A little later, when Ismene reports the prophecy that if Oedipus dies hostile to the Thebans his tomb will be an affliction to them, the old man, in deep self-consciousness of his inward power, says drily: "A man might know that by his wits, without a god's help." [26] Indifferent to what the gods may seem to do, Oedipus trusts his intellect still; he does not really fancy the gods care about him at all. [27] His exaltation cannot be interpreted as an act of grace, as Ismene suggests. It is a product from within, born of Oedipus' own equipment.

It has long since been recognized that Oedipus, in fundamental character, is still the same as ever. His mind, the quality which made him "small and great," has only been deepened, not discredited by time. No less his famous wrath is vigorous as of old, and perhaps even a little more savage, as the insight and authority which motivate it grow. Innocent sufferer though he may be, he shows none of the religious transfiguration or humble self-abnegation of the Christian martyr. [28] Half of his exalted function is to bless Attica, but the other half is to have personal revenge on his enemies, and the terrible explosions which Creon and Polyneices endure show the ferocity of his hatred and anger; even Theseus gets a rather sharp answer. [29] Christian sentiment may recoil from the sheer violence of these outbursts; but the hypocrisy which they rebuke need find no sympathy. Oedipus is more right than ever in his anger, for his honesty has only grown fiercer with the years. The compromise which all expected of a condemned and polluted exile has not been forthcoming.

For all that, it is never for a moment forgotten that Oedipus is polluted, that he is the man who slew his father and married his mother. Not only his character but also his external fate remains unchanged. To emphasize this point, Sophocles has symbolized it nicely in the first part of the play by making him once more stumble into defilement. The first thing he does is to step on the consecrated ground and sit on a sacred stone. Thus throughout the prologue, first chorus, and first episode, he is technically guilty of sacrilege against the Eumenides. Eventually he makes amends, or rather sends his daughter to make them; but he is in no hurry, and in the end, it is into the most sacred and forbidden part of the grove that he turns. By this light touch the poet recalls and reasserts the same old fate of Oedipus the king — his almost innate luck of touching things which are forbidden, without knowing it. He is the man who treads blindly and innocently upon taboos. Yet even as Oedipus had formerly committed sacrilege and survived in greater wisdom and strength, so now the revelation of his error does not cause him to start up in alarm; he only asks on what land he is trespassing:

STRANGER

Here the dread
Goddesses dwell, daughters of Earth and Darkness.

OEDIPUS

Let me hear by what name I should address them.

STRANGER

The people of this land call them the all-seeing
Eumenides; elsewhere they've other names.

OEDIPUS

Graciously let them take their suppliant,
For from this place I never shall depart.

STRANGER

What does this mean?

OEDIPUS

The token of my fate.[30]

The last line, like so many of Oedipus' remarks, is spoken as an aside and goes uncomprehended by the stranger, who at once changes the subject. But it is clear that Oedipus has passed beyond the phase where technical defilement matters. If it had been his fate alone of all men to defile what was most sacred and to suffer for it, his suffering has invested him with certain rights; for now he alone of all men may walk in the Athenian grove of the Furies and not suffer.

And what strange Furies these are, who receive their suppliant graciously — and such a suppliant — and whose grove echoes with the song of nightingales.[31] These are purely Athenian Furies;[32] only after the first consistory of the Areopagus were the Furies given night- ingale voices, when an earlier exile, "hated of the gods," Orestes, found relief and dignity again in the equable air of Athens. Now Oedipus comes to Athens, and there is no yelping of "insatiable, bronze-footed bloodhounds," but only the music of the birds, as if all the past evil of the Theban house were transformed by the mysterious forces of time and suffering into a present of tranquil beauty and a prospect of hope. Quite after his own fashion, Sophocles has borrowed the gentle goddesses of pain from Aeschylus and spun them magically into his many-leveled, symbolic scheme of the heroic life. Here, in the grove of these paradoxically sweet dread goddesses, Oedipus could recognize a token of his fate; and Athens too could see herself once more, as at the trial of Orestes, the defender of the weak, mediator between the suppliant and justice, the restorer of the fallen — the great role she loved to play. With characteristic finish, Sophocles brings in these nightingales again in the great ode on Athens, so that the whole episode of Oedipus' coming and acceptance is rounded off with the music of nightingales.

Error and exaltation, pollution and the song of nightingales! No union of opposites could be more Sophoclean. Nothing is denied or remitted; all the old misery, the horror of the fate of Oedipus remains unchanged and unrationalized. Nothing has been invented to show that the gods really meant well. Within and without Oedipus is the same man, save that he has added a new dimension of fortitude and knowledge. He continues to act his role with ever increasing self-consciousness.[33] He knows the "token of his fate," and therein creates a historical self. He is the blind man who knows; he is the "hated of God" who is innocent and noble. In this role he will win recognition.

Oedipus' battle for significance finds its core in the defense of his nobility. Those about him on the whole believe that no one could do the things which he did and yet be a good man. The lack of distinction which antiquity, until the time of Socrates, made between inner and outer values is well expressed in the famous *scolion* of Simonides:

> No man can help being bad
> Whom hopeless misfortune seizes;
> For every man who fares well is good,
> But if he fares ill, he is bad; and the best on the whole
> Are those the gods love.[34]

The gods had not loved Oedipus; he had been seized with hopeless misfortune. Hence the chorus is suspicious of him from the first. When they hear who he is, their reaction shows clearly how they have formulated their feelings about him. He must be guilty, for if his murder of Laius had been the moral equivalent of mere manslaughter in self-defense, the gods would not have punished him:

> No fated punishment comes to him
> Who avenges what he first has suffered.[35]

The gods afflict him, he must be evil; let him get out. Antigone attempts to correct this attitude by presenting her father in the light of one undeservingly oppressed by the gods' arbitrary will:

> Among all men you will not find
> One who, if a god leads on,
> Has power to escape.[36]

In these two views the fate of Oedipus is summarized respectively as a tragedy of fault and a tragedy of fate. Antigone's appeal is meant to lighten the burden of guilt, but only Oedipus himself understands fully his own innocence.

The *Oedipus Rex* can hardly have failed to stir ambiguous reactions in Athens. The passages just quoted illustrate the interpretations which his story prompts; indeed, it is even possible that between 429 and Sophocles' resumption of the myth, the much debated question of the guilt or innocence of Oedipus had already begun to divide readers into bristling camps. Sophocles may have wished to settle it once and for all by the heavy emphasis he lays in this play upon his hero's innocence.[37] In his very opening speech, Oedipus mentions "suffering, time, and third, nobility" as the things which have given him his strength. The emphasis upon "nobility" is beyond question.[38] Time and suffering will do nothing for the ignoble man, except make him bitter. Even as in the *Oedipus Rex*, when he faced the imminent revelation of his parricide and incest, he knew that no external fortune could destroy his soul, so now in his old age he maintains his basic excellence. Later, when Antigone's appeal has quieted the chorus, in a speech of formal defense, he states quite explicitly that his deeds were unwilled, and that his griefs are due to no evil in his nature:

> And will you then
> Uproot me from this seat and drive me forth,
> Fearing a name alone? You cannot fear
> Either my body or my deeds; for these
> My deeds were not committed; they were suffered,
> If, as you must, you mean my history,
> My father and my mother, for which tales

> You fear me. Ah, full well I know it is!
> And yet, how am I evil in my nature,
> I who, when struck, struck back, so that had I
> Even known my victim, I'd not be condemned.[39]

The legal claim that he killed in self-defense and ignorance is backed by the moral claim that even if he had known that his assailant was his father, he would not be morally guilty. It will be remembered that Laius had hit him over the head with an ox-goad, for no reason other than that he was in the way, a fact which perhaps lends weight to Oedipus' claim. Be that as it may, the real innocence rests, in his own eyes, upon his inward conviction of integrity. Later he says to Creon:

> For not in me, not in myself, could you
> Discover any stain of sin, whereby
> I sinned against myself and mine.[40]

Oedipus' rejection of the word "hamartia" here clearly has an inward reference, while his outer misdeeds are undeniable. In a similar spirit he can use the old figure of the "gift of the gods," always a dangerous thing to receive:

> CHORUS: You have done —
> OEDIPUS: I have not done.
> CHORUS: What then?
> OEDIPUS: I have received a gift. . .[41]

The gods and their gifts, the misery of his life; these are all externals, and ineluctable. But he is himself, and the gods can do nothing to break the strong moral good he wills. Oedipus is a landmark in Greek morality, for he presents the first really clear exposition of the independence of the inner life, that doctrine which in Socrates and his followers became the cornerstone of a whole new phase of civilization.

Yet for this moral independence to be significant — to be real, one might say — it had to be recognized. Herein the feelings of the fifth-century poet differed from the mysticism of Plato, the reality of whose inner world was prior and causal. For Sophocles, the hero must win in this world; whether in such a death as Antigone's or in such a life as Oedipus', the heroic victory had all its reference and significance in the purely human sphere. Hence the rising action of the *Oedipus at Colonus* shows the hero's triumph over person after person. He already has Antigone, in whom for the first time a Sophoclean protagonist has a real companion. Antigone is not a foil, she is a counterpart to Oedipus; Sophocles kept in mind the character he had given her almost forty years before and here endowed her with no little of her father's endurance.[42] Ismene shares her position to some extent, so that in the three of them, in the scenes where the old man praises his daughters,[43] one detects the nucleus of a world in which Oedipus is acceptable and honored. With them, Oedipus stands on his own terms, commanding and receiving freely their love and honor.

It is not long before the stranger of the prologue adopts a respectful tone.[44] The chorus similarly, in spite of its misgivings, is forced "to feel awe at his pronouncements." [45] But the climax of Oedipus' triumph over society appears in the scene with Theseus, who recognizes him at once as a superior being.[46] It is the essentially Athenian interpretation of arete which underlies this scene and makes it moving. Theseus represents Athens; without hesitation he penetrates all the disguises of fortune and circumstance and arrives at the true man. Drawn in the aristocratic colors of a legendary king, he is none the less the embodiment of the most enlightened kind of democratic individualism. Mutual recognition of virtue, as in the case of Philoctetes and Neoptolemus, can bring the great man back to the world, or, more accurately, can bring the world back to the great man, whose ethos has remained unchanged. The value of the true man, whatever his state, attains a just estimate in the liberal air of Athens. Theseus comes and listens respectfully before Oedipus, and Oedipus acknowledges his excellence.[47] Hero recognizes hero as a fellow stranger in this world, knowing its uncertainty, and basing standards of behavior on its immanent sorrow.[48] Oedipus makes for himself a world of the souls that can respect him in his tribulations, and when he departs, he is no longer isolated, but prized.

Thus, like Philoctetes, Oedipus is set free to bestow the value of himself upon the world. But those who would avail themselves of his blessing must accept the blind beggar himself and not try to use his greatness without understanding him. So too, Philoctetes' magic bow could not be separated from its lame and offensive owner. The paradox of human value must be taken whole; there is no short way.

Philoctetes and disease are one; Oedipus and pollution are one. The hero's external daimon and internal daimon, that is, the inner and outer divine forces of his life, are inextricably interwoven until the great moment comes when the external yields, and the hero's inwardness may burst out and become a reality. And this is not so much a mystic process as a social one. Theseus and the Athenians could perceive that reality through the shell. They are therefore a little like Oedipus, who is blind but full of true insight: "All he says has eyes." [49] His murmured remark, "When I am nothing, then am I a man?" conveys the whole secret. His triumph is prepared within himself, almost in defiance of the very gods themselves, and the Athenians, when they accept his paradox, are made worthy to share in his triumph.

But his triumph does not come without a struggle. The two scenes in which Oedipus sets his face against Thebes forever have occasioned much criticism. Their relevance has either been missed altogether,[50] or else explained merely in connection with the original saga, the *fabula sacra*.[51] But part of the saga is not necessarily part of the play. For the Greek dramatist, there was no *fabula sacra*; he was as free as Homer to exclude whatever detail he felt to be irrelevant. As examples of Oedipus' growing heroic powers, wherewith he settles his accounts in the world, the episodes of Creon and Polyneices clearly contribute something to the character of the protagonist;[52] but their significance is greater than that. The moral essence of these scenes is derived from the problem of the *Philoctetes*, where an individual of heroic proportions, rejected long since and cast away by his comrades, becomes once more the object of their specific personal concern.

Over and over again we are told that the Thebans, and Creon in particular, had exiled Oedipus long after the latter had ceased to feel that exile was necessary or appropriate to his misfortunes; up till that time they had kept him against his will.[53] Precisely why is a question. Euripides, in the closing scene of the *Phoenissae*, makes the exile of Oedipus begin after the expedition of the Seven is over; it is therefore an act of the new king, Creon, who perhaps may be thought to have planned it in order to consolidate his power.[54] In Sophocles' play, however, Oedipus was exiled while Creon was merely regent, during the minority of the princes. The latter, apparently, had been quite passive in the matter. In the absence of conclusive evidence, it is perhaps safe to assume that the disposal of Oedipus in some way affected the various claimants' interest in the throne.⁵⁵ In any case, the very doubtfulness of the motivation suggests Sophocles' real intention: the Thebans had used the legally justifiable reason for exile, blood guilt, as a kind of political cover for more selfish motives. Oedipus himself seems to feel that he ought to be received into Thebes and buried there.⁵⁶ Yet technically, as a parricide, Oedipus could not possibly return. The Thebans certainly had no intention of bringing him into the city, but only of keeping him near at hand.⁵⁷ One might well ask how it had been possible for him to stay in the first place, and why he thought he might return at all, if ritual pollution had really such a solemn significance.

But the fact is, such pollution was open to flexible treatment, and the sons of Oedipus and Creon had made political capital of it. And now, like Odysseus in the *Philoctetes*, Creon and Polyneices both wish to use the great man's power without accepting the man himself. The oracle told them they would conquer if they could get him back,⁵⁸ but there is yet some question of how a hero must be received. The great contrast with the pragmatic scheme of the Thebans is the frank and generous attitude of Theseus. Not only does he feel a personal respect and kinship for Oedipus; he gives him the full rights of a citizen and even offers to take him to his own house.⁵⁹ With Theseus' example before them, even the choristers seem no longer to fear the pollution which attends the old man, and they defend him valiantly against Creon's attack.⁶⁰ To be sure, the Athenians are to gain much from him, but they have not tried to achieve it by the half-and-half plan of Creon.

In the scene with Creon, the political substance of the play becomes most clear, and brings the elements of festival drama into the foreground. All that the Athenian mind felt to be politically good clashes openly with the spiritual blindness of Creon. Creon arrives in guile and departs in violence. He behaves like a tyrant — indeed, he calls himself one ⁶¹ — and he carries off women, as tyrants are supposed to do.⁶² But he is also much subtler, and like most fifth-century stage tyrants, he possesses less in common with the economic dictators of history than with the clever, sophistically trained oligarchs of the war years. His obsequious carefulness before the Athenian choristers who, by a curious anachronism, are at once the subjects of Theseus and liberal exponents of democracy, includes not only respectful compliments, but even a passing intimation that he represents a majority vote.[63] With deft political skill he answers the arraignment of Theseus by trying to use Athenian institutions and the famous piety of Athens to his own advantage: he says smoothly that he is sure that Athens would never receive an unholy incestuous parricide; the Areopagus would never allow it.[64] Creon seems to know well the principle formulated later by Aristotle, that "we should know the moral qualities characteristic of each form of government, for the special moral character of each is found to provide us with our most effective means of persuasion in dealing with it." [65]

Aristotle further states that the end of tyranny is protection of the tyrant, while the end of aristocracy is the maintenance of education and national institutions. Clearly Creon is here a tyrant speaking in his own defense; but with great skill he uses as his principal argument the moral end of the aristocratic Theseus, namely the maintenance of Athenian piety and the court of the Areopagus. A definite political antinomy, therefore, is only thinly veiled in this scene. It appears even more clearly in Theseus' reproof, which enters almost unnecessarily into Theban manners. Creon, says Theseus, is not only unworthy of Athens, but unworthy of Thebes herself, and the Theban tradition of breeding gentlemen.[66]

By contrast with Creon, the failed aristocrat, the mythic figure of Theseus, characterized both as the true aristocrat and the man of the polis, with its ideal of legality and true piety, points the religious question implicit in the political antinomy. Creon's well-planned references to Athenian piety miss fire. Theseus deigns no answer, but Oedipus in towering wrath bursts out in one of his terrible cannonades. He defends himself from the scornful, personal taunts of Creon,[67] strips the veil from his pretense of justice, and then says:

> How fine for you to flatter Theseus' name
> And Athens, calling her well administered!
> But in your commendations you miss much;
> If any land knows how to honor gods

> With reverence, this land leads all the rest.
> Wherefrom you, plundering these girls and me,
> The aged suppliant, try to drag us off! [68]

Creon's breach of the most holy right of the aged and the suppliant fits oddly with his otherwise scrupulous observance of religious forms in treating a parricide. He will bring Oedipus into the vicinity of Thebes as a useful object, but will not admit his technical pollution within the walls. The Thebans are thus represented as standing on the forms of piety without regarding their essence, while Athens "knows how to honor the gods with reverence," by receiving the suppliant generously with no reservations. Far from dallying over mere religious formalities, Theseus leaves a sacrifice half-finished in order to go to battle for his guests [69] — the sort of religious enlightenment which Sparta, for instance, would not risk in the crucial year of Marathon.

These details are too closely allied to the play's principal action to be regarded as merely adventitious. The paradox of seeming and being, which informs the character of the hero, is here extended to include a commentary on the spirit and the letter, in the culture and political ethics of Greece herself. In this scene, even more fully than in the great ode on Athens, Sophocles has poured out his love for the city and his faith in her as the genuine polis, where not merely the nightingales sing and the sacred olives flourish, but where also the individual man, that irreducible minimum of political or any other kind of greatness, holds his place by arete alone, and "whatever good he may do the city." [70]

Scholars have long since recognized references to the Peloponnesian War in this play.[71] The shadow of bitter hatred between Athens and Thebes overhangs the whole, and with reason, for in the late years of the war, Thebes showed herself Athens' most implacable enemy, ransacking her outlying fields for anything movable,[72] and clamoring later at the peace table for demolition of her walls and enslavement of her inhabitants.[73] In the years just preceding Arginusae (406), when the *Oedipus at Colonus* was written, Athens was in desperate condition. The treasury was empty, the statues stripped of their gold; her leaders were incompetent, her population starving, every nerve was strained to the breaking point. If Thucydides, writing probably at about this same time, could call Athens "the education of Greece," because she represented the greatest opportunity for an individual to be self-sufficient and at his best,[74] it is not so surprising that Sophocles too, with his profundity of poetic insight, should have been able to see his city historically and create a vision of her which would be as timeless as the heroism of the old Oedipus. When he speaks of Athens in the play, he never mentions her sufferings. He speaks of her as if she were inviolable, as if the sacred olive trees were not burned stumps and the land ravaged and ruined. Athens herself in those days was a pattern of heroic tlemosyne; and if Sophocles could see beyond the ruins and the stumps, it was because he saw whence Athens derived her almost incredible fortitude. The value of man was implicit in it all, and embodied in the figure of Oedipus. The man whose intellect has brought him to divine insight has come to the place where only the true counts. The ideal Athenian setting is more than a patriotic motif: in it Sophocles symbolizes the world of man's metaphysical value, the world which is the only home for Oedipus. The picture is, of course, confessedly and purposely idealized, but it is not fiction. It is myth, which is to say, it is history distilled into meaning.

The scene with Polyneices completes the picture of society's misguided attempt to regain the great individual for its own ends. Once more, as in the *Philoctetes*, the attempt through guile and force yields to the attempt through persuasion and appeal, and once more the same refusal follows. Polyneices is no mere politician like Creon; he is very sympathetically drawn. Even though he is perhaps still too self-involved to rise above his practical need of Oedipus into a full understanding of the old man's worth, nevertheless his full admission of guilt, and especially his recognition that has come too late,[75] stamp him at once as a serious and wellnigh tragic character.[76] Therefore the appalling execrations which the old man calls down on him are the more surprising. But Polyneices really is too late, and it is only out of empty hope that he can suggest how he may make up for his sins.[77]

For Polyneices' faults are in his nature and in the nature of his will. He has put himself where he cannot turn back,[78] but he has done so not because of any moral standard, but because he wanted the throne. He is therefore in a tragic situation, perhaps, but he is not a tragic character; however genuine his penitence may be, it implies little understanding and no real morality. Fundamentally he needs Oedipus for precisely the same reason as Creon does, and he would never have come otherwise.[79] Oedipus' refusal of him rests on the same absolute standard he had always espoused. Since now Oedipus is himself all but a god, it may be said that his refusal rests on a divine standard.

The curse may seem another matter. Many scholars have argued that Oedipus was wrong to curse his son;[80] others that the curse merely illustrates Oedipus' great exaltation.[81] Still others have collected much juridical evidence to prove that Polyneices, as the very image of a bad son, by all contemporary standards deserved damnation.[82] Yet in a play about inner and outer religious standards, Sophocles would hardly allow Polyneices to be condemned on merely legalistic grounds. Polyneices is undoubtedly a bad son; yet he is drawn in touchingly human colors: in his parting from Antigone, in his rather high conception of generalship, and in the loneliness of his sorrow as he bravely accepts his fate, he carries away a good deal of our sympathy.[83] The simply bad son might be forgiven, one feels, if Antigone could intercede for him. If Sophocles meant us to remember only his past deeds, he should have made him appear more like them. But instead, he has deliberately given his cause some justice by making him the elder, instead of the younger brother.[84]

It has been wisely noted that in the epic source the curse on the sons of Oedipus precedes and apparently causes their strife,[85] but in Sophocles the strife came first, arising "from some god and their own sinful mind." [86] By the time Oedipus utters his curse, Polyneices is already on his way to the war, and is too fatally involved to turn back, as his words to Antigone show. So the curse, which once had a supernatural causative force, is here simply a statement of fact, though Polyneices still refers to the Furies as the ones who will bring it to pass, as one always speaks of a god in connection with what is true.[87] Obviously it is Polyneices who will bring it to pass, for he is already doing it, and Sophocles has made it doubly pointed by letting Antigone beg him so movingly to desist. But Polyneices, whose name means the "man of the heavy curse," knows who he is. Quite aside from his past cruelty to his father and sister, and even apart from the fact that he is still only trying to use Oedipus, Polyneices deserves the curse because he is accursed, as Esau was accursed long before the actual denunciation came.[88] Oedipus, like an oracle, has simply told the truth. Once more, the supernatural element enters in such a way that it can only be symbolic. Appropriately enough, the last of the three gods whom Oedipus invokes to destroy Polyneices is the War itself, the really destructive element "which has cast such heavy strife" between the brothers.[89]

The Creon and Polyneices scenes are not loosely or poorly integrated, from the moral point of view. From the mere standpoint of plot they revive and restate the conflicts of the *Philoctetes*, illustrating with infinitely subtle turns the world with which the great individual must deal, in his struggle for weight, dignity, and reality. Individualism in terms of such values means more than ordinary individualism; it is a norm of heroic being. And the basic difference between Oedipus and Polyneices is that Oedipus asserts his heroic right to be, while Polyneices asserts only his right to have. Therefore the one is oracular and blessed, the other accursed and pathetically confused in his humanity.

With the retreat of Polyneices, Oedipus' moral triumph is complete, and the mastery which he has shown throughout the play is now symbolized in the final scene of divine mastery. The last and most impressive of the supernatural happenings in Sophocles has this in common with all the others: the supernatural "cause" follows its effect. Oedipus officially "becomes a hero," with the power of blessing and cursing. But manifestly, the transformation which takes place in the depth of the sacred grove adds little in itself to the power of Oedipus. The blind and aged hero has already repulsed Creon and cursed Polyneices; before he leaves, he pronounces the eternal blessing upon Theseus and Attica. To the Greek, a person could become a hero only if he really was one, and Oedipus has already exercised his full prerogatives. Viewed in their simplest and most profound light, these prerogatives are no more than the ability to see through the veils of circumstance into essential fact. Oedipus' words all "have eyes." His insight attains its perfect symbol when he himself leads the way into the grove, unguided except by what he calls "the present deity"; nor does he hesitate to identify himself subtly with that divine force.[90] The inward man has at last come true.

It is a grave mistake to overlook the moral qualities which have made Oedipus a hero, and to regard his apotheosis as a simple act of grace on the part of the gods, or as amends made by them for the sufferings which he has endured.[91] The choristers, indeed, interpret it thus:

> Out of the many woes that came
> Without cause, now the god in justice
> Would lift him up.[92]

On the other hand, they have already prayed on their own behalf, when they heard the thunder and saw Oedipus' fate coming, to be delivered from any share in such "gainless grace."[93] It is clear that they regard the gods as the actors here, and the whole process as fraught with danger, not only for Oedipus, but also for the passive spectators. These good Athenians, with their simple, human limitations and their sophrosyne, know that the gods can be almost as perilous friends as they are enemies, and they would prefer to stand apart and pray. Oedipus himself rejects any such interpretation, however. He uses the word "grace," but always of the blessing he himself is to bestow on Athens.[94]

It will be remembered with what contempt he treated the suggestion of Ismene, in an earlier scene, when she remarked that the gods who formerly destroyed him were now about to reinstate him.[95] Oedipus, with his customary brutal truthfulness, called it a cheap favor. Indeed, the gods did little for Oedipus; he had to prove himself every inch of the way, and it is no wonder that he omits all sanctimonious expressions of gratitude. He speaks seriously of the gods and the world at large only to Theseus, for the latter is the only other character of sufficiently heroic proportions to understand him in his own terms. By the same token, Theseus alone is permitted to witness the last hour of Oedipus. Only the large soul can fully understand how "the gods look well but late," how time penetrates all things, or how the noblest in man is rooted in his essential weakness and subjection to change.[96] Others may grasp the words when they are spoken, but Theseus comprehends out of his own being. And Theseus, champion of the true Athenian religiosity, regards Oedipus himself as the grace-bringer, not the gods. There was no Messiah in Greek theology; if man was to come near to the divine, he must get there himself. How this can be achieved is known only to him who has in some sense already achieved it; the rest of the world will view it with limited, and doubtless frightened, eyes. As Hölderlin once wrote:

> Only those who themselves are
> Godlike ever believe in gods.[97]

Oedipus brings us to a vision of godhead, whose content and significance are Oedipus himself. Sophocles says nothing of the gods who greet him, but he has shown all he could of the man who, after long sorrow, greeted the gods.

The end, therefore, is no great change, except that it releases Oedipus from the struggle of asserting himself and the suffering which pursued the moral activity of his soul. He had exalted himself by his endurance in that activity, and the final scene shows only the universal of which the play was the particular. That universal is all important, but one must not forget how it came about. It is the result of "time, suffering, and his own nobility." How perfectly his last words to his daughters sum up the trial of values by which he has triumphed:

> Children, it now behoves you leave this place,
> Enduring, in nobility of mind.[98]

Endurance, nobility, mind: these are the laws of the human soul. So stated, they sound very simple, and in essence perhaps they are. But in action, which is life and the only context in which human beings can know them, they are the stuff of tragedy, the divine scheme or *ananke*, which binds the magnanimous man to himself and puzzles and outrages the philistine world, until it finally can ratify itself in a form that can no longer be denied.

To the audience which first witnessed the *Oedipus at Colonus* the conviction must have inevitably come that this was not the end of the hero, but his real beginning. The eye involuntarily follows him out of sight, and creates its own image of what happened thereafter. The simple fact that Oedipus became one of the lesser, though doubt-

less more revered, local deities can never account for Sophocles' having written this long complex work, with its keenly dramatized distinctions between inner and outer, and its iridescent interplay of
godlike and manlike qualities in the central figure. Sophocles must
seek what the process of becoming a hero included for Oedipus himself; how and why the fallen — for Oedipus is in this play, as much
as before, Everyman — can still achieve an inch of significance and
grow before our eyes, though the weight of the unyielding, and to
ancient eyes, divine forces seemed forever pressing downward.

The *Oedipus at Colonus* ends with an apocalypse which, together
with some other lines in Sophocles, illustrates to some extent the fifth
century's outlook on both hero cults and death in general. There is,
for instance, a passage in the *Electra*, where the chorus, attempting
to console the heroine for her brother's supposed death, says:

> I know that the king Amphiaraus,
> Betrayed by the golden wiles of woman, lies buried;
> And now under the earth
> All-shade he rules.[99]

In this difficult passage, the reference to Amphiaraus is clear
enough, but there is considerable question of its relevance. The famous
warrior-prophet, who was betrayed into joining the Seven against
Thebes by his wife Eriphyle, seems to have little to do with Orestes.
And what does the last line mean — "All-shade he rules"? The word
translated "all-shade" (πάμψυχος) occurs only here, and the scholiast,
confused but generous, offers three explanations: "Either," he says,
taking it as "all-soul" rather than "all-shade," "he rules over all the
souls, which stand in need of his prophetic art" — referring presumably to the souls of the living who consulted his oracle near Thebes;
for the shades of the dead have little need of prophecy — "or, he is
'all-soul' because he saved his whole soul; or, because throughout
everything he keeps his soul, which is immortal." [100] The idea that
famous heroes become rulers among the dead is as old as Homer; [101]
hence the scholiast's first suggestion is the one generally accepted.
Although this does not seem quite right, still the general meaning of
the lines is clear. It is a contrast between the fact of death and the
fact of ruling. Death has not deprived Amphiaraus of his eminence,

but has given him an eternal though shadowy royalty. Therefore, it is implied that, in a similar way, though Orestes is dead, his arete still holds its place in the world of the shades.[102]

Does this imply the immortality of the soul? The scholiast barely suggested the idea, and few would care to defend it. Yet the juxtaposition of death and power implies something; the paradox is pregnant with faith in the indestructible value of human nobility. Added to the other passages in which the inner divinity of the protagonist shows itself, these lines form one more link in the chain of Sophoclean humanism which sees godhead operative in the moral being of man. The Niobe passages of Antigone and Electra, the latter's reference to the present deity in Orestes, Philoctetes' vision of his patron god, the passage on Amphiaraus, and old Oedipus' departure from the stage unguided save by "the present god" — all these, and perhaps more, point steadily in one direction: toward a verity in human life which is, or at least becomes, immutable — a particular which becomes general and attains to the authority of a historical truth.

And for this truth, in what was perhaps the last line of poetry he ever wrote, Sophocles used the word *kyros* (κῦρος), which indicates a universally ratified authority: "Weep not, for altogether these things have authority [*kyros*]." That which is conceived to be at once authoritative and universal was to the Greeks divine: the gods were divine, law was divine; certain aspects of nature, even aside from conscious or developed animism, had their own divinity — the sea, the earth, the sun. Not superstition but religious intuition lies in such terminology, for it is almost a way of saying that these things really exist and are wonderful — even as the Ionian philosophers equated real being with "the divine" or "godhead." [103] Therefore when Sophocles says that the fate of Oedipus has complete *kyros*, he means that he has passed into the realm of what is universal, true, and authoritative, and so divine. His inner divinity is forever ratified and preserved. For Electra and Antigone, the universal symbol was Niobe; for Philoctetes, Heracles; for Orestes, perhaps Amphiaraus, in a lesser way. The ancient classic example, or *paradeigma*, was thus extended into a religious token or symbol. In the *Ajax*, this technique was not yet developed, and in the *Trachiniae* the faith that impelled it was lost. But Oedipus, who even in the earlier play could call himself the brother of the months, in the end dwarfs all the earlier heroes by becoming his own symbol. It had taken Sophocles ninety years of spiritual struggle, probing the depths of human evil, to see man finally in such a light.

Without the aid of doctrine, dogma, or formal creed, and without the weighty deliberation of ecumenical councils, a poet is not apt to evolve a system. Sophocles did not. His work is the truer therefore; all the paradoxes remain; nothing is oversimplified, and equally, nothing is explained by the cathedral-like rationale of a static theology. Experience for the poet remains fluid and valid; it crystallizes, if at all, only into myth and poetry, both of which are imperishable but plastic. Wherever the experience of the individual soul becomes important, there the value of society's systems is called in question and eventually relegated to a position of merely formal, social importance, if not altogether overthrown. The Italian Renaissance, of course, is the perfect illustration, and the works of Sophocles, seen in the light of their spiritual and humanistic import, gain still a new degree of incandescence when set beside the emotional stirrings of the Renaissance. There again faith in the individual becomes heroic, experience becomes at once illuminated and mysterious, the state religion recedes coldly before the intuition of human beauty and excellence and only glows for the last time when a fair lady guides an intensely personal and sensuous poet through its labyrinthine levels.

It is never easy to say what exactly is the content of humanistic faith. It is as broad as human experience; its core is moral, and it becomes authoritative and universal. But it is hard to say more. In Sophocles' plays, various specific elements have presented themselves; but as a whole, the underlying humanistic faith is an emotional and poetic one, most akin to the intuitive passion of the Renaissance. And indeed it is not surprising, on the brink of a great Enlightenment, where the blankest superstition may stand side by side with utter skepticism, that the men who most fully embody the spirit of their age should give themselves to neither, but on their own behalf seek out and evolve, not cautious middle ground, but a truly perspicuous faith. It is more wonderful that so plastic a religious attitude, at once passionate and refined, should be able for a brief period to flood the interstices of early disintegration in a culture where the canons of a

powerful and once-satisfying orthodoxy and the aspirations of the
individual's destiny have begun to diverge. Perhaps the finest commentary available on the work of Sophocles, and on the victory of
Oedipus in particular, is to be found in the famous work on the
Dignity of Man by Pico, Count of Mirandola. It would be dangerous
to assume a direct connection; but in 1423, Giovanni Aurispa sent the
great Laurentian manuscript of Sophocles to Niccolo de' Niccoli, a
famous Florentine bibliophile, and three quarters of a century later,
Pico wrote:

> I created thee (God is speaking to man) a being neither heavenly nor
> earthly, neither mortal nor immortal only, that thou mightest be free to shape
> and to overcome thyself. Thou mightest sink into a beast, and be born anew
> to the divine likeness. The brutes bring from their mother's body what they
> will carry with them as long as they live; the higher spirits are from the begin-
> ning, or soon after, what they will be for ever. To thee alone is given a growth
> and a development depending on thine own free will. Thou bearest in thee the
> germs of a universal life.[104]

It is the germ of this universal life which in *Oedipus at Colonus* has
come to full flower. The status of the chthonian hero, the dead *numen*
in the earth, aptly symbolizes, as doubtless it did from the beginning,
man's special partaking of death and life, of the transient and eternal.

PART FIVE

THE HEROIC WORLD

I will form man.
Let him be burdened by the toil of the gods,
That they may fully breathe.
                              — Enuma Elish VI

XI

SOPHOCLES AND THE FIFTH CENTURY

THE close of the *Oedipus at Colonus* presents the daemonic moral force of man in its fullest development.
To comprehend this force is not entirely a matter of
intellect; its very existence depends perhaps upon religious intuition, or faith, and it certainly did for Sophocles. Therefore, although it would be easy, with the aid of modern psychology,
to explain it away into a number of independent "drives," the service
to Sophocles would be slight. For to Sophocles, man's moral strength,
though various in its manifestations, was a unified essence implicit in
his nature, and the problem before the critic is to perceive, if possible,
the way the poet felt. The primary evidence of the plays themselves
has already been analyzed. There now arises the question of the historical circumstances in which Sophocles shaped and developed his
faith. For behind the turbulent events of the fifth century, it is possible to see the rise, progress, and decay of certain cultural aspirations
which gave their impetus to the greatest period of Athenian art and
life. As a city, Athens can scarcely be said, despite her magnificence,
to have achieved all her ideals. That, however, is irrelevant. The ideals
were there, and Sophocles, far from being alone in his religious humanism, was only the subtlest and most profound exponent of the heroic
idea.

The modern world derives so many of its conceptual patterns of
thought from the time of Plato, that it finds great difficulty in integrat-
ing the culture of a century such as the fifth, in which conceptual
thinking was not yet paramount. The Periclean Age, therefore, *lauda-
tur et alget*. Moreover, there is the consideration that that great era
is one of the most poorly documented in all Greek history. It has
bequeathed to us so much of its spirit and so little of its letter that
any estimate of it must necessarily involve much that will appear in-
sufficiently, if at all, supported. That the greatest poet of this period

has been ignored as a source is not surprising, in view of the traditional prejudice that he objected to his times and held himself aloof from them. Yet it may well be inquired what he objected to, if he did object, and if he held himself aloof, exactly why and how he did so. In the pursuit of answers to these questions, it will appear perhaps that Sophocles' difference from his countrymen was other than has been supposed, and that in any case he can tell us much about his times. His works, indeed, add little or nothing to our factual knowledge of the fifth century; rather they may be classed with the *Funeral Oration* of Thucydides, as testaments of the spiritual tenets and aspirations available to the contemporary Athenians.

The tendency of Greek culture to departmentalize itself into distinct genres sometimes obscures the historical concurrency and interplay of these genres. Particularly in the fifth century, when so many forms of culture, new and old, attained their own separate peaks of achievement, it is important to recall that such contrasting figures as Parmenides, Heraclitus, Anaxagoras, Xenophanes, Socrates, and even Plato all belonged, in some degree or other, to this age; that Aeschylus and Pindar simultaneously conceived within their opposing frameworks a scheme of international and exalted man; that Sophocles experienced both Salamis and the Sicilian Expedition and observed Athenian statesmen from Themistocles to Cleophon. The diverse sculptures of Aegina, Olympia, and the Acropolis were all made within a few years of each other; while in Euripides the currents of a rationalism as old as Homer clashed constantly with the passional psychology and sheer natural dynamism of the Sophistic. The authority of the supreme oracle at Delphi shared honors with the agnosticism of Protagoras. The godless Alcibiades was general with the pious Nicias. The graceful prolixity of Herodotus and Thucydides' pungent involutions are equally fifth-century products. In some ways the policy of Cimon, that Athens and Sparta were "yoke-fellows" — neither complete without the other — was entirely in keeping with the spirit of the fifth century; for in this hundred years, all the elements of Greek culture met and coexisted for a brief while in the most exquisite counterpoise, whose decay began with the death of Pericles and was complete with that of Sophocles. Dionysus did well to escort his poet's funeral. The other gods might have done likewise, for the infinite variety of Greece, from which they drew their being, went to its grave with this, the last of the builders of the fifth century.

It was Athens, and Athens only, that united for the brief space of some fifty years the various currents of Greek culture into a single stream. Thucydides makes Pericles say that the Athenian could enjoy the goods of all places in the known world without stirring from home; [1] but it was not only material goods that Athens drew together. Her intellectual commerce was equally broad, so that, whereas there were typically Ionian and typically Eleatic schools of thought, everything Athenian shows many sides, the facets of a marvelously poised design cohering through the opposition of its dynamic elements. Only in Athens could a tyranny assist the birth of a constitution, or a dynastic family like the Alcmaeonids ally itself with the essential designs of liberal government. The specifically Athenian blend of personal aristocracy with a democratic universal becomes familiar, of course, in the ideal Athenian hero, Theseus, who appears not merely in the *Oedipus at Colonus* but also in Euripides, as the representative of truly Hellenic justice and civilization.

One may well ask what it was which enabled Athens to smelt down such rigid opposites and recast them in new and transfigured shapes. The mere coexistence of many kinds of thought is not necessarily so productive, unless there be a unifying fire which brings them all to life — a religion, in fact, broad and humane enough, as well as lofty enough, to dignify the multiformity of human effort and make it glow with a divine aura. If Greece at large in the fifth century provided the multiformity, Athens herself provided the religion — in the form of the heroic idea of man. And the chief prophet of this idea was Sophocles.

In the seven plays seven heroes — or perhaps better, six — go their way, each led by his own individual arete, into suffering, and through suffering to moral triumph. In every case, the kind of arete is different, for no two individuals can have exactly the same excellence; hence the variety of the plays. Furthermore, the final triumph sometimes is achieved only in death, and sometimes it is a barren and inglorious victory, whose only trophy is that the hero has not faltered. But in every case, Sophocles draws his hero's will as free of all restrictions save the moral one. All morality is in the nature of a restriction, but in its heroic form it is so extreme as to restrict life itself and destroy it; yet such restriction is also creative and expansive, and as it destroys the mortal, it creates the god. Out of the dead Antigone arises the timeless symbol of the deified Niobe, and the chorus can sing:

> Great fame it is
> To share the lot of those equal to gods
> In life, and thereafter in death.[2]

In this whole pattern of moral suffering and triumph, if it can be called a pattern, Deianeira is the one exception — and that for a special reason — to the implication that through his inner flame a mortal may meet the gods.

Sophocles was not the first to envision godhead overhanging a tragic death through action. Like everything Greek, the idea begins in Homer and appears most fully in the death of Patroclus. When Achilles sent Patroclus into the field he warned him not to fight Hector or to go too near the walls of Troy. Patroclus was not fated for these victories; he was not the man whose precise skill was required. Hector must fall to Achilles, Troy to the son of Achilles and Philoctetes, as all knew. But Patroclus forgot. In the fire of battle he outdid himself, and the Achaeans at his heels, as Homer says, would have taken Troy "in despite of fate" had not Apollo intervened. But, as it was, when Patroclus' valor was at its height, the god came through the press and struck him from behind, stunning him and knocking his helmet from his head, so that he stood helpless and dazed before Hector. The moralist finds that Patroclus committed hybris when he tried to scale the wall, and remarks that had he remembered Achilles' warning, all would have been well with him — wellnigh as if thus he would have been living to this day. It is possible to look upon Apollo's destruction of him as an example of the envy of the gods, or as the punishment for presumption. But it is a great deal more than either, as the title of the sixteenth *Iliad* shows. It is the *Patrocleia*, which means literally "The Story of Patroclus"; but it implies an *aristeia*, or display of personal greatness, which indeed it is. We might almost translate it, "The Great Hour of Patroclus," for it was the hour in which he cracked the limits set upon him, and having transcended himself in this world, met the god face to face and was gathered gloriously into history. The death of Patroclus is an illustration of the tragic pattern, where man in his illimitable potential strikes so high he reaches toward and makes his pressure felt by godhead, and is destroyed. This is the heroic Eucharist, not gained through humility and prayer, but through defiant self-expectation and exalted courage.

Yet it must be remembered that Patroclus, Ajax, and Oedipus were no common beings, although each in his own way may represent man in the large. Their ethic scheme is not necessarily designed for every individual. In the works of Sophocles and Homer one meets the moral aristocrats of antiquity. The standard by which these heroes lived and died was higher and different from the standards of ordinary mortality; and it is for this reason that they are heroes. The poets of the great tradition were not concerned with the commonness of man, but with his uncommonness — though Sophocles, at least, was aware that at any moment, from any unexpected quarter, the moral hero might appear, ready to take up the gage of action because of what he felt himself to be. For, somewhat like the mythic figure of Theseus, the heroic idea, though it certainly originated in the early aristocracy, became in Athens during the fifth century a kind of human norm, achievable no doubt by very few, and perhaps by none, but constantly present for contemplation. The value which Homer set upon his heroes, seeing them as he did constantly in the light of their attendant divinities, if not exactly the potential birthright of every Athenian citizen, was yet implicit in the culture of the city. Athenian institutions at their best aimed at the individual's best, and for the Greeks, an individual's best might reach very high indeed. Athens might rock on her foundations with debates about the existence or meaning of the gods, but no one had as yet questioned the value or dignity of man. Poets might call him a shadow, but only in an attempt to frame a paradox. Man was one thing the Greeks were sure of.

Such a humanism, religious both in its intensity and in the obligation it placed upon the individual, and rooted in the antique authority of Homer, formed the core of the Athenian genius in the age of Sophocles. Scarcely less important, however, than the "grand tradition," and equally founded upon Homer, was the tradition of religious rationalism. Its characteristic concern was the nature of the gods them-

selves, and its chief aim was to achieve a scheme of theodicy whereby
the evil in experience could be rationalized and adjusted to the idea
of Divine Justice. At no time were the Greeks entirely content to
leave the gods remote and inscrutable; the object of the rationalistic
spirit, which bred the Ionian "physicists" and attained such phenomenal heights of abstraction in the fourth century, had been in its
earliest, and even in many of its later phases, a religious one — the
problem of God's comprehensibility. The attempt to know God was
in itself, as Professor Werner Jaeger has so ably demonstrated, a religious act.[3] It was this kind of religiosity which built the framework
of the *Odyssey*, in which Zeus and Athena figure as gods absorbed in
creating moral order. No less does Hesiod emphasize, both in the
Theogony and the *Works and Days*, the strict justice of Zeus who is
constantly at war with darker powers, whether they be unruly Titans
or human greed. And this same spirit of religious rationalism came to
Athens in the person of Solon, whose long first elegy is a powerful,
though somewhat disjointed and archaic, attempt to embrace the un-
predictable chaos of experience within a scheme of eventual Divine
Order. This poem is important to the history of the drama, for its
chief concerns — inherited guilt, unlooked-for disaster, and a World
Justice which functions through time — became at length, almost
without change, the foundation of the tragic design of Aeschylus.
In the *Oresteia*, Zeus, who brings justice slowly but surely and provides for the institution of the courts of the polis to represent him on
earth, was the climax of Athenian rational theology.

But the stream had many channels, and while Aeschylus labored
to bring just and comprehensible gods out of the traditional myths,
the intellectual successors of the Ionian philosophers continued the
search for divinity in nature.[4] Parmenides and Heraclitus ushered in
the philosophical thought of the fifth century with the two polarities
of pure Being and pure Becoming, respectively, while in the next
generation Archelaus and Anaxagoras, both Athenians by adoption,
continued the older method of the formulation of natural causes. It
should be, if it is not yet, an admitted fact that these so-called "physicists" were in reality theologians concerned with establishing, through
rational observation of the phenomenal world, the unchanging form
of its divine essence. One finds, therefore, among them — particularly

in their enthusiastic herald Xenophanes — a total reaction against the anthropomorphism of mythology. Xenophanes' relation to the "physicists" is an interesting one; for while they overlooked, on the whole, the question of the morality of God, he made a considerable issue of it by satirizing gods who lied, stole, and committed adultery like human beings.[5] He insisted, in short, that the true God must be good, an idea which appears more than once in the work of Euripides. The whole effort of early philosophic speculation was to divest divinity of its human attributes and know it as divinity.

The new Sophists, on the other hand, regarded divinity as, by and large, a human projection. Sometimes only a fine line divides religious questioning from outright agnosticism. As the philosophers studied the natural universe in a purely theoretical spirit, the Sophists, having in view primarily the practical uses of things, gave up the nature of divinity, or of the world at large, and turned exclusively to human nature. Protagoras, it is well known, found the existence of the gods a moot question and stated that man was the measure of all things. Others went further than he, until in the later years of the Sophistic, Critias, the cultivated and somewhat notorious kinsman of Plato, could suggest in his satyr play, *Sisyphus*, that the gods were invented by a skillful politician in order to frighten the mob into obedience.[6] With divinity so neatly disposed of, justice could then be defined in disillusioned, practical terms of power and advantage.[7] Plato's defiant insistence on the hopeless opposition of the "true philosopher" and the Sophist was indeed just: for the philosophers from the beginning had regarded divinity as the inevitable predicate of the functioning of the natural world (*physis*), immanent in it and directing it; whereas the Sophists generally treated divinity as one of the outgrowths of the far-reaching world of convention (*nomos*), and thereby attained an irreligiosity less notable for its denunciation of religion than for its practical ability to do without it altogether, except insofar as it could be useful in furthering personal or political aims.

The effect of the Sophistic Enlightenment on the generations of Sophocles and Euripides was, of course, tremendous. Before this violent counterblast to centuries of religious thought, the mind of Euripides was driven and battered; his plays abound in the nature-versus-convention debate, and in all the stock-in-trade arguments from "advantage," "likelihood," and the "right of the stronger." He accepts the Sophistic teaching about human nature and presents his disillusioned world bitterly in these terms; yet he cannot let the gods rest, but hammers them with indefatigable criticism in the Xenophanean vein, examples of which would run on to tedious length. It is usually said that he did this in order to break down superstition and replace it with reason. But that is not really the case.

Euripides was neither a Sophist nor a great rationalist.[8] His passionately religious instinct caused him constantly to rebel in agony against Sophistic doctrines which, however, he could not deny. In reality he was no less concerned than Aeschylus was to see some kind of justice in the world and to identify it with God. But in the bright glare of the Enlightenment it was not easy. The gods, with all their human attributes, certainly looked like a human invention, and even the Aeschylean Zeus became a little transparent when the Athenian institutions, through whose medium he had seemed so comprehensible and true in 458, were examined in the days of Cleon and Hyperbolus. Euripides was really a little archaic. He worked at the problem of divinity without ever having fully digested or thought out the ideas of his time, turning hopelessly from one horn of the dilemma to the other. If he faced the facts of irrational evil and looked at the gods as mere impersonal forces of nature, they were, indeed, supreme, but cruel and revolting; if, on the other hand, he regarded them as rational powers, or even persons, capable of goodness, it was manifest that they were neither consistently good nor even particularly competent — "out upon the gods." [9] The two goddesses of the *Hippolytus* sum up his ambivalence: Aphrodite is the naked and merciless drive of sex, but Artemis has the touch of myth upon her; she is kind and beautiful, even exalted, but remote and not all-powerful, and capable of an equally cruel vengeance as Aphrodite's.[10] Neither naturalism nor myth could satisfy. In the end, Euripides gave it all up and wrote in the incomparable *Bacchae* a shattering paean of unreason, a hymn to the god of the beautiful but meaningless world.

But if the Sophistic rationalism destroyed Euripides, its effect on Sophocles was quite the reverse. Confronted with the same religious dilemmas as his fellow dramatist, Sophocles stood his ground and thought through the implications of religion as a human invention and man as the measure of all things. The grace and power with which his intellect moved amid and transcended the rabid theorizing of the *avant-garde* is one of the miracles of artistic history and almost justifies the classic impression of Sophocles as one who stood quite apart from his time. But he did not stand apart. A full-sized study could be made of passages wherein he touches on ideas current among his contemporaries, and throughout the foregoing analysis of his plays an attempt has been made to align certain basic conceptions with corresponding phases of fifth-century thought. But the most important of these is the relation of his religion as a whole to the Sophistic. Sophocles offered no objection whatever to the theory that divinity was man made. He simply adhered to the conviction that it was man's greatest and most wonderful creation, and demonstrated in the heroic actions of his plays the tragic steps by which man created it. Like all the men of his time, except perhaps Euripides, Sophocles ceased to look for justice from Zeus, the gods, or the inanimate world in general. He found it in man's own soul. He wove no complex rational system to explain evil as part of a larger divine plan. A very clear analogy exists between the relation of Aeschylus to Sophocles, and the relation of the early physical philosophers to the Sophists: for Aeschylus, like the philosophers, sought for the all-embracing plan, the rationale of godhead, while Sophocles abandoned the theoretical for the psychological and turned from theology to morality, from transcendent to immanent divinity. Thus he shared the focus of his period and could speak adequately to his audiences. But his emphasis is distinct and quite his own; to a society in which religious decay was having its fullest centrifugal effect, he tried constantly to reveal again the outlines of the heroic idea, in whose light "the gains of virtue are alone secure." His emphasis is an inward one, centered wholly upon the individual, who has in him the divinity to create divinity.

Yet he did not merely praise man as the contriver of religion. The generation of Sophocles felt confronted by a challenge to prove, if possible, the existence of Deity. If Sophocles found that divinity was in man, and was in some sense the creation of his own moral being, that did not mean that divinity was an idle dream. It was an extension of the heroic tradition which was still so strong in Athens until the death of Pericles, and it has certain points of contact with other religious thought of the fifth century. Once man had been declared the measure of all things, man rose to the occasion magnificently. In no century before or after did he so thoroughly and directly thrash out his differences with God. The question of God's existence gave rise among the philosophers of nature to a teleological method of study whereby existing things could be explained with reference to a purpose, or divine plan. Hence we find the doctrine implicit in Anaxagoras that the mind of man is the divine in him, enabling him to comprehend the Divine Mind which arranged all things at the beginning.[11] Similarly in Diogenes of Apollonia the "measure of nature," by which its excellent arrangement is preserved, is taken as evidence, together with the works of nature and the functional design of the human body, of Divinity at work.[12]

Sophocles was, of course, no teleologist, but these examples show that ideas of immanent divinity were not altogether repellent to the age. How much he may even have been directly indebted to these thinkers is a serious and probably unanswerable question. It would seem, however, that he accepted no complete doctrine from anybody, philosopher or Sophist. True, in the "yielding" speech of the *Ajax*, there appears to be a distinct reference to the "measure of nature," [13] but whether or not the idea is derived from Diogenes, it is clear that Ajax at least does not believe it. The idea is woven in with popular wisdom about not indulging friendships too far,[14] and all are together rejected as the kind of world in which Ajax is unwilling to live.

There is more than mere artistry in the way in which Sophocles, though he makes use of such ideas to his purpose, manages to avoid any explicit or frigid intellectualizing. Ajax may perhaps quote Diogenes, but he remains Ajax; the dramatic validity of the character is never for an instant submerged in the poet's personal concern. The reason for this is doubtless that the poet's concern was the character, in whom he felt the complete moral cosmos existed. Had Sophocles been the simple, old-fashioned pietist he has been imagined, had he felt that the moral and religious answer to life lay in the remote and inscrutable gods themselves, he could never have been able to seek and find so fully rounded a dramatic vehicle in the lonely tragic hero. He would have been forced to reason of the gods themselves, apart from man, and would have had to walk in some of the paths laid out by the theological rationalism of his predecessors, especially Aeschylus. But the Sophistic wing of rationalism had in some sense freed him from all that. For a poet driven to such moral inwardness as Sophocles was, the question of anthropomorphism for instance could have had little significance. He never, in fact, says anything about it at all. His silence on the subject gains wider importance when one reflects that the reaction against mythology which first found voice in Xenophanes in reality did not make the gods less anthropomorphic. For when Xenophanes decided that it was "unfitting" for gods to commit human sins, he was only imposing his own judgment about what it was fitting for gods to do.

Similarly, when Euripides, in a fragment quoted earlier, said, "If the gods do evil, they are not the gods," he had nothing but his own feelings to support him, and Homer would surely have laughed. With the development of civic ideals in the polis, justice had become the leading motif of Greek civilization, and it was hence, after a fashion, foisted upon the heavenly pantheon; Critias, though doubtless his aims were destructive, yet made no mistake when he showed that the most moral conception of God was only a vast projection of human conscience. In the whole movement to moralize the gods, the most evident result is merely that one degree of anthropomorphism yielded to another. Euripides seems not to have understood this; but the Sophists did, and so did Sophocles.

It seems inescapable that Socrates knew it too. The man who associated constantly with the Sophists and was blamed as the "teacher" of Critias for the latter's political misdeeds could hardly have failed to understand that the belief in the transcendency of moral order was exactly that — a belief. No one, of course, if Plato's account be true, could have proclaimed that belief with greater ardor than Socrates, but that it was admittedly a matter of faith with him is clear from a sentence in the *Crito*: "I know that few people agree to these things, or ever will; for between those who believe this and those who do not, there is no common counsel, but rather inevitable mutual contempt, when they perceive each other's doctrines." [15] Even Socrates had to admit that dialectic was helpless when it came to the most basic point of all — faith. It is interesting to observe in juxtaposition these two deeply religious and hopelessly misunderstood men: Socrates, who was executed on charges amounting to impiety and moral corruption, and Sophocles, who left the greatest reputation for simple piety of any man of his age. The contemporaries of Socrates knew scarcely more than we do about his views on the gods themselves; and the same must have been true, to some extent, in the case of Sophocles. Yet both men were completely typical of their time, Socrates the philosopher adhering closely to the theocentric focus of the rationalistic tradition and evolving thereby a universal idea of God which was to revolutionize Western civilization; Sophocles the poet probing the everlastingly fertile idea of the heroic individual — a concept which continued to embody the most deeply felt cultural aspiration of Athens until the end of the century, when the effects of the war on an over-emancipated generation managed to destroy it forever.

The personalities of these two men could hardly have been more different, yet in one important respect they resemble each other: that is in their inwardness. Both men laid their emphasis on the relation between morality and self-knowledge and zealously upheld the ethic sufficiency of man's inner being. Socrates, however, to whom society seemed misled by materialistic ends, invoked the perfect goodness of God as the necessary condition for universal cosmos, paving with his faith the way for the systematic ontological realism of Plato, wherein divine perfection becomes fully objectified. And thus the religion of Socrates, as Plato at least represents it, anticipates by four hundred years or more the dawn of a revealed creed which was destined to give substance and authority to the belief in God's illimitable benignity. The religion of Sophocles looks backward three hundred years to the *Iliad*, whose gods feel few moral obligations, and asserts for the last time the moral creativity of the individual as himself a cosmos, in his very ability, one might say, to have faith, to strive and die for the superhuman stature which he symbolized in the figures of the gods. To the last poet of the pagan grand tradition, morality and justice were the normal property of the magnanimous man, not of the gods. The gods had power, and no one knew how much. But their powers could be limited by the moral tenacity of the great man. And probably the greatest living example of such moral tenacity and creativity in the fifth century was Socrates himself.[16]

After the battle of Aegospotami, Greece underwent a century of metamorphosis, in the course of which the basic unity of individual and society, which formed one of the principal foundation stones of the city-state, was dissolved. In earlier periods, the Greek individual had been able to find his ethical validity within the existent polis: for Plato it was no longer possible. The *Antigone* unquestionably reflects one of the earliest phases of the rift between city and citizen; Creon, drawn in tyrannical or oligarchic colors, embodies the moral atrophy of civic institutions, while the heroine herself presents the ideal of individual moral perception. Her tragedy is a tragedy which Sophocles, writing at the peak of Athenian greatness, could envision as a possibility. Yet, though he may foreshadow the problems, he does not reject the assumption of the city-state; the whole drama is cast in terms of it. The *Antigone* is "political" through and through, in the broad Greek sense of "pertaining to the polis." For the religious adherences of Sophocles are profoundly interwoven with the whole concept of the city-state, and neither could exist without the other. Somewhat as the Sophoclean hero stands alone by his own moral force, the city-state looked to its own inner, organic structure for its justification; it could live only through the individual political conscience of its statesmen and citizens, and it would last only so long as there was someone strong enough to understand it. Demosthenes, appearing against the background of Athens' last days of political significance, seems almost like a post mortem epiphany of the old spirit. Actually, it had been dead, or all but dead, for some time. Throughout the fourth century the problem of individual salvation had had less and less to do with the city. There were all manner of channels in which it might be sought — philosophical, rhetorical, scientific — but the variety of the fourth century, though it preserved the concept of the city-state, had no functioning social unit to draw it together.

Not only were man and the state divided, but also man was divided, in some sense, from himself. The Platonic dualism of soul and body is symbolic of its age. Once more, in Sophocles one can see the initial stages of this dualism in the paradoxical distinctions between inner and outer in the *Philoctetes* and especially in the *Oedipus at Colonus*. Nevertheless, for Sophocles it was a paradox, a single truth with opposing implications: man has an inner and an outer being, which may contrast strongly, but they are deeply necessary to each other. As yet there is no real dualism. Philoctetes' excellence, symbolized by the bow, and Philoctetes' social repugnance, symbolized by the festering wound, cannot be separated. Oedipus the "hated of god" and Oedipus the hero are one man. No less in Socrates, in contrast to his followers, was there a characteristic essence which unified his many-faceted nature with its ugly exterior and inner beauty and endowed him with the genuinely fifth-century ability to live as a citizen and play the role to the very end, in the most heroic sense of the grand tradition.[17] But the fourth century struggled to resolve its paradoxes: inner and outer became separate and discrete, the one divine and the other human. For Sophocles in the fifth century, the interdependence of the two was itself evidence of and a commentary on divinity. The divinity which was man's belonged to the whole man. Given merely a soul, with no flesh and blood to deal with, man for Sophocles could have had no moral fibre; the stakes would have been taken out of the tragic game. For Sophocles much wonder lies in the fact that all this heroic strength grows in so weak a vessel.

The heroic aspiration found its natural expression in the myths. In the earliest days of the city-state, Homer was the first to set them forth in artistic form, extracting from them, by selection and emphasis, the meanings which had been there from the beginning. The emergence of the Homeric epic and the rise of the city-state cannot be totally independent phenomena; no more can Sophoclean tragedy be considered as independent of the Sophistic Age, the greatness and decline of Athens. The history of the city-state is bounded by these two poets who could see the heroic and the social, the aristocratic and the democratic in terms of each other. No other poets handle myth as they do. Neither in Sophocles nor in Homer is there an overlay of meaning. They had no need of it, for both could penetrate to that essential understanding of the individual in the world, whereof each myth is an aspect and each god a symbolic entity who lends timeless dimension and reality to action and circumstance. Myth offered both breadth and loftiness: within its scheme, if a poet resisted the temptation to superpose an immediate or timely concern, it was possible to see the naked truths of experience, stripped of detail and dated function. Wherever the tale might fit the present, as it may have done in the case of the *Ajax*, Sophocles allowed it to do so.

But primarily he sought and found what had always been the heart of Hellenic folklore — the dignity of man against the indignity of his fate. For this reason, and not because he was a "primitivist," the myths provided him with much to retell and little to change. They still contained the heroic core. They could still carry him through all strata of experience, seeking for that which might be called divine; [18] at the same time, with such media, he could move freely among the theoretical tendencies of his time, estimating them without commitment, and judging them without rancor. The saws of the people, the argumentative finesse of the Sophists, political antinomies with their ethic roots, the speculations of the naturalists — all these have their meaning for Sophocles, but no one of them is his meaning. Only the myth contained life whole.

Tragedy dealt less dogmatically and more analytically with the problems of divinity, morality, and justice than did any other form of Greek literature. In those years when it seemed necessary to find a just god in heaven or lose moral order entirely, Euripides made his Amphitryon, in peril of his life, exclaim:

> In virtue I, a mortal, conquer you, great god! [19]

And to Euripides that was a bitter fact. But to Sophocles it was both a bitter and a triumphal fact, for he alone had transcended even that form of anthropomorphism which demands that the gods satisfy human moral norms. Sophocles was more ready to identify the gods with irrational evil than with eternal justice. Yet it would be absurd to tag him therefore as merely a pessimist. True indeed, he could say on occasion that it was better not to be born; [20] yet his heroes are far removed from any such popular quietism. Each wears his own peculiar radiance which affirms life in the large for the hero who has the faith to conceive it morally in the face of all the circumstances which tend to deny its value. Ajax would rather die than yield; Antigone is determined to suffer for her right, Oedipus will know himself; the love of Deianeira, the hatred of Electra, and the independence of Philoctetes are invincible. What knowledge or suspicion of eternity and value in themselves gives them the power to affirm such confidence and self-respect?

The answer to this question lies in the cultural temper of the Age of Pericles. The heroic tradition of faith in man reached a climax in its resistance to the forces which were already building the postwar world of the fourth century, and found its most complete expression in the works of Sophocles. The idea of arete could receive such direct symbolic presentation in Sophocles chiefly because the time was ripe. Even so familiar a work of art as the procession of knights from the Parthenon, wherein each figure is an ideal norm subtly individualized by its own personal beauty, shows how germane it was to the age to see in each individual the immanent, and in some degree, normative and divine cosmos. From the very beginning, arete had embraced this combination of the general and the particular. In Sophocles, the hero's particular morality grows to the stature of a type without ever losing the hero's name and personality. After him, this never happens again. In Plato's hands, the meaning of arete changed radically and lost its personal affiliations, becoming instead purely general; the old idea was dead. Sophocles' poetry is the *stele* which records its mystery for all time.

The association of divinity with arete showed itself most clearly in the *Oedipus at Colonus*, in the spectacle of a man who became a god through adherence to what he knew to be the moral truth about himself. Similarly, the close of the *Philoctetes*, with its reference to "immortal arete," reveals the peculiarly Sophoclean intuition of the indestructible value of a great man. In earlier plays, the idea is less pronounced, but it appears in such tentative and suggestive symbols as the Niobe and Amphiaraus passages of the *Antigone* and *Electra*. The notion of "becoming a god" through arete is confined, in these terms, to the fifth century, though the idea of an eternal extension of a hero's value after death is as old as the heroic ideal itself, and is at least partially implicit in the "divine" and "godlike" honorifics of Homer. Indeed, in one place, Homer makes all men pray to "Zeus among gods and Nestor among men" [21] — a rather unusual line. But in the fifth century, one finds traces of a widespread acquiescence to the conception — if it may be called such — of "immortal arete." The encomia and lapidary epigrams of Simonides offer well-known examples:

> Of these who died in Thermopylae,
> Far renowned in their fortune, glorious their fate;
> Their tomb is an altar; for them no mourning, but
>   memory; for them no dirge but praise.
> And such an epitaph
> Not rust nor conquering time shall waste away.
> This tomb of noble men takes for its minister
> The glory of Greece. Witness hereof is Leonidas,
> The Spartan king, who left behind the great splendor
>   [*kosmos*] of arete,
> And fame forever fresh.[22]

Again:

> If to die well is virtue's [*arete*] greatest part,
> To us of all men Fate has granted this:
> Zealous to garland Greece with liberty,
> We lie in death, enjoying ageless fame.[23]

And perhaps most clearly:

> These, reckoning glory in their country's cause
> Quenchless, are wrapped in the dark cloud of death;
> They died, but are not dead; up from the house
> Of death transfiguring virtue [*arete*] leads them back.[24]

In these lines, Simonides is not necessarily displaying any great originality; the style is typical: Aeschylus himself, speaking of those who fell in a battle in Thessaly, uses almost the same language:

> A dark fatality slew also these
> Staunch men, defenders of their country's flocks.
> But living is the dead men's fame, who wrapped
> In pain the dust of Ossa round their limbs.[25]

Most significant of all, perhaps, so far as the wide diffusion of the idea is concerned, is the fifth-century Attic drinking song:

> Beloved Harmodius, you are not dead. . .[26]

Such expressions have, of course, become commonplaces of eulogistic oratory, and it might be maintained that even in antiquity they were mere modes of praise. But the fact is that commonplaces have

their origins in true feelings, and such statements as these rarely ante-
date the fifth century. When Homer's heroes die, their fame indeed
lives, but the clear conviction of historic value, of a kind of personal
deathlessness, is lacking. As Achilles intimates, there is no consolation
for the dead.[27] For though the departed shade may continue in Hades
some of the pursuits or attitudes which characterized the living person,
yet only life in the flesh is real life; after death, all is simply image and
shadow, with no substance but memory. Once Tyrtaeus says that a
man who falls in battle for his country becomes "immortal under the
earth"; but while this isolated line seems to arise from the Spartan
ideal of well-ordered society rather than from belief in the individual,
in the fifth century, the sense of the timelessness of values had given
birth to a strongly personal intuition of eternity in the context of
heroism, and the idea found its way into many of the diverse channels
of current thought, even into the cryptic sayings of Heraclitus.[28] It
was, therefore, to a broad and deeply felt basis of religious humanism
that Sophocles appealed with his lines on the "immortal arete" and
"present deity" of heroes; nor was it merely a manner of speaking
when Pericles himself, in a funeral oration for those who fell in the
Samian War (where Sophocles was his fellow general), added the
following explicit statement: "They [the fallen] are immortal as the
gods: for we do not see them themselves, but only by the honors we
pay them, and by the benefits they do us, attribute to them immortality; and the like attributes belong also to those that die in the service
of their country." [29]

The question of exactly what this whole belief entailed, in the
way of formal eschatology, is a hard one. Even if more evidence were
forthcoming, it would be highly dubious whether a precise philosophy
of the afterlife could be derived from it, for the very elasticity of
the idea was a condition of its existence. Furthermore, it depended in
great part on individual experience and action. It had little to do with
the other world, or the soul, as such, and everything to do with the
dynamic Athenian approach to life in this world. Hence it could
never become, even in the remotest sense, a dogma. Yet, for sheer
audacity and defiant insistence on human dignity, this vision of
"divine man" puts to shame all doctrines of the soul's immortality.

The immortality of the soul is an idea which gains acceptance only in an age of spiritual dividedness such as the fourth century, when the circumstances of life and education forced the soul into seclusion from the body for survival. As it appears in Plato, it is a philosophical theory, mystically conceived, dialectically supported, and fundamentally dependent upon the hope that the unseen is the real and true. The fifth-century idea of "immortal arete" is a moral estimate of man entire, as a being whose existence is partly in time and partly out of it, but in no sense disunified. It resembles Homeric kleos, except that it is even more lofty and indestructible, for it embraces an infinitely broader ethic and implies the achievement of a greater kind of reality.

The only true vehicle for such an outlook is tragedy, wherein man can be presented both analytically and synthetically. The Sophoclean hero passes from the world of his own struggle, led by the daimon of his moral strength, into a kind of divine historical existence; or, more briefly, that which was always divine within him makes him wholly divine. He does not correspond with God; he "becomes a god." His triumph consists in the achievement of an eternal aspect of being, through his exceeding moral fiber. To conceive a great individual as a moral landmark and then view him historically is a kind of prophecy; and in this sense Sophocles was a prophet. In this sense too his prophetic role was identical with his role as the poet of the Periclean city-state, which Thucydides characterized as not exactly democracy but the "rule of the first man." [30] The Athenian democracy rested upon the unity of classes under arete, and the validity of the human mind in perceiving justice and law. No limit was set to the potential of the individual, and Pericles, who most truly represented the moral consistency of the city, enjoyed almost unlimited power. His position was implicit in democratic theory, as he and every Alcmaeonid knew; its justification was genius. Only in a city which fostered and believed in the illimitable scope of human genius could such a work as the *Oedipus at Colonus*, to take the most striking example, have been written. But the other plays are equally representative: it is Sophocles the Athenian — one might almost say, the Periclean — who reveals man as able to understand his duty to himself, like Ajax, or to real authority, like Antigone; able to seek and find himself, like Oedipus and Deianeira, and to take the consequences of self-knowledge; able, like Electra and Philoctetes, to live through the problem of living amid the abuses of the world and society.

The plays of Sophocles are not the works of one who stood apart from his age. As primary documents of the Periclean Age, they constitute an epic paean of the Athenian spirit. Pericles himself once said that such a record was unnecessary; [31] but perhaps it had become necessary by the latter years of the war. In any case, it is of infinite value to history.

XII

THE METAPHYSIC OF HUMANISM

THROUGHOUT the preceding chapters the emphasis has fallen on what has been termed "inward divinity," the arete of the heroic tradition, which in the fifth century prevailed in the Athenian mind as a unifying and motivating assumption, a religious humanism that lay behind the vast cultural, political, and artistic projections of the age. It now remains to formulate, if possible, the metaphysical implications of this humanism, to describe at least the boundaries, if not the nature, of the divine outside of man. For inward divinity was never, to the Greek mind, the only divinity, though it may have been the only knowable form, the only form which could be observed in the phenomenal life of man in the world. To a certain degree all things were divine; and when Oedipus becomes a god, his inward being takes its place among other immutables which are detached from time. Since tragedy deals with humanity, critical emphasis upon the inward aspect of the divine is predetermined; yet, since Oedipus goes to the gods, some speculation on what the process meant to Sophocles and his audience is equally inescapable.

For this, an excellent starting point is provided by Aristotle, in certain passages mentioned earlier,[1] where the philosopher speaks of "divine virtue" and "noble incontinence." These two phrases are both, in a way, pointed and deliberate contradictions in term, whose import for the tragic paradox has been all but overlooked. At the very commencement of the seventh book of the *Nicomachean Ethics*, Aristotle, "making," as he says, "a new beginning," poses a categorical triad of things to be avoided: vice, incontinence, and brutishness. The opposites of these form a triad of things to be **sought**, two of which have well known names: the opposite of vice **is virtue** (arete), and the opposite of incontinence is continence. To brutishness, however, is opposed "a kind of superhuman virtue, heroic and divine . . . so that, if, as they

say, men become gods through an excess of virtue, such would obviously be the habit opposed to brutishness: for as the brute has neither
vice nor virtue, similarly neither has God." [2] The statement about men
becoming gods through an excess of virtue seems to be quoted from
popular parlance; to make clear what he means, Aristotle gives Hector
as an example and quotes Homer.[3]

Closely allied to this idea, though never actually identified with
it, is the recognition that continence is not always good. It may for
instance lead one to the suppression of good appetites; conversely,
incontinence may lead one to the indulgence of good appetites and
may therefore be good. At this point, significantly enough, Aristotle
cites Sophocles' character of Neoptolemus as an example of noble incontinence, because he indulged a noble pleasure — the pleasure of
telling the truth.[4] This may seem a little naïve, since Neoptolemus
himself expressed the most adequate possible moral reasons for telling
the truth to Philoctetes; indeed, one could find better examples of
noble incontinence, and later, Aristotle himself does so. Niobe, he
asserts, followed the noble pleasure of mother-love to an excessive degree, yet without moral guilt.[5] Her act, he concludes, was not exactly
incontinence; if it is to be called incontinence, a qualification must
be added: incontinence in respect of something. Niobe, therefore, one
might say, was incontinent in respect of mother-love — a virtue —
and hence, excessive in virtue.

It is clear from the example of Niobe that "noble incontinence"
and "heroic and divine arete" resemble each other closely. Aristotle's
choice of examples is interesting, also, for they are all taken from
tragic or heroic poetry. Niobe, who is doubtless drawn from Aeschylus, has a particular significance when one recalls that Sophocles
twice refers to her directly as a goddess, though the point of her story
had originally been her all too human attachments. For Aristotle to
present her in the light of one guilty of "noble incontinence" — that
excess of virtue through which men become gods — indicates that
not only for Sophocles, perhaps, was Niobe a symbol of the everlasting value of the human spirit.[6]

This whole portion of the *Nicomachean Ethics* is a little surprising.
The values here introduced seem to have little to do with the rest of
the treatise wherein virtue is regularly discovered as lying in the mean

between two extremes; neither is it entirely clear what, if any, connection exists between these tragic examples of excessive virtue and the well-known statement in the *Poetics* that the tragic hero should not be a man of exceeding virtue and justice. One thing, however, is clear: virtue (arete) in this part of the *Ethics* does not have the univocal meaning which it achieved in the Academy. As Aristotle uses the word here, it has reference to contexts familiar in the fifth century rather than the fourth, which accounts for the examples drawn from poetry. Clearly the philosopher is taking into account that heroic aspect of human nature found in the older poets, before "arete" was narrowed to a single meaning. For Aristotle, the philosopher of the norm or mean, to attempt to reckon with this kind of tragic but noble departure from the norm argues an honest desire for completeness, even at the expense of the consistent scheme. It must furthermore be associated with his interests as a historian of culture. Plato was occupied with his spiritual revolt from fifth-century culture and with the establishment of a new ideal in education. To Aristotle, a generation younger, the civilization of earlier eras was already a field for research and study; he was therefore sympathetically more free, perhaps, to interpret the monuments of the Periclean Age than his master had been. If the discussion of "noble incontinence" and "heroic virtue" seems a little disjointed from the rest of Aristotle's ethical thinking, it is doubtless because it is just such an interpretation, involving an ideal which he could approach historically, but which was difficult, and perhaps impossible, to fit into the rest of his design. That he personally felt a deep emotional appeal in these heroic values is proven by the language of his *Hymn to Arete*. It is a scholar's poem, a little frigid, but modeled on the old hymnic style and containing one of the most explicit statements of the immortalizing function of heroic arete.[7]

In view of this whole context, Aristotle's schematic triad of virtue, continence, and heroic virtue may now legitimately be applied to tragedy, at least in part. The remark, for instance, that the gods have neither virtue nor vice, because they are above them as the beast is below them, may seem axiomatic, but it is of assistance in formulating the levels of moral activity among which the plot creates the tragic tensions. These levels may be roughly, though by no means perfectly,

classified as four in number: first, the sheer immorality of the clearly
bad characters, mostly of a tyrannical sort — Creon, Clytaemnestra,
Aegisthus; second, the everyday, maxim-guided chorus, based firmly
on immovable, decent, though limited principles of moderation and
safety; with these may go Ismene, Tecmessa, and the neutral messengers. In these two lower classes we see the world very much as it is,
of mingled crime and honesty, the rather helpless melting pot of raw
human equipment. And fundamentally these two are one, even as
the picture of war and peace on the shield of Achilles are in the same
category. This is the world of sophrosyne and hybris, of knowledge
and ignorance, the merely human backdrop, itself a part of fate.

The third level is the level of the hero himself, the center of
Sophocles' tragic world. The hero's arete, as the most active moral
force in nature, differs qualitatively from the values of the first two
levels by being both divine and human at once. It is human because
it is moral, but its existence creates a process of becoming divine. Because of its qualitative difference from the world, it conflicts below
with the first two levels and moves toward the fourth, which is Deity
itself, or, in more Hellenic terms, the divine substance of all things.
Yet because the fourth level is above morality as it is above humanity,
the relationship is one of keen life-and-death conflict. And herein of
course lies both the moral glory of tragedy and its human poignancy.

It is precisely to make clear these interlocking conflicts that Sophocles used oracles, epiphanies, curses, and the rest of the supernatural
machinery, as symbols of the timeless facts which the play's action
proves. Sophocles may have believed in some oracles, or partly believed, with others of his time, like Pericles, who did not let them
deter him from his purpose;[8] but as they are used in the drama, these
tragic "properties" cannot be taken as evidence of superstition. The
inward, functional, and organic divinity woven in the tragic nexus of
life cannot be conveyed in explicit words, but it can be symbolized.
Such transcendent statements as those from Delphi, or the gods, cut
across the mental limitations of each moral level, though the hero, in
his highest development, may not need them. As old Oedipus says in
answer to an oracle, when he himself is verging on timeless godhead,
"A man may gather as much by his own insight."[9] He might have
added, that if the hero's special arete were something other than

"insight" (*gnome*, the special virtue of Oedipus), it would serve almost as well. The real word is "action." For Oedipus, action was *gnome*, but each hero has his own arete, through whose activation he comes to be what the oracle says he is. What happens from within is only summarized in what seems to be prophesied from without.[10]

The struggle of the hero with the lower levels is generally explicit: in each of the plays its issues are set forth clearly in such antitypes as Antigone versus Creon, Deianeira versus Lichas, or Electra versus her mother. Between the hero and the upper or supramoral level of the gods, the struggle is implicit and must be approached either through the supernatural symbols or through provocative motifs, such as Oedipus' picture of himself as "the brother of the months," or his cry that Apollo had destroyed him, though he himself struck the blow. All such motifs center around the basic feeling that the gods are unjust. This is, of course, natural and inevitable, for in his dealings with the fourth level the hero faces a supramoral realm not responsible to the values by which he is forced to live. In their answers to the problem of evil, the Greeks tried constantly to embrace this irrational aspect, but only Sophocles, it seems, saw the supramorality of God as a plain ontological fact. He could, at times, cry out against it, as if it were not supramorality but immorality, as he did in the close of the *Trachiniae*. His dark middle period teems with the negative aspect. But for the most part he could leave the gods to their own existence, be it whatever it was, and by concentration on human arete discover therein another form of divinity. Thereby a metaphysic was established, for divinity could appear in the world, and man, by setting up his moral essence in contrast to the gods, could give it the dignity it deserved. For though divinity outside of man had no need for morality, divinity in man was morality, and the interaction of the kinds of divinity is the key to Sophocles' world order.

The prevailing theory is that the world order of Sophocles involves two realms, one of humanity and one of the gods, between which lies an impassable gulf; any attempt by man to cross the gulf and know the gods better is overweening and hybristic, for actually man is a nothingness and only the gods are real.[11] Sometimes it is added that a scheme of universal justice, similar to that of Aeschylus, is somehow inherent in this rigid design.[12] Such an account directly contravenes the moral validity of man, that is, of the hero, which the action of the plays illustrates. Yet some foundation for this interpretation seems to exist in Sophocles' frequent uses of the theme of shadow and substance, illusion and reality. These passages, for the most part, have been noted as they occur,[13] but a summary estimate of their meaning here will not be amiss. The idea was, of course, a commonplace: Homer, Mimnermus, Pindar, and even Aeschylus had used it, undeniably with the implication of the nothingness of man.[14] In his famous speech in the prologue of the *Ajax*, Odysseus means no more by it than the deceptiveness of apparent greatness and happiness. Yet on the whole the recurrence of this theme in Sophocles is more in the nature of an oblique reference to, than a direct statement of, the world order.

When Sophocles calls man a nothing or an image (*eidolon*), or says darkness is light or the world a dream, the motif has clearly to do with knowledge and being; with what we know or think we know, and with what we are, or think we are. Faced with the sight of Ajax mad, Odysseus heaves a sigh of disillusion; but before the body of Ajax dead in his glory, he takes a strong positive stand in defence of the man who was "the best of all the Greeks . . . except Achilles." In both the early plays, the fate of the protagonist has the effect of distinguishing truth from seeming: the arete of Ajax or Antigone emerges as a solid reality which all must recognize. In the later works, the implications are even clearer. Through a long series of deceptive appearances, Electra comes to the central paradox that she is really the strong one, though she seems weak. Her arrival at full self-knowledge is the climax of the play. Similarly in the *Philoctetes* the hero cries:

> . . . What do you want with me,
> Who am nothing, and long since was dead to you?[15]

The truth, however, turns out to be that he is not "nothing" — the veil of appearance breaks under the force of his will. Finally, it is Oedipus himself who gives the paradox of human substance and shadow most simply in the form of a question:

> When I am nothing, then am I a man?[16]

Through such themes Sophocles drives steadily at the inner reality of moral being.[17] The action of the moral will is alone valid, amid a host of deceptions; it alone is true, and must, whether it triumph by intension over death or by extension over time, be acknowledged as an eternal verity — a divine reality. Such acknowledgment is missing only in the case of Deianeira, in whose fate, it must be admitted, shadow seems to conquer substance. She breaks the nets of delusion, but she herself vanishes with them. For a few bitter years, Sophocles may well have seen life as wholly deceptive, and human excellence as meaningless.

The last lines of the *Oedipus at Colonus*, where the hero's fate is sealed with the word *kyros*, belong naturally with the passages on shadow and substance. Kyros, the authority of a ratified law, is in a sense the reality of the law, and in the Sophoclean context the word might be translated "reality." The almost visionary world of the last plays, especially the very last, embodies a profound study of the reality of man. Working for the most part indirectly, Sophocles chose often to state the problem negatively in terms of illusion and seeming, and only in his parting lines offered an unpretentious, though explicit, positive. Yet his implications are clear. Man's moral being is the only thing about him which is timeless. Like all other divinity, inner divinity is indestructible. Clear at last of the shadows and illusions, Oedipus' arete is immortal, like that of Amphiaraus and Heracles, and is gathered into the historic life of things which have real weight and authority. The world order that these haunting passages suggest is not one in which man, a nothing, is morally forbidden to cross the gulf that separates him from God. Rather his fate is that he must cross the boundary in defiance of all warnings, and by suffering and death dissolve the shadow and make his essence as timeless as the deity he contends with.

The world order of Sophocles depends far more on the nearness of God and man — their coexistence, in fact — than on their separation. Within the framework of a religion which lacks any form of Messianic mediation, something in the nature of the heroic soul is necessary in order that God may appear in human life at all. As Pericles said, "We do not see the gods themselves" — no more do we in Sophocles, but we see divinity in man achieving kyros; that is, becoming more and more real as it emerges from time, dream, and shadow. The Homeric heroes console themselves for the transitoriness of life by winning immortal kleos, which was a kind of greater, or mythic life in which the hero existed for all history. The kyros which the Sophoclean hero achieves is also eternal and personal, but as moral fact it is also universal and directly associated with divinity. For each, except Deianeira, this greater life is symbolized by a divine figure; for Antigone and Electra, it is Niobe; for Philoctetes, Heracles; Ajax and Oedipus, as established cult heroes, can be their own symbols. This process of crossing the gulf, and of "becoming divine" through moral action, is deeply essential to Greek humanism. It is the evidence of the divine existence in a world where "the gods themselves" are so remote; and since it fills the place of Messianic revelation, it entails an anthropocentric conviction — though perhaps not explicitly stated — that man is as necessary to God as God is to man.

If the divine and the human be represented as two secant circles, the one amoral and the other moral, it is in the intersecting part that the heroic soul exists; it is only the hero who can really come into contact with God, for only in the hero is moral law sufficiently binding to force him out of the realm of safety, where the chorus waits in piety and sophrosyne, into the realm of moral action. This general metaphysic was never, of course, actually formulated by Sophocles, although he came near to doing so in the *Oedipus at Colonus*. Yet certain inferences are inescapably clear. Godhead in itself — whether looked upon as singular or plural — has being and reality, but is apart from (or, as Aristotle said, above) the moral sphere. Morality, however, is also a divine thing; though it is part of man, it is also a part of God (the universal divinity of real things) without which God would be incomplete. Man and God therefore are interdependent for the completeness of the world's being: neither would have any effect, or kyros, without the other.

Action also is solely the prerogative of humanity; for in a religion where an act of grace is impossible, if man is to draw near to God, he must do it by his own efforts. Apart from man, God cannot act; apart from God, man cannot be. That which the inner and outer divinity share is Being. Outside of man it is pure. Within man it functions through the heroic will. As itself alone Being is supramoral, actionless, and transcendent; in heroic man it is moral, functional, and immanent. This is not of course to say that the gods outside man are morally evil — though that is the implication at the close of the *Trachiniae*. The divinity which exists outside man permits both good and evil — permits indeed so much evil that it can be truly said that evil is the condition of man's life.[18] But it is also the condition of his greatness. If there were no evil, he would have no more need of moral goodness than the gods. And similarly, if God possessed moral goodness in addition to his omnipotence, he would be compelled by it to forestall and prevent man's moral strength from action by saving him in advance from suffering, or at least by using suffering as a punishment for sin. But such a doctrine, though it may exist plausibly within the framework of a Christian theology of primal sin and final judgment, is unsuitable to the Greeks and especially to Sophocles. An arbiter of morality in heaven deprives man's moral goodness of originality and freedom, while at the same time it binds God to a system essentially man made and inappropriate to divinity. In Sophocles, both God and man are free. Where their two circles intersect and the amoral existence of God crosses man's world of action, the irrational evil of the universe takes on the especially tragic appearance of the injustice of the gods. Where the moral and supramoral meet, the conflict destroys human life. A purely moral position, in that it asserts the hero's pure being, more resembles the timeless than it does the human sphere; hence the hero makes himself inappropriate to life. The paradox is that in fulfillment of his human function of moral action, he separates himself from humanity. By identifying himself with absolute morality, he becomes appropriate to the Absolute.

The two forms of divinity thus interact, and neither can dispense with the other; for only through its presence in man can divinity be comprehensible, and only by the existence of and conflict with an external and completely amoral form can the divinity in man emerge and become forever real.

Hence it is clear, in the last analysis, that a third circle embraces the other two, the circle of Divinity as a whole, which is identical with the realm of Being. The two lesser circles are forever merging and forever apart, for that is the paradox of the human and heavenly natures. Religious humanism demands the acknowledgment of two fundamental forms of divinity, which may be considered as a unit but which operate in opposite ways. Within the two forms, smaller ones may appear. External divinity may show itself in all the shapes and phenomena of the world and become identified with the "gods"; internal or human divinity may appear in all the varieties of arete. The full expression in Sophocles of the activity and function of the human side defines almost by exclusion the activity and function of the external divine. Their differences are thus made known. But they have in common, obviously, a timeless durability; neither "the gods" nor the hero's will is breakable. In this quality their respective divinities coincide and exist forever; the eternity of God receives stamped upon it the impress of the moral power of man. Thus there is a kind of unity in the duality, perhaps best symbolized by the figure of the third circle of Being itself — that which is and remains.

As for the Divine apart from man, little can be said about it in the plays of Sophocles. It is utterly divested of all human attributes and should, perhaps, be looked upon only as in the nature of a living core, intuitively suspected in all things existent, but hardly describable in the large, since it does not make itself felt except as the greatness of the hero brings him into conflict with it. It possesses no conscious will toward man, but since it may be found in any circumstance involving heroic action, it may be considered as imposing a certain circumscription upon man's will. The Greeks were capable of finding in some circumstance, in some of the kaleidoscopic configurations of life, a "divine chance," and man's lot had long since been deified as the goddess Moira.[19] These configurations of life, in which the Divine essence makes itself felt, put a limit upon man; and it is perhaps the most central paradox in Sophocles that the hero, who by his arete breaks the limits set upon him by life at large does so because the virtue of his own free will sets an even stricter limit on him than Divinity is able to do. The moral limit is the most stringent of all. Only the gods are free from time, death, and old age, says the old Oedipus; all other things are subject to the sway of time.[20] If the gods are that which fashions temporal life in its fullness; if one may speak of them figuratively as "willing a limit" for man, and as fashioning life so as to effect that purpose; then it must be recognized that man's knowledge of self-limitation — that is, of moral restriction — imposes a narrower limit and pulls the rein even closer, at cost of life if necessary. And thus, but only thus, it may be argued that man's will becomes harmonized with that of "the gods." Man's volitional freedom consists in the tragic ability to live in moral limits more compelling than those of circumstance, unavailable to the timeless and actionless "gods" and created by himself.

There is no virtue in trying to schematize too closely what was plastic and visionary to the poet. Love, and a sense of wonder, illuminated the suffering with which Sophocles gazed into the ultimate mysteries, and no effort of prosaic criticism will ever outline, even dimly, the profundity of his religious insight. The figure of the three circles here offered pretends neither to exactness nor inevitability; it is most imperfect, but it tends to preserve at least that refined balance which in Greek thought could always recognize "divine things," as well as "The Divine." A certain vagueness and mystery may indeed be inevitable to the essence of humanism. For the humanist looks at the many wonderful things and finds "none more wonderful than man"; he is the codeterminant of the world order; yet if the other half were not silence and mystery, man would never be what he is.

Sophoclean tragedy is both bitter and triumphant. Each hero's fate is an illustration, or better still, a re-creation of a world order, wherein the gulf between shadowy man and eternal reality is transcended by the heroic moral fire. That is the triumphant part. The bitter or tragic part lies in the split between the hero and the rest of the world, for whom heroic arete is as inscrutable as the gods themselves. The living hero is always too large for the world. But all his consciousness of greatness, all his steadfastness and loyalty to inner law cannot console him; there is no happiness involved, but only the bleak and barren mountain peaks of grandeur. Achilles, as Homer knew, was the saddest man at Troy, and Sophocles' heroes take leave of life, or invoke their fate in laments which show the fullness of their consciousness of loss and evil. These outpourings are not weakness, but the strength of true knowledge. Only in his last play does Sophocles seem to have achieved and to have given his greatest character a sufficient abundance of that knowledge so that he can be at his departure "without groans, nor racked with pains, but, if ever mortal was, wonderful." [21]

NOTES

I. The Classic View

1. Note, for instance, the classic view of Sophocles in the well-known sepulchral epigram of Simmias, *Anth. Pal.* VII, 22; or again, in the Lateran statue.
2. *Frogs* 1043f.
3. Cf. Eur. *Troad.* 884ff.; *fg.* 596 (Nauck).
4. Cf. G. Perrotta, *Sofocle* (Messina, 1935), p. 618.
5. What little Wilamowitz did say, however, in the preface to his translations and the supplementary chapter of his son's book, deserves attention; for although he was also affected by the classic picture of Sophocles, he does broach some of the moral and historical problems in passing, and in general shows much greater freedom of approach than do most others of the period.
6. εὔκολος, *Frogs* 82.
7. *Rep.* 430e6–432a9.
8. *Il.* I, 4.
9. See Perrotta, p. 1, n. 2, for a brief summary.
10. Cf. Eudoxus' success in promulgating the theory of pleasure as the highest good, through the excellence of his own character, Arist. *Eth. Nic.* 1172b9–16.
11. *Vita Sophoclis* 12; Cicero, *De divin.* I, 54.
12. Plut. *Mor.* 1103b1f.; *Et. Mag. s. v.* Δεξίων.
13. Perrotta, p. 53.
14. W. S. Ferguson, "The Attic Orgeones," *Harvard Theological Review,* XXXVII, 61ff.
15. Plut. *Numa* 4.
16. *Vita* 17; cf. U. v. Wilamowitz, *Der Glaube der Hellenen,* II, 224f. On the whole subject of the cult of Amynos, Asclepius, and Dexion and the exact nature of Sophocles' heroization, see Ferguson, "The Attic Orgeones," and A. D. Nock, "The Cult of the Heroes," *Harvard Theological Review,* XXXVII, 2, 61–166, especially 86–91.
17. *Rep.* 329b–d (Jowett).
18. *De officiis* I, 40. Cf. Plut. *Per.* 8.
19. Diehl, *Anth. Lyr. Gr.,* I, XVIIII, 3.
20. Ion of Chios, *fg.* 67 (Köpke).
21. *Vita* 1. Cf. Perrotta, p. 3, nn. 2f.
22. Phrynichus, *Musae, fg.* 31 (Kock). Cf. *Argumentum ad Oed. Col.*
23. U. v. Wilamowitz, *Einleitung in die griechische Tragödie,* chapter i.
24. Perrotta, p. 3, suggests the urban Colonus, rather than the rural deme.
25. See Chapter IV, note 51.
26. See Max Pohlenz, *Die griechische Tragödie* (Leipzig and Berlin, 1930), p. 161.
27. For the connection of Archelaus, Cimon, and Sophocles, see: Diels, *Vorsokr.*[5] 60A5a, on an elegy written by Sophocles to Archelaus; Jaeger, *Paideia* II, 375, n. 30, for the view that Cimon was more or less the philosopher's patron; and Plut. *Cim.* 4 or Diels, 60B1, mentioning a poem possibly written by Archelaus to Cimon.
28. For example, *El.* 417ff. and *Oed. Col.* 337ff. Cf. Herod. I, 107–108, and II, 35. See Plut. *Mor.* 785b, for an ode written by Sophocles to Herodotus. Cf. Perrotta, pp. 25f. and 26 n. 1.
29. By Rasch, *Sophocles quid debeat Herodoto,* Leipzig Diss., 1913.
30. As Edmund Wilson aptly remarks (*The Wound and the Bow,* p. 293), "Somewhere even in the fortunate Sophocles there had been a sick and raving Philoctetes."
31. L. R. Farnell, *The Higher Aspects of Greek Religion,* pp. 1f.; cf. pp. 125ff.

32. Xenoph. *fg.* 10 (Diehl).
33. Thuc. I, 6, 3–4.
34. Cf. Pohlenz, pp. 14–16.
35. *Paideia* I, 255.
36. Pohlenz, pp. 8f.
37. *Ibid.*, pp. 153f.
38. *Ibid.*, p. 155, for the view that Sophocles won his popularity through the conservatism of the people. Cf. succeeding section for a general summary of Pohlenz' beliefs.
39. Fr. Lübker, *Die Sophokleische Theologie und Ethik*, 1st half (Kiel, 1851), p. 2. Lübker however does not quite succeed in showing how this excellent observation fits Sophocles.

II. Scholarship and Hamartia

1. R. C. Jebb, "The Age of Pericles," *Essays and Addresses* (Cambridge, 1907). Reprinted in Lane Cooper's *The Greek Genius and Its Influence* (New Haven, 1917), pp. 63–76. See especially p. 75.
2. T. v. Wilamowitz, *Die dramatische Technik des Sophokles* (Berlin, 1917), pp. 39f.
3. *Ibid.*, p. 64; cf. *passim*, esp. pp. 49f., 86.
4. *Ibid.*, p. 40.
5. W. Schadewaldt, "Sophokles Aias und Antigone," *Neue Wege zur Antike*, VIII, 61–109, especially 67–69, 79–82.
6. *Ibid.*, p. 79.
7. κλέος, τὸ καλόν, τὸ γενναῖον, as opposed to νοῦς, φρονεῖν, εὐβουλία, σωφρονεῖν.
8. Schadewaldt, pp. 102–105.
9. Max Pohlenz, *Die griechische Tragödie* (Leipzig and Berlin, 1930), p. 163. Cf. p. 155.
10. *Ibid.*, p. 237.
11. *Ibid.*, pp. 238f. See below, Chapters IV and V.
12. For instance, *Sophokles* (Frankfurt am Main, 1933), p. 46, where he interprets the *Trachiniae* as a "double isolation" of the two main characters. The moral issue is ignored.
13. H. Weinstock, *Sophokles* (Leipzig and Berlin, 1931), p. 6.
14. *Sofocle*, p. 633.
15. *Ibid.*, p. 631.
16. *Sophoclean Tragedy* (Oxford, 1944), p. 367. Cf. p. 285 on a similar passage in the *Philoctetes*. Bowra fails to note, however, that a good many criticisms of the gods pass without disapproval even from the chorus; for instance, *Phil.* 446ff.
17. *Ibid.*, p. 9.
18. See G. B. Shaw, *Saint Joan* (New York, 1924), Preface, p. lxxv.
19. E. Abbott, "Theology and Ethics of Sophocles," *Hellenica*, pp. 58ff., 65f.
20. *Ibid.*, p. 56.
21. J. A. Moore, *Sophocles and Arete* (Cambridge, Mass., 1938), p. 8. Cf. p. 51.
22. *Poetics* 1453a7–10. It must be noted that crimes are called ἁμαρτίαι in *Agam.* 1197, and *Choeph.* 519. The usage does not, however, correspond to Aristotle's definition.
23. The Christian conception of pride differs from hybris in that it directly relates to one's attitude toward God. A man is guilty of pride if he puts any love before the love of God. But hybris has far more to do with how a stronger man treats a weaker. If a Greek boasted that he was better than a god, it was folly, impiety, and presumption. It was also very dangerous, but it was not hybris. Eur. *Hipp.* 474 gives, not a definition, but a deliberate extension of the term to embrace a special sense.

24. *Poetics* 1452b34–36.

25. See U. v. Wilamowitz, *Griechische Tragödien ubersetzt* (Berlin, 1899–1929), I, 9, 14f.

26. Horace, *Ars Poetica* 196–201.

27. *Ant.* 471f.; *Oed. Rex* 616f.; *Phil.* 1045f.

28. *Ajax* 481–484; *El.* 217–220.

29. *Trach.* 121–126.

30. J. A. Moore, p. 56.

31. As Moore, p. 57, nicely puts it: "What is the meaning of saying that a person does wrong, if he has no opportunity to do right?"

32. S. H. Butcher, *Aristotle's Theory of Poetry and Fine Art* (London, 1902), pp. 317–332. Butcher actually allows for a wide range of meaning. This essay seems to be the best possible exposition of the function of hamartia in tragedy.

33. In *Poetics* 1453a16, hamartia is again referred to as μεγάλη, a "great frailty" (Butcher).

34. I. Bywater, *Aristotle on the Art of Poetry* (Oxford, 1909), p. 215.

35. Cf. P. W. Harsh, "Ἁμαρτία Again," *TAPA*, LXXVI (1946), 47–58, from whom much of this argument is derived. The article is extremely sound, so far as its discussion of Aristotle is concerned.

36. *Eth. Nic.* 1135b11–25.

37. *Poetics* 1451a36–b11. Harsh makes this point irrefutably clear, and it is very important, for the intellectual interpretation of hamartia would certainly reduce tragedy not only to the particular, but to the insignificant.

38. *Oed. Col.* 966ff. Cf. αἰσχρὸν ὄνειδος, *Phil.* 842, showing how the moral implications of the present passage are made inescapable by the use of ὄνειδος. However, in *Prom.* 266, the very tone in which Prometheus boasts of his "sin" (ἥμαρτον) implies not admission of moral guilt, as Harsh suggests, but rather consciousness of a moral step taken against unrighteous power.

39. *Poetics* 1452b36. There is a very serious problem involved in reconciling the *Poetics* with the *Eth. Nic.* VII, where certain tragic heroes are specifically analyzed, but in very different terms. The *Poetics* seem not to have been Aristotle's final, or only word on tragedy. See Chapter XII.

40. *Rep.* 392a13–b6.

41. *Poetics* 1453a12–15.

42. Cf. Moore, pp. 56–58, on the Hegelian theory.

43. *Soph. Trag.*, pp. 373f., 368, 292, 166.

44. Cf. E. Abbott, *Hellenica*, pp. 53–55.

45. Cf. Weinstock, *Sophokles*, pp. 35ff., on the *ananke* of justice which necessitates the matricide in the *Electra*.

46. Cf. Perrotta, p. 633.

47. *Paideia* I², 21; on Ate generally, see W. C. Greene, *Moira: Fate, Good, and Evil in Greek Thought.*

48. Words implying sin in Aeschylus: ὕβρις, μέγα θρονεῖν, ἀλιταίνω, ἁμαρτάνω, ἁμαρτία.

49. *Oed. Rex* 1213.

50. *Oed. Col.* 1536.

51. It must be admitted that Aeschylus in the *Persians* did compress divine justice into one play. But this is not usual, and it was made possible only by the unusual circumstances. As the Battle of Salamis was in a sense a military miracle, so Aeschylus celebrates the fall of Xerxes as a divine miracle, a rare example of the gods' interference, and a departure from the usual long-term way of justice.

52. Diels, *Vorsokr.* II⁵, 80B4.

53. Suffering which is ὑπὲρ μόρον, *Od.* I, 34.

III. Chronology

1. *Arg. ad Phil.*, archonship of Glaucippus 410/409. *Arg. ad Oed. Col.* archonship of Micon, 402/1.

2. E.g., cf. Reinhardt's date for the *Trachiniae* (before 442) *Sophokles*, pp. 45–48, 51–58, 66, with Perrotta's (410/409), *Sofocle*, pp. 526–558; cf. pp. 548–549, on Euripidean influence in *Electra*, *Philoctetes*, and *Oed. Col.* Similarly, cf. Perrotta's date for *Oed. Rex* (412 or later), App. II, pp. 257ff., with Bruhn's (late fifties, the oldest extant play), *Oed. Einleitung*, pp. 33ff. See. T. v. Wilamowitz's answer, *Dram. Tech.*, p. 69n.

3. Plut. *Mor.* 79b.

4. J. H. Finley, "The Origins of Thucydides' Style," *HSCP* (1939), pp. 57–59. Cf. also Reinhardt, *Sophokles*, p. 96, on the antithetical structure of larger elements in the play.

5. By Jebb, *Ajax*, Introduction, pp. li–liv; by U. v. Wilamowitz, *Analecta Euripidea*, 195. Cf. *Ajax* 1102 with Eur. *Telephus*, fg. 722 (Nauck), for basis of the argument sometimes offered that *Ajax* is dependent on Euripides' plays of 438; by T. v. Wilamowitz, *Dram. Tech.*, p. 51; by Perrotta, App. I, pp. 163ff.

6. Jebb also mentions the use of anapests in *Antigone* as archaistic. But the *Ajax* also has anapests interrupting the parodos (201–220, 233–244, 257–262), and even introducing it (134ff.), a truly Aeschylean practice. For other entrances marked by anapests, cf. *Trach.* 974ff. and *Phil.* 1409. Finally, if it is archaic to use anapests in the middle of an epeisodion as part of the dialogue, as is done at *Antigone* 929–943, then *Ajax* 1163–1167 must be equally archaic.

7. H. D. Kitto, "Sophocles, Statistics, and the Trachiniae," *AJP* (April 1939), pp. 178–193. Sophocles' various stylistic devices have been elaborately studied by F. R. Earp in his book, *The Style of Sophocles*, but he has attempted no dogmatic conclusions on the basis of them. However, Siess, *Wiener Studien* (1915), pp. 244ff., does try to settle the question in this way, and is answered by Kitto.

8. Grace H. Macurdy, *The Chronology of the Extant Plays of Euripides* (Columbia Diss., 1905).

9. *Ajax*, Introduction, p. lii.

10. Earp, pp. 56–72.

11. *Ajax* 7–8.

12. *Ajax* 17.

13. Cf. the fragments of the early *Triptolemus*, fgs. 596–617 (Pearson), esp. 598.

14. For instance, the last invocation of *Ajax*, lines 855–865, with its clear echoes of the great monologue of Prometheus.

15. On ἔκπληξις cf. Medicean *Vita* of Aeschylus, 7.

16. *Fg.* 44 (Sidgwick).

17. Reinhardt, pp. 22–23.

18. For a good summary of these points, see Pohlenz, *Gr. Tr., Erläut.*, pp. 49–51.

19. *Ajax* 127ff., 758–777.

20. Jebb offers 442 or 441 as possibilities for the date of the *Antigone*, Introduction, pp. xlii ff. Perrotta (p. 23, n. 5) contends rather plausibly for 442.

21. Bowra, pp. 49–50.

22. Plut. *Them.* 31, puts Themistocles' death about 460.

23. *Ajax* 1097ff.

24. Pindar *Nem.* VII, 22–27, on the ὅπλων κρίσις, where the character of Odysseus seems distinctly associated with the blindness of the masses.

25. *Ajax* 1382.

26. Herod. VI, 35, 4; Paus. I, 35, 2; II, 29, 4; Didymus, see Schol. ad Pindar., *Nem.* II, 19.

27. Cf. Finley, "Euripides and Thucydides," *HSCP* (1938), pp. 35–37; and "The Origins," *HSCP* (1939), p. 55. Cf. also Chapter IV.

28. *Ajax* 1328–1329, and the speech at 1332ff., summarize Odysseus' transcendence of class distinctions. He represents the best interests of all. Cf. Thuc. II, 60, 2; 65, 4, on the σύμπασα πόλις.

29. The principal ones are U. v. Wilamowitz (see *Herakles*, I², 152f.); T. v. Wilamowitz (see *Dram. Tech.*, pp. 90ff., 116, 145); and Albrecht Dieterich "Schlaf-scene auf den attischen Bühne," *Rheinisches Mus.*, 46 (1891), pp. 25–46.

30. For example, cf. *Trach.* 542 with *Her.* 1373; *Trach.* 1101 with *Her.* 1353; *Trach.* 1096 with *Her.* 181; *Trach.* 1112 with *Her.* 877; *Trach.* 1058 with *Her.* 178; *Trach.* 1009ff., 1061 with *Her.* 222ff.; *Trach.* 1070ff. with *Her.* 1354 (1412); *Trach.* 1149 with *Her.* 339. Dieterich and Steiger produce others.

31. T. Zielinski, in his "Excurse zu den Trachinierinnen," *Philologus*, 55 (1896), pp. 491–633, shows very convincingly that Euripides, if anyone, is the borrower. Cf. Dieterich, who finds the parallels indifferent.

32. Zielinski, esp. pp. 628–632. Doubtless Zielinski went to extremes in making Sophocles an expert clinical analyst of disease, though he was connected with the cult of Asclepius. See the vitriolic answer to this point by M. L. Earle, "Studies in Sophocles' Trachiniae," *TAPA*, 33 (1902), pp. 5–29. Perrotta, p. 53, gives a collection of the facts about Sophocles' relation to the Asclepiadae.

33. Reinhardt, pp. 45–58, 63, 66, stresses the "archaic" structure, and stylistic similarities in the *Ajax*; he finds an Aeschylean reminiscence in the chorus at *Trach.* 497ff. He feels the play to be an example of "passive" tragedy, where the speeches are mere reactions to fate, rather than causally connected with it. Reinhardt finds this passive quality in the speech evidence of an archaic disunity of external and internal motiva-tion, which is borne out by the somewhat unskillful use of oracles and other tragic properties. Given external properties in the *Oedipus*, Sophocles does draw them in such a way as to make them seem practically identified with the psychological springs of the action. But on the other hand, the plot of the *Trachiniae*, like the *Oedipus*, deals with a certain set of baffling and fatal circumstances, and compels a dichotomy between inner and outer. If the *Oedipus* is richer in symbols, the *Trachiniae* is not therefore "Aeschylean." The similarity of the kinds of evil treated in the two plays tends to associate the two.

34. T. v. Wilamowitz, p. 155.

35. Perrotta, p. 479.

36. *Gr. Tr.* IV, p. 357; cf. Reinhardt's answer, pp. 44–45.

37. *Alc.* 286; 324.

38. *Trach.* 441; 25, 465, 547ff.; 531ff., 672ff.; 61–63.

39. Cf. Reinhardt, p. 44.

40. Pohlenz, *Erläut.*, p. 58. Pohlenz dates *Trachiniae* in 430/29, or just a year or so before *Oedipus Rex*. The immense technical superiority of the *Oedipus*, however, seems to demand that we allow a few more years to elapse between the two. Granted their similarity of tragic shape, *Oed. Rex* shows a much clearer and more mature grasp of the kind of problem.

41. Cf. T. v. Wilamowitz, p. 116.

42. See for instance the exchange of courtesies between Jocasta and the Corinthian messenger, *Oed. Rex* 929–932; the beginning of the scene between Oedipus and Ismene, *Oed. Col.* 324ff., and the Antigone-Polyneices scene, *ibid.* 1414–1446.

43. The most interesting, of course, is the farewell to the nuptial couch, cf. gen-erally, *Trach.* 915–922 with *Alc.* 175–184. These narratives as a whole, however, have a certain similarity that seems hardly accidental: cf. *Trach.* 904ff. with *Alc.* 170ff., *Trach.* 908 with *Alc.* 192; *Trach.* 913 with *Alc.* 175; *Trach.* 938 with *Alc.* 403, 366; *Trach.* 942 with *Alc.* 396. There may also be some imitation traceable in *Trach.*

862–895; cf. *Alc.* 86–140; the Sophocles scene may be distilled from the Euripides. Note also the possible verbal echo in *Trach.* 869, from *Alc.* 777.

44. Zielinski, "Excurse," pp. 624f.

45. Other evidences for an early date have been offered: Earp, p. 63, suggests that the *Trachiniae* may be earlier than the *Antigone* on the grounds that it contains more epic and Aeschylean language. Cf. *ibid.*, pp. 129–132. Pohlenz, *Erläut.*, p. 58, urges the immaturity of the *Dreigespräch*. Kitto's article, I think, puts all purely metrical arguments out of court.

46. *Hipp.* 545ff.

47. Cf. above, note 40.

48. Pohlenz, p. 226.

49. Jebb, on *Oed. Rex* 180ff., compares Thuc. II, 50; but so far as the actual nature of the plague itself is concerned, it seems to derive from an earlier literary source, the threefold plague in Herod. VI, 139. Cf. Jebb's note to *Oed. Rex* 25ff. Still, this does not indicate anything more than that Herodotus' *History* was written and Thucydides' was not. Even with a real plague to observe, Sophocles could have used Herodotus as a help to description. If the play was produced during or soon after the plague, there was all the more reason to avoid too much detailed realism.

50. Cf. *Oed. Rex*, prologue and 863–910, with Thuc. II, 52, 3.

51. τί δεῖ με χορεύειν; *Oed. Rex* 896.

52. Thuc. II, 53, esp. para. 4.

53. *Oed. Rex* 964.

54. Indeed, if Sophocles' actual description of the plague were detailed and corresponded minutely to the description by Thucydides, the natural inference would have to be a later date for *Oedipus Rex*. For the assumption would then be that the first four books of the *History* were actually published after the Peace of Nicias and that Sophocles used them as a source. The fact, however, that they correspond in their general psychological outlines, but scarcely at all in details seems a strong indication that the *Oedipus* came during or right after the plague. See H. Hagelüken, *Quo tempore Sophoclis Oedipus Rex acta sit*, Rostoch Diss. (1873), pp. 9–13, for an interesting analysis of the background, and the conclusion that the play was written after Pericles' death, between 429 and 424.

55. "Excurse," *Philologus*, 55 (1896), p. 523, n. 7.

56. The parallels are: *Oed. Rex.* 646ff. and *Hipp.* 1037; *Oed. Rex* 583ff. and *Hipp.* 1013ff.; *Oed. Rex* 614ff. and *Hipp.* 1051; *Oed. Rex* 965f. and *Hipp.* 1058. More likely evidence for a *terminus ante quem* is the apparent parody of *Oed. Rex* 629, ὦ πόλις πόλις, which occurs in Aristoph. *Ach.* 27, produced in 426/5. But the phrase may be a common exclamation.

57. See Finley, "Eur. and Thuc.," *HSCP* (1938), p. 34, and "The Origins," *HSCP* (1939), pp. 42f., 50, for a discussion of this argument and other examples in Euripides.

58. Other datings always rest on hopelessly minute points, or on criteria assumed *ad hoc.* Bruhn's thesis and T. v. Wilamowitz' answer has already been noted, note 2. Perrotta's defense of 412 for the *Oedipus Rex* remains unanswered. Among many arguments, his most provocative one (see *Sofocle*, App. II, pp. 257ff.) is that the use of trochaic tetrameters to close the play was due to a resurrection of that meter by Euripides around 420 in the *Heracles*. Thereafter, tetrameters become more frequent in Euripides, hence apparently more popular; and by interpolating *Oedipus* in a scheme of metrical statistics, Perrotta arrives at a date, 412. Like all metrical criteria, this suffers from our lack of full knowledge of the matter, and once more needs Kitto's corrective. Furthermore, the almost identical closing lines of the *Oedipus* and the *Phoenissae* in the tetrameter meter and containing old traditional sentiments, may indicate that there is an older source — the *Oedipus* of Aeschylus? — from which both poets derived it. And Sophocles, even in 429, could have indulged this slight

archaism even to the extent of writing the whole last scene in tetrameters, without waiting for the example of Euripides. The meter need not have been popular when the scene was written. It need not even have been successful. After all, the play did not get the prize.

59. Perrotta, App. IV, esp. p. 402, does offer 410/409, thus placing the play in very close connection with the *Philoctetes*, and, in his view, also with the *Trachiniae*.

60. *Hermes*, XVIII (1883), 214–263. Actually Gruppe was the first, with his *Ariadne* (Berlin, 1834), pp. 453–461. For a brief history of the problem up to 1890, see F. Kraus, *Utrum Sophoclis an Euripidis Electra Aetate sit prior*. (1890), pp. 3–9.

61. *Philologus*, 56 (1897), pp. 561–600.

62. *Hermes*, XXXIV (1899), 57, n. 2.

63. pp. 37ff. Cf. his earlier book, *Lucubrationes Euripideae*, in *Fleckeisens Jahrbücher für Klassische Philologie*, XV (supp.), 308–324.

64. *Dram. Tech.* pp. 228ff.

65. Pohlenz, *Gr. Trag.* p. 326. On the other hand, compare his remarks in the *Erläut.*, pp. 89ff.

66. Cf. Bruhn, *Introduction to Electra*, p. 29; also Gruppe, *loc. cit.*

67. Eur. *El.* 1245ff.

68. *Ion* 1595.

69. *Iph. T.* 1774.

70. See Steiger, pp. 588–600.

71. Cf. Eur. *El.* 895–904 with Soph. *El.* 1487ff.

72. Eur. *El.* 1245–46; 1301–04.

73. Steiger, pp. 586ff.

74. *Ibid.*, p. 582, n. 39.

75. *Ibid.*, p. 582.

76. Linde, *Sophokles' Elektra im Verhältnis zu der des Euripides* (Königshütte, O.-S., 1910), p. 14.

77. Steiger, p. 597.

78. *Ibid.*, p. 598. Cf. Linde, pp. 12–13.

79. Cf. Soph. *El.* 549 with Eur. *El.* 1106; Soph. *El.* 554f. with Eur. *El.* 1055f.; Soph. *El.* 582f. with Eur. *El.* 1093ff.; Soph. *El.* 86f. with Eur. *El.* 54; Soph. *El.* 1422f. with Eur. *El.* 1172–76.

80. The most recent treatment of the priority question is in J. D. Denniston's edition of Euripides' *Electra* (Oxford, 1939), pp. xxxiii ff., where the priority of Sophocles is generally, though not very determinedly upheld.

81. Bury, *History of Greece* (Modern Library ed.), p. 336.

82. Soph. *El.* 9.

83. Cf. Soph. *El.* 4 and Eur. *El.* 1, with Gilbert Murray's note. The Euripides passage seems to be another quotation from Sophocles, and Jebb is no doubt wrong to capitalize ἄργος in the Sophoclean text. In the line following, ἄλσος stands in apposition to it, which indicates pretty clearly that neither the city nor the Peloponnesus, as in Homer, is meant.

84. See note 1 of this chapter. The date of composition of the *Oedipus at Colonus* has been a matter of some dispute. Perrotta, p. 47, claims that it was being composed in 417, the date he alleges for Iophon's suit, on the basis of a passage in Arist. *Rhet.* III, 15. That it was, however, composed after 409 and in part influenced by the *Phoenissae* of that year is sufficiently proved by Jebb, ed. *Oed. Col.*, p. 198, and by the elaborate dissertation by Templin, *De fabulae Sophocleae Oedipus Coloneus quae inscribitur tempore*. Cf. U. v. Wilamowitz in Tycho's *Dram. Tech.*, pp. 317f., 367, 371.

IV. The Matrix of Heroism: *Ajax*

1. *Il.* I, 414–418.
2. *Il.* IX, 410ff.
3. The idea of passing beyond one's own limits, and therefore the limits of Zeus himself, seems indicated in the phrase ὑπὲρ αἶσαν in *Il.* XVI, 780; XVII, 321f. Achilles' speech, *Il.* XXI, 106–113, is an example of supreme victory over himself, and to some degree also Hector's monologue, XXII, 297–305.
4. *Il.* XVI, 780–817. Cf. other such familiar examples as *Il.* XII, 450; XV, 694–695; XX, 97–98.
5. *Il.* I, 194; II, 1ff.; cf. VII, 44; XII, 252–257; XIII, 72–75, 810–823; XV, 242; XVII, 456.
6. *Il.* XVI, 843ff.
7. *Il.* XXIV, 194–199.
8. Pausanias, I, 35, 3.
9. For a summary, see Pohlenz, *Erläut.*, p. 47.
10. Arist. *Poetics* 1459b2–7.
11. Cf. Pohlenz, p. 138.
12. Cf. Weinstock, *Sophokles*, pp. 40–41.
13. *Odyssey* XI, 543–567.
14. *Ajax* 154–157 (cf. Pindar, *Nem.* VIII, 22–25; *Pyth.* XI, 29, etc.); 138ff. (cf. Pindar, *Nem.* VIII, 32–34; *Pyth.* II, 76f.); 158–161; 167–171 (cf. Pindar, *Pyth.* I, 81f.); 191f.
15. *Ajax* 148–153.
16. *Il.* XVI, 630; XIX, 215–220.
17. *Il.* XII, 195–250; XVIII, 249–252.
18. Thuc. I, 86; II, 40, 2–3. Cf. Finley, *Thucydides*, pp. 132ff., and "Eur. and Thuc.," *HSCP* (1938), pp. 34ff. Cf. the passage cited from Pindar's description of Ajax as ἄγλωσσον μέν, ἦτορ δ'ἄλκιμον, *Nem.* VIII, 24. Cf. also the funerary epigram on Ajax, *Ex peplo Aristot.* 7 (Diehl), of uncertain date, but notably in the Doric dialect.
19. See *Ajax* 1374f. with its reference to γνώμη. Cf. Thuc. I, 138, 3, where the word is closely associated with statesmanlike foreknowledge and political skill. Cf. Finley, *Thucydides*, pp. 95ff.
20. Cf. Bowra, p. 19, where it is stated that Ajax is adjusted by Sophocles to fifth-century ideals of greatness. This cannot be true. Manifestly, Ajax cannot be adjusted to any ideal except his own old heroic, aristocratic one, with which he was associated from the beginning. To turn him into anything else renders the play pointless; and not even Sophocles could have managed to do it.
21. *Ajax* 125f.
22. *Ajax* 127ff.
23. E. Abbott, *Ethics and Theology*, pp. 44, 52.
24. Cf. Greene, *Moira*, p. 149.
25. *Ajax* 767ff.
26. Pohlenz, pp. 184, 233.
27. Some conceivable connection may exist in the fact that in the *Odyssey*, XI, 547, Athena acted as judge of the ὅπλων κρίσις. But Sophocles had every opportunity to remind his audience of that fact, if he had intended it to have any significance. In any case, Ajax' greeting to her in the prologue implies nothing of the sort.
28. *Ajax* 44–54. Cf. Pohlenz, p. 180, who also claims that Athena's plan for saving the chiefs is Sophocles' invention, and was not in the myth.
29. *Ajax* 756.
30. Cf. Vergil, *Aeneid* I, 39–45.

NOTES: AJAX

261

31. Cf. Bowra, pp. 39–44, 46, who says Ajax learns his lesson but immediately forgets it, goes mad, and kills himself. So much for sophrosyne! Cf. Reinhardt, p. 26, who compares Ajax to Croesus.

32. Bowra, pp. 33ff.

33. *Ibid.*, p. 36.

34. See Pohlenz on Sophocles generally. Cf. Weinstock and Reinhardt. On this scene of the *Ajax*, see Pohlenz, p. 174. Also cf. above, Chapter I.

35. *Ajax* 1415–1416. As for "shadows," Athena herself is called a "shadow," *Ajax* 301.

36. Cf. Bowra, p. 27, where it appears that Odysseus hated Ajax for moral reasons, and only forgave him when he had atoned for his pride. The interpretation of *Ajax* 1347 on which Bowra bases this amazing statement simply cannot be tenable. Odysseus only means it is no longer καλόν for him to hate Ajax because he is dead, and there can be no further hatred; cf. lines 1343–1345. Odysseus originally hated Ajax out of fear and jealousy, cf. *Ajax* 74–82. If he changed his mind, it was partly because he (not Ajax) had learned a lesson, cf. lines 1355–1361, and partly because there was nothing more to fear when Ajax was dead.

37. Pindar, *Pyth.* VIII, 96f.

38. Cf. *Ajax* 758–760.

39. *Ajax* 1340f.

40. *Sophokles*, pp. 12, 14, 24, 36–39, 45, *et passim.*

41. Cf. Nietzsche's remark, "The gods justify the life of man by living it." Such is perhaps the epic emphasis; in tragedy the case is reversed.

42. *Ajax* 646ff.

43. *Ajax* 669–677.

44. See F. G. Welcker, "Über den Aias des Sophokles," *Rheinisches Mus.* (1829), pp. 229–239; and Jebb, Introduction to *Ajax*, pp. xxxiv, xxxviii.

45. Schadewaldt's interpretation, *Neue Wege zum Antike*, VIII (1929), 70ff. is fundamentally the same, but more subtle. He believes the speech to be a λόγος ἐσχηματισμένος (cf. Welcker's κεκρυμμένη βάξις) in which Ajax really yields, but in a different way from what he says. Thus Ajax arrives at a norm. Yet Schadewaldt recognizes the sarcasm of lines 668ff. (p. 73), and it is never quite clear whether Ajax really behaves as he says he will, or grows "hard" again.

46. *Ajax* 824–844.

47. *Ajax* 651.

48. Bowra's, for instance, cf. above, n. 31.

49. See T. v. Wilamowitz, pp. 63–65; but Wilamowitz does not state why Ajax must do it, but assumes merely that it was part of the story.

50. Cf. two excellent analyses of this speech in Reinhardt, pp. 33ff., and Weinstock, p. 50. That Ajax was really speaking a deeper truth behind his deception was recognized by U. v. Wilamowitz, *Lesefrüchte*, CLXXXI, 1; *Hermes*, LIX (1924), 249ff. Cf. also Pohlenz, pp. 176f., and the *Erläut. ad loc.*

51. *Ajax* 669–676. This passage is thought by Perrotta, p. 20, to reflect the ideas of Archelaus, the contemporary φυσικός. If this is true, then Archelaus was in the tradition of the Milesian Anaximander, as the general doctrine, and the surprising use of τιμαῖς in line 670 recall the theory of universal τίσις which Anaximander evolved as the central process of φύσις. However, any ethical or political concept derived from the Anaximandrian view would depend necessarily on the physical or natural law of τίσις whereas we know that Archelaus believed justice and other moral values to exist οὐ φύσει ἀλλὰ νόμῳ (Diels, *Vorsokr.* II⁵60A1. I think these facts are hard to reconcile. As to the use of the doctrine in the *Ajax*, the fact that Ajax treats it so cavalierly implies not the antinomy between νόμος and φύσις, but the familiar aristo-

cratic antinomy between the common existences which have no standards (here perhaps summed up in φύσις), and the life of arete and breeding, φυά. See Chapter XI and note 13.

52. *Ajax* 430ff.
53. *Ajax* 470–473; 476–480.
54. Cf. Jaeger, *Paideia* I², 11.
55. *Ajax* 485ff.
56. *Ajax* 652–654.
57. *Ajax* 589–590.
58. *Ajax* 594–595.
59. *Ajax* 967–968.
60. Cf. Perrotta, pp. 129ff.; L. Campbell, *Mélanges Weil*, pp. 17ff.
61. See Reinhardt's remark, p. 42: "Gegen das Unrecht des Grossen, welches Recht der Kleinen!" However, I am not so convinced of Ajax' *Unrecht*. Cf. Reinhardt's further sentiments on useless survivors, pp. 104f.
62. Arist. *Polit.* 1279b5.
63. *Ajax* 1071–2; 1073–1086. Cf. *Ajax* 1102. Contrast Thuc. II, 37, 3, and compare Thuc. I, 84, 3–4; see Finley, "Eur. and Thuc.," p. 35, where he notes the comparison and cites other examples. Cf. Aristotle on Spartan mistrust of human nature, *Polit.* II, 9 (1271a20).
64. Horace, *Sat.* II, 3, 188. Horace's little scene is perhaps derived from this of Sophocles. At least, it is in keeping with the Sophoclean version that Agamemnon is accused of stupidity (210), a regard for vain titles (212) and a *tumidum cor* (213) — all earmarks of the true authoritarian.
65. *Ajax* 1253–1254.
66. *Ajax* 970; 1036ff.
67. Pohlenz, pp. 198–202. Cf. the theory of Schadewaldt, described in Chapter II.
68. Pohlenz, p. 234, who also derives their surety and directness from the serene nature of Sophocles. This argument makes a syllogism whose conclusion is that Sophocles must have been as wrong-headed in his serenity as his heroes were!
69. Thuc. II, 37.
70. *Ajax* 1357.
71. ἀείμνηστον, *Ajax* 1166. This phrase is not merely a reference to the cult of Ajax, but also a true evaluation, of which even the chorus, now that he is dead, is capable. Cf. particularly Thuc. II, 43, 2–3, on the universal moral example involved in the ideas κλέος and δόξα. On the immortality of the nobly dead, in Pericles' eyes, cf. Plut. *Per.* 8. As an example of the respect and love which Ajax commanded from those who held to the heroic ideal, it is interesting to note that the most aristocratic of the Black Figure painters, Execias, painted no less than five pictures of Ajax which have come down to us. Cf. Beazley, *Attic Black Figure*, pp. 20–21. The numerous references in Pindar are well known.

V. Man the Measure: *Antigone*

1. Cf. Weinstock, p. 43.
2. Pohlenz, pp. 199–202.
3. Hegel, *The Philosophy of Fine Art*, trans. Osmaston (London, 1920), I, 293; cf. II, 215. Cf. C. Robert, *Oidipus*, I, 332, for a development of this idea, with a study of the γένος-right.
4. μεγαλοψυχία vs. σωφροσύνη; see W. Schmid, *Philologus*, 62 (1903), pp. 1–34. He is answered by Allègre, *Sophocle*, pp. 398ff., who finds the central message of the play to be the sanctity of the family right and the religion of the dead, a view anthropologically, perhaps, correct, but poetically and morally sterile.

5. See Weinstock, chapter on *Antigone*.

6. *Sophokles*, pp. 75, 88, 97.

7. *Ant.* 449–460.

8. *Ibid.* 570.

9. Eckermann, Mar. 28, 1827.

10. See Chapter III, and n. 28.

11. See Jaeger, *Paideia* I²240f., on how "civic arete" underlay the genius of the fifty years after Salamis.

12. *Ant.* 96–97, 463–470; cf. *Ajax* 479–480; cf. also Aesch. *fg.* 453 (Sidgwick), possibly spurious.

13. *Ant.* 69–74; 80f.; 83; 502ff.; 553, 555, 557–560.

14. *Ant.* 502ff., 536–547.

15. *Ant.* 49ff.

16. See a good defense of her in Schadewaldt, pp. 89–91.

17. U. v. Wilamowitz, *Gr. Tr.*, XIV, 112f.

18. Cf. *Ajax* 1118–1119, where the chorus is in a similar position and says, irrelevantly: "You may be right, but your tone is objectionable." The Sophoclean chorus preserves the amenities first, and more fundamental values (if at all) later. Its usual misunderstanding of the heroic protagonist is simply one more layer of Sophoclean irony, and contributes greatly to the isolation of the hero — a point which Reinhardt has ably studied in his book.

19. *Ant.* 875.

20. Pp. 93–97; this view Schadewaldt apparently derived from A. Boeckh, *Des Sophokles Antigone* (Berlin, 1843), pp. 161ff.

21. *Ant.* 477ff.; cf. *Ajax* 1253f.

22. See Bowra, pp. 72ff. Cf. Pohlenz, p. 196, and Weinstock, p. 250, who says Creon is "immoderation personified." Weinstock unfortunately, however, proceeds to compare him to Ajax. The parallel with the Atreidae is almost too clear to be missed.

23. *Ant.* 280; 726; 289ff., 302ff., 1055; 484, 678, 740, 746; 478f., 666f., 738. In Creon the personal characteristics of the tyrant are superimposed on the political platform of oligarchy and Spartanism. For the fifth-century Athenian, tyrants were oligarchs; cf. the Thirty. Creon's lines, 639ff., should be carefully compared with Archidamus' speech in Thuc. I, 84, 3–4, on the submission to law and the necessity of control and obedience. The underlying conception of this political view is εὐταξία, cf. Aristotle, *Pol.* 1321a3. For the oligarchic fixation on the peril of false friends, cf. *Ant.* 651f. with Theognis' frequent warnings to Cyrnus. The perfect hoplite ideal of Tyrtaeus occurs also, *Ant.* 667–671.

24. See Weinstock, p. 103. Cf. Reinhardt, p. 99 and n. 2, on the double meanings of κέρδος in the Creon-Teiresias scene.

25. For instance, Bowra, chapter iii, generally. Bowra indeed does not think Creon tragic, but believes that he does illustrate the principle of pride and fall.

26. *Ant.* 332ff.

27. *Ant.* 211ff.

28. *Ant.* 1259f.; 1270.

29. This scene seemed to U. v. Wilamowitz to be out of character; see *Gr. Tr.*, XIV, 50, n. 1.

30. Cf. Schadewaldt, pp. 83–93, who feels that her defense here lacks assurance because she now feels Creon is partly right. Thus Hegel slips in by the back door.

31. This passage of the *Antigone* is certainly a tortured question. It is unquestionably derived from Herodotus III, 119, but that fact does not prove its genuinity. Jebb, ed. *Antigone*, App., pp. 258ff., brackets the whole passage and adduces some very cogent arguments therefore, partly derived from Jacob, *Sophocleae Quaestiones*,

pp. 362ff. Most scholars since then, however, disagree. E. Bruhn, ed. *Antigone*, p. 40, and Perrotta, pp. 24, 118ff., think it was meant for a compliment to Herodotus. T. v. Wilamowitz, pp. 45-49, defends it as genuine, while granting its irrelevance, on the grounds of Sophocles' delight in pure rhetoric. I should like more examples of such a delight. Pohlenz, *Erläut*. pp. 53-55, finds these lines an answer to the chorus' criticisms. Weinstock, pp. 102-103, thinks they show the sanctity of the blood relationship in antiquity, but Reinhardt, p. 88, thinks that the ἄγραπτοι νόμοι do not apply merely to the dead, and that Antigone's meaning cannot be limited by any mere anthropological facts. Others have defended the passage on the grounds that Antigone's interest in Polyneices was incestuous, as was only appropriate to the daughter of Oedipus; but the text will not bear the weight of such beguiling Freudianism. The two facts which are incontrovertible are (1) the argument is basically sophistic, whether in Herodotus or Sophocles; and (2) there is nothing in all the rest of Sophocles which is so deadly ψυχρόν. The fact that Aristotle had it in his text (cf. *Rhetoric* III, 19, 9) does not mean that it could not be an actor's interpolation (cf. Denys Page, *Actors' Interpolations in Greek Tragedy*, pp. 2, 14), and its sophistic quality would imply an early interpolation. The matter cannot be definitely settled without the discovery of a new manuscript tradition, but all in all, Jebb's arguments for rejecting the lines seem better than anybody's for retaining them.

32. *Ant.* 823ff., especially 834.

33. See Chapter III on Aeschylus' *Niobe* as a possible model for the *Ajax*.

34. *El.* 150.

35. *Eth. Nic.* 1148a34.

36. σπουδαία ἀκρασία; *ibid.*, 1151b18.

37. *Ant.* 837-838.

38. *Ant.* 1348ff.

39. Line 451 seems to be an equally symbolic θεολογούμενον. Δίκη is never represented as among the nether gods; she dwells with Zeus. Yet, from her own situation, Antigone projects her among the dead, because for Antigone justice lies only in the grave. Similar, too, is the storm, the θεία νόσος, which hides Antigone until the deed is done. If the gods meant to protect her with it, they should have done better. If they meant her to be destroyed, they could have dispensed with it, for she was guilty already. Either way it makes no sense as divine interference. As a symbolic use of "pathetic fallacy," however, to cast the deed in a cosmic light, it is perfectly discreet and comprehensible.

40. *Sophokles*, p. 12.

41. Cf. J. A. Moore, p. 74.

42. Cf. Schadewaldt, pp. 103f., for the theory that guilt and terror are always associated with greatness. See also above, Chapter IV, and note 38.

43. E.g., Solon 1, 9-13 (Diehl); and *Agam.* 750-762.

44. *Ajax* 758ff.

45. See Dodds, "Euripides the Irrationalist," *Classical Review*, 43 (1929), pp. 97-104.

46. *Poetics*, chapter 25. See Perrotta, p. 41; cf. Moore, p. 65.

47. See Jaeger, *The Theology of the Early Greek Philosophers* (Oxford, 1947), chapter x. See below, Chapters XI and XII, for a further discussion of Sophocles in the light of Professor Jaeger's analysis of the Sophistic theology.

48. Diels, *Vorsokr.* II⁶80B4.

49. Such as the political types with their theories of government; deliberative debates about one's τύχη, as in *Ajax* 430ff.; "dialectical" passages such as *Ajax* 265ff.; *Ant.* 904ff. (if genuine); *Trach.* 734ff.

50. See Pohlenz, pp. 156, 160, 237, 342; and Perrotta, p. 68, where it is asserted that the first stasimon of the *Antigone* is a refutation of the doctrine of Man the Measure.

51. Eur. *fg.* 294, 7 (Nauck).

52. αἰσχρὸν γὰρ οὐδὲν ὧν ὑφηγοῦνται θεοί, Soph. *fg.* 247 (Pearson).

53. See A. D. Nock's remark, "Religious Attitudes of the Greeks," *Proceedings of the American Philosophical Society*, 85 (1942), p. 481: "Man was the measure: but what he sought to measure seemed larger than himself." It was Sophocles who showed wherein man was indeed large enough to be the measure of the universe — that is, morally.

VI. Late Learning: *The Trachiniae*

1. *Soph. Trag.*, p. 377. Others have occasionally noted certain distinctions in spirit: Perrotta, for instance, who thinks Sophocles thoroughly pessimistic, admits the "heroic beauty" of the *Ajax* and *Antigone*, which he says conquers their gloom. *Sofocle*, pp. 21f.

2. Weinstock, p. 7, actually states that no development can be noted, because all the extant plays were written after Sophocles was fifty years old. Weinstock also gives up the dating problem, so it is hard to see how he arrived at that conclusion.

3. Cf. Grace Macurdy's remark about Euripides: "Indeed, three groups of plays, separated by stylistic differences, are easily discernible among the surviving plays, in spite of the fact that the earliest of them, the *Alcestis*, was composed when Euripides was already more than forty years old" (*The Extant Plays of Euripides*, p. 1).

4. The words ὀψὲ μαθεῖν, whether separately or together, are constantly used with tragic implications throughout Greek poetry from Homer down: e.g., Soph. *Ant.* 1270, 1353; Eur. *Or.* 99; Aesch. *Agam.* 1425; cf. Pind. *Pyth.* V, 28ff. (ὀψίνοος). See also an example of it in Aeschines, 157 (544, Reisk), where the orator is indulging a bit of the tragic style Demosthenes ridiculed him for.

5. *Il.* IV, 160f.; Solon, I, 25ff. (Diehl).

6. *Ajax* 646.

7. See Reinhardt, pp. 100, 102, and Schadewaldt, p. 97. Reinhardt says well, "He loses what he has, not what he is." See also preceding chapter.

8. *Poetics* 13. Cf. T. v. Wilamowitz, p. 88, who says if the main characters were fully delineated, the *Oedipus Rex* would be unbearable.

9. *Trach.* 669, 694, 710, 934, 1118, 1171.

10. *Trach.* 1–5.

11. *Trach.* 945f.

12. *Trach.* 155–168.

13. *Trach.* 74–81.

14. *Trach.* 1159–1162.

15. *Trach.* 1264–1278.

16. The argument from εἰκός, "what is the defendant likely to have done," is familiar to all readers of Greek Sophistic or legal reasoning. Its speciousness is clear.

17. *Trach.* 28–30.

18. τίκτει, κατευνάζει, *Trach.* 94f.

19. *Trach.* 131f.

20. *Trach.* 144–150. Cf. other passages on the harm of being a wife, the danger of beauty, etc., lines 25, 143, 465, 536.

21. *Trach.* 459.

22. *Trach.* 472–474.

23. *Trach.* 592. Note the use of δρῶσαν; δράω is always associated with decisive, or fatal action.

24. *Trach.* 707–716.

25. *Trach.* 1159.

26. Plut. *Per.* 8. Cf. Plato, *Rep.* 329b-d. Cf. Chapter I.

27. Even to the sending of the son to find his father, *Trach.* 65ff.

28. *Trach.* 543f., 552f.; 461–467, 627f.; 61ff.

29. *Trach.* 293–306.

30. *Trach.* 307–309.

31. *Trach.* 630ff. English is at a disadvantage here, since it lacks anything corresponding to the sorrowful restraint of the formal τὸν πόθον τὸν ἐξ ἐμοῦ, and the *pluralis modestiae* of the ποθούμεθα, almost like a correction for having said ἐμοῦ.

32. Abbott, p. 57, for instance.

33. Cf. Bowra, pp. 147–148; he cites Antiphon I, 9, and Arist. *Magna Moralia*, 1188b31ff., for innocence in case of death by love-philter poisoning. On p. 128, however, Bowra seems to say the opposite.

34. As to the notion that Deianeira owed it, as a good Athenian wife, to Heracles to accept his concubines, it would be easy to produce Attic law to the contrary. Hipparete, the wife of Alcibiades, sued for divorce on just such grounds, and the defendant did not risk a trial, but carried her home by force, while Athens, no doubt, smiled (Plut. *Alcibiades* 8). But the very mention of this case shows how absurd it is to treat Deianeira as an Athenian; she is in a larger world where social *mores* are not so fixed.

The idea that she is an Athenian type occurs in Wilamowitz, *Gr. Tr.* IV, p. 357. He thought there was a "Dissonanz" between her and Heracles, who appeared to him the archaic heroic Heracles of the saga. Bowra seems to have adopted this strange attitude. Actually, it is Heracles who is the more contemporary figure, while Deianeira resembles the women of the chivalric days of Homer.

35. Bowra, pp. 125–128. The statement that Theocritus' Simaetha is not a model for a good wife is perhaps true, but it should be apparent that Simaetha has not a stitch of pride.

36. *Joseph in Egypt* (London, 1944), pp. 611–623.

37. *Trach.* 596f. These lines have been dreadfully misunderstood as a full confession of guilt, by all scholars except J. A. Moore, p. 57. Moore, however, thinks she has no reference in these lines to what she is doing, but she must, or there is no point in them. What has not been understood is that πράσσῃς with the neuter plural adjective here means "suffer," not "do." Cf. Eur. *Or.* 538, for an exact parallel, and *Oed. Rex* 1006, where τι is added to the usual idiom of εὖ πράσσειν as a direct object, yet the meaning is passive. Also *Ajax* 905, where πράσσειν is used without either adverb or object, but with a passive meaning. Also *Ant.* 625, where πράσσειν means "fare" or "exist." Αἰσχρὰ πράσσῃς therefore doubtless means αἰσχρῶς πράσσῃς. More important, however, is the fact that the general word αἰσχρὰ does not necessarily imply moral guilt, but an act which Deianeira is ashamed to have to do.

38. *Trach.* 540–551.

39. *Trach.* 354f., 431ff.

40. *Trach.* 476ff.

41. *Trach.* 860ff.; cf. Sophocles, *fgs.* 149, 941 (Pearson) on Eros.

42. *Trach.* 445, 491, 544. Cf. the ironical use of νόσῳ in Lichas' speech, 235.

43. *Trach.* 784.

44. *Trach.* 497ff. Cf. Achelous, lines 15ff.

45. *Trach.* 565.

46. *Trach.* 545ff.

47. *Trach.* 436–440; 449–453; 457–462.

48. Reinhardt, pp. 51–58. Cf. T. v. Wilamowitz, p. 150.

49. Zielinski, "Excurse," pp. 511–518. The distinction is absurdly anachronistic. Why not also mention that Heracles became the saint of the Stoics, the prototype of perfect self control? As to the other question, Deianeira did not use the philter

before because she had never before been asked to live with one of her husband's concubines; see *Trach.* 545.

50. *Trach.* 543–544.
51. See Perrotta, p. 501, for further arguments against the deceit of Deianeira.
52. Reinhardt feels this whole scene is detached from the plot, and forms a kind of passive attempt to avoid fate, oracles, etc. But plot and fate are not so separate, nor is Deianeira's attitude passive. She is as assertive and positive as possible. This scene actually is the plot, and is in truth identical with the activity of Deianeira's will.
53. Once more in the political sphere, the same contrast is visible in the Thucydidean contrast of Spartan quietism (ἡσυχία, ἀνδραγαθίζεσθαι) and Athenian enterprise (πολυπραγμοσύνη, δρᾶν τι); cf. Thuc. II, 63, 64. See also earlier part of this chapter.
54. See Pohlenz, pp. 211–212, who thinks that if Heracles were drawn sympathetically, the ending would be too horrible. I fail to see it. The end of the *Hipp.* is far more merciful than that of the *Trach.*
55. Bowra, pp. 132ff., is alone in thinking Heracles noble. Contrast T. v. Wilamowitz, p. 155; and Pohlenz, p. 211, where he says the play shows the weakness of human heroism; but he forgets that Deianeira is the hero.
56. See Dio Chrysostom, *Or.* 60, who indulges in shameless allegorizing of the poisoned robe. Allegory and symbol, however, differ; the latter is certainly present here.
57. *Trach.* 140f.
58. *Trach.* 1264–1278.
59. *Trach.* 1270.
60. Pohlenz, pp. 212f.
61. Bowra, p. 158 and note 2.
62. Perrotta, p. 525.
63. *Ajax* 1036ff.
64. For another example, possibly written in this period, though it is impossible to know definitely, see Fritsch, *Neue Fragmente des Aischylos und Sophokles*, No. 7, col. 2, ll. 10ff.

VII. Irrational Evil: *Oedipus Rex*

1. Reinhardt, *Sophokles*, p. 108, who says the oracle is of the "historical" not "mythical" type. What it really resembles is the two ultimata exchanged by Athens and Sparta in 431, to cleanse their lands of their respective pollutions; see Thuc. I, 126, 2; 128, 1.
2. *Oed. Rex* 1527–1530 (Francklin).
3. Perrotta, however, differs (pp. 252–253), but I think for the wrong reason.
4. *Oed. Rex* 774–833.
5. *Oed. Rex* 8. The καλούμενος is modest, as in *Trach.* 541, where it certainly means "so-called" and not, as Jebb, *ad loc.*, takes it, the heroic utterance of a μεγαλόψυχος. Oedipus assuredly values himself highly, but he need not have said καλούμενος at all, except to tone it down a little.
6. *Oed. Rex* 31–34.
7. *Oed. Rex* 37–39.
8. γνώμη. Thuc. II, 65, 8–9.
9. *Oed. Rex* 58–60. Oedipus regards his own intellectual gift highly, and reckons it above a mere τέχνη, such as prophecy; cf. *Oed. Rex* 357, 380ff.
10. *Oed. Rex* 69–71; cf. 65f. and 77; cf. on the *Trachiniae*, and note 23.
11. *Oed. Rex* 132, 136, 141.
12. *Sophokles*, pp. 145f. See his distinction between "tragic error" and "tragic seeming," *ibid.*, pp. 116ff.

13. For instance, compare some of Bowra's conclusions: Oedipus is morally and legally innocent, since he acted in ignorance (*Soph. Trag.*, p. 168); he is capable of a frenzy of pride (p. 165), which, however, has nothing to do with his fall (p. 175), except that it is the instrument by which the gods, who have predestined his fall, destroy him (pp. 192ff., 209); at the same time, he is the victim of his own curse, which was an act of free will (pp. 172ff.); he is also guilty of living in a "private universe" out of which the real "common universe" of the gods rouses him (p. 209). Bowra verges on the puzzling theory advanced long ago by Sudhaus, *König Oedipus' Schuld*, pp. 12ff., that Oedipus was guilty of hybris, but that hybris had nothing to do with his fall.

14. Such, e.g., is the position of U. v. Wilamowitz, *Gr. Tr.*, I, 14, who states that Sophocles could not have intended the *Oedipus* to be so overwhelmingly gloomy as it now seems. Wilamowitz believed in the innocence of Oedipus (pp. 9ff., and "Excurse zum Oedipus des Sophokles," *Hermes* [1899], pp. 55ff.), but felt that Sophocles was so exalted by his simple faith that the fall of his hero was bearable to him.

15. Cf. E. Rohde, *Psyche*, pp. 525-529.

16. The most completely Aristotelian interpretation of the *Oedipus* is to be found in Marjorie Barstow's "Oedipus Rex: A Typical Greek Tragedy," *Classical Weekly*, October, 1912 (reprinted in Lane Cooper's *The Greek Genius*, pp. 156ff.). According to this article, Oedipus' temper is his hamartia; but this is apparently so serious that it can hardly be called either a "frailty" or an "error." The conclusion is, Oedipus' "lack of the 'intellectual virtues' of Aristotle is paralleled only by his inability to keep the norm in the 'moral virtues'" (L. Cooper, p. 159).

17. Cf. Perrotta, pp. 188ff., esp. 192.

18. See U. v. Wilamowitz, *Gr. Tr.*, I, 11ff.

19. For what it is worth, there seems to be a majority among those who believe that Oedipus' will was free and that he was morally innocent of parricide and incest. In favor of free will, besides Perrotta, are Croiset, *Oedipe roi*, p. 101; Petersen, *Att. Trag.*, pp. 173ff.; Pohlenz, p. 223. His innocence is defended by Rohde, Wilamowitz, Perrotta, Pohlenz (*locc. citt.*), C. Robert, *Oidipus* I, 295ff.; Sheppard, *Oedipus*, Introd., pp. xxiv ff.; A. Kleemann, *Wiener Studien* (1924-25), pp. 33ff. His guilt is maintained by Sudhaus (*loc. cit.*); and Petersen, pp. 173ff., who also holds out for free will — a consistent stand, at least.

20. Aristotle says (*Poetics* XIII, 4) the tragic hero should be great and glorious, like Oedipus or Thyestes. If Oedipus is an example too of one who had a hamartia, so must Thyestes be. What is Thyestes' "trifling flaw" — the seduction of Aerope, the attempted murder of Atreus, the incest with Pelopia, or the παιδοφαγία?

21. Bowra, p. 190.

22. *Ibid.*

23. Cf. *ibid.*, p. 192, on the subject of Oedipus' θυμός.

24. *Oed. Rex* 483ff., 505ff.

25. See Thuc. II, 53, and note 1 of this chapter.

26. *Oed. Rex* 700f.

27. *Oed. Rex* 76f., to give one instance.

28. Cf. Pohlenz, pp. 215f., 219f., who also asserted that the angry counterattack on Laius was not rash temper, but a justifiable self-defense. Cf. *ibid.*, pp. 230f., for a good discussion of Teiresias' kind of mantic art.

29. *Oed. Rex* 378. Schadewaldt, p. 67, also interprets this line as a sign of shrewdness, not folly.

30. See the section in Chapter III on the *Oedipus Rex*.

31. U. v. Wilamowitz, *Gr. Tr.*, I, 10, points out that in letting Creon off so easily, Oedipus would win approval from the audience who expected worse of kings. I think the lively Athenians would also approve of his shrewdness in smelling a plot.

32. *Oed. Rex* 1420f.

33. Cf. U. v. Wilamowitz, *Gr. Tr.*, I, 16. See also Sudhaus, generally, for Oedipus as an example of the Athenian *Aufklärungzeit*, against which Sophocles is supposed to have written the play. See especially p. 14, for other faults.

34. Bowra even goes so far as to say (p. 206) that her skepticism comes of having lived in a "false world."

35. Cf. *Oed. Rex* 723f., with 911ff.

36. "Excurse zum Oed.," *Hermes*, 34 (1899), p. 59; cf. A. W. Schlegel, *Lectures on Dramatic Art and Literature*, translated by J. Black (New York, 1892), p. 102; see a refutation by Reinhardt, pp. 128, 132, 136–138.

37. See Thuc. II, 8, 2; 21, 2; 54, 2–5; perhaps a similar situation in Aristoph. *fg.* 230; the oracle monger of the *Birds* is later, of course, but of the same feather.

38. *Oed. Rex* 883–910. For the sake of its literal accuracy, I have given Jebb's translation. See Jebb, *ad loc.*, and Pohlenz, *Gr. Trag.*, pp. 226, 239, and *Erläut.*, p. 62, who takes the ode as a protest against the whole "free-thinking" movement, and the words τί δεῖ με χορεύειν as a very personal remark from Sophocles himself about the fate of tragedy (χορεύειν) if religion should fail!

39. U. v. Wilamowitz, *Gr. Tr.*, I, 16. For similar interpretations see Pohlenz, pp. 222f., and Perrotta, pp. 185ff.

40. See Chapter III and notes 49–54; cf. also the explicit statement of the irrationality of life by Pericles, Thuc. I, 140, 1.

41. *Oed. Rex* 503ff., 510f.

42. *Oed. Rex* 897–910. So, at least, I take these lines. The prayer seems to be more directly for the fulfillment of the oracles given to Laius (and therefore to Oedipus) than for the mere discovery of the murderer. See Jebb, *ad loc.*, and cf. *El.* 499 for a similar prayer for the fulfillment of an omen.

43. Cf. Aesch. *Suppl.* 154–161, and 455–466. Note, however, the difference in the kind of threat: the Danaides threaten Zeus with pollution of his altars, which implies nothing about the validity of his worship but much about the form and essence of his godhead. The Sophoclean chorus threatens with disbelief, which has to do with the very existence of the gods. The change is analogous to that which W. Jaeger finds between the theology of the early pre-Socratics who speculated on the "form of the divine," and that of the Sophists who inquired into its existence. Cf. Jaeger, *Theology*, chapter x.

44. Cf. the first stasimon, esp. line 486, on the blind fluttering hopes. Ἐλπὶς appears several times in Sophocles in connection with the common run of humanity and the mere ability to get through life without trying to assess the future. Cf. *Ajax* 478; *Trach.* 137, 724; *Oed. Rex* 835; *fg.* 948. (Pearson). The destructiveness of such hope appears in *Antigone* 221 and *Trach.* 667. The contrast between hope and true knowledge appears often in Thucydides (III, 45; I, 5; V, 103); but the idea of hope as a blissfully ignorant basis for living, when full knowledge, or at least full realization of one's position, would be unendurable seems to go back to Hesiod, *Erga* 96ff. Cf. Aesch. *Prom.* 248–251. There seems to be in *Oed. Rex* the same contrast between the hope of the chorus, who will life, and the γνώμη of Oedipus himself, who wills knowledge, as there is between the hope of the people in Thucydides and the γνώμη of Pericles.

45. So at least I take τὸ καλῶς δ'ἔχον πόλει πάλαισμα, 879f.

46. I cannot believe the interpretation of Pohlenz, pp. 225f., that this ode is almost forcibly dragged in as a protest against *Freigeisterei*. The very fact that it seems dragged in in this context is against it. Critics, not Sophocles, drag things in. T. v. Wilamowitz feels that Jocasta's return to the subject of μαντικὴ in line 851 is unmotivated because nobody had so far believed the prophecy of the seer, and that she only reopens the matter in order to make an excuse for the ode of protest. This, he

feels, is an example of the fine artfulness of Sophocles; see his *Dram. Tech.*, pp. 81f. But it makes no sense. If nobody had believed Teiresias, why should the chorus suddenly believe now?

47. Pohlenz, p. 225.
48. *Oed. Rex* 979.
49. Plut. *Per.* 24; πειθώ, γνώμη, and λόγος determine a surprising proportion of the late fifth-century intellect.
50. Herod. V, 63; I, 60; Plut. *Them.* X, 1.
51. Plut. *Per.* 6, *ad init.*
52. *Oed. Rex* 724f.
53. A. D. Nock, "Religious Attitudes of the Greeks," pp. 472–482. See especially pp. 474f. on this very passage of the *Oedipus*.
54. *Oed. Rex* 646ff.
55. *Oed. Rex* 705ff.
56. *Oed. Rex* 754f.
57. See W. C. Greene, *The Murderers of Laius*, for a study of the interplay of singular and plural in the references to the murderer of the king.
58. *Oed. Rex* 848f., 861f.
59. *Oed. Rex* 851–854.
60. *Oed. Rex* 964ff., 977ff.
61. *Oed. Rex* 716, 738, 754.
62. *Oed. Rex* 848f.
63. *Oed. Rex* 842–847; 859f.
64. *Oed. Rex* 316–325.
65. *Oed. Rex* 1060f.
66. *Oed. Rex* 1169f.
67. Thuc. II, 60, 5. γνῶναί τε τὰ δέοντα καὶ ἑρμηνεῦσαι ταῦτα, φιλόπολίς τε εἶναι καὶ χρημάτων κρείσσων.
68. Perrotta, pp. 252f.
69. *Oed. Rex* 1064. Note the strong verb, μὴ δρᾶ τάδε.
70. *Oed. Rex* 744f.
71. *Soph. Trag.*, pp. 172ff.
72. U. v. Wilamowitz, *Gr. Tr.*, I, 12f.
73. *Soph. Trag.*, pp. 177–185.
74. *Oed. Rex* 1329f.
75. *Oed. Rex* 1331ff.
76. Cf. Pohlenz, p. 224.
77. σκότος ἐμὸν φάος, *Ajax* 394. ἐν σκότῳ τὸ λοιπὸν . . . ὀψοίαθ', *Oed. Rex* 1273f.
78. *Oed. Rex* 1189–1192.
79. Cf. Pohlenz, *Gr. Tr.*, pp. 213f., and *Erläut.*, p. 61. Cf. U. v. Wilamowitz, *Homerische Untersuchungen*, p. 195, and n. 37.
80. For a reconstruction of the plot, see Pearson, *Fragments of Sophocles*, II, 105–110. It is interesting to observe that *fg.* 461 seems to be an accusation of Zeus, perhaps in the same spirit as the end of the *Trachiniae*.
81. Aristotle apparently is referring to this play in *Poetics* XIV, 13, where, in describing this kind of catastrophe (πρᾶξαι τὸ δεινόν, εἶθ' ὕστερον ἀναγνωρίσαι), he mentions the *Oedipus* and the 'Οδυσσεὺς Τραυματίας. See Pearson, *Fragments of Sophocles*, II, 105f.
82. See Soph. *fg.* 247 and Pearson's note.
83. Pearson, *Fragments*, I, 91.
84. For instance, the examples already quoted: Fritsch, *Neue Fragmente*, 7; and Pearson, *fg.* 461.
85. Thuc. II, 47, 4; 51, 4; 52, 3–4; 53.

86. *Oed. Rex* 1076–1085.
87. *Oed. Rex* 1414f., 1458. The first of these has double meaning, (1) that the chorus cannot derive pollution from him, and (2) that only he is strong enough to bear these evils (οἷός τε φέρειν). The loneliness of suffering is apparent throughout Sophocles, especially in the later plays. Jebb recognizes the first meaning and Campbell the second.

VIII. Trial by Time: *Electra*

1. Note a characteristic passage in *Il.* XIX, 215–219. Even more interesting is the famous meeting of Achilles and Odysseus in Hades, where the poet makes both heroes deplore the disappointments of their respective ways of life. Their words are, of course, partly a tactful boast, Odysseus showing his greatness by the duration of his troubles, and Achilles doubling his fame by showing how the price of it cut him off utterly from all hope.
2. Cf. *Od.* I, 3–4.
3. Pindar, *Nem.* VIII, 24–27. Cf. his character in Sophocles' own *Philoctetes*. Nevertheless, in endowing his three later protagonists with tlemosyne, the Odysseus virtue, Sophocles has, needless to say, plunged below the political level and sought out the moral springs (cf. Chapter IV on the *Ajax*). No populism, of course, is implied in the late plays.
4. Cf. Archilochus 6 (Diehl).
5. *Ajax* 125f. Cf. Chapter IV.
6. It may be pure coincidence, but the word ἔκηλος (tranquil) occurs only in these last three plays: *El.* 786, 826; *Phil.* 9, 769, 826; *Oed. Col.* 1039.
7. Soph. *fg.* 247 (Pearson).
8. *Poetics* XIII, 3.
9. *El.* 308f.
10. *El.* 379f.
11. *El.* 528–546.
12. *El.* 577–584. Perrotta, p. 310, like many others, takes this speech as expressive of Sophocles' own sentiments about the vendetta system, and feels they are dragged in and mar the play. But Sophocles, in the fifth century, did not have to crusade against vendetta.
13. *El.* 417ff. Cf. n. 43 of this chapter.
14. See Chapter III on the dating of Sophocles' and Euripides' *Electra* and Hugo Steiger's article, "Warum schrieb Euripides seine Elektra," *Philologus*, 56 (1897).
15. Cf. Allègre, *Sophocle*, p. 200, and Perrotta, pp. 320–329, who finds the *Electra* irreligious and aesthetically faulty. The ending he calls "prolix and ineffective"; and he finds it a mistake to have Clytaemnestra killed first. Perrotta's reactions are exemplary of the extreme confusion over this play: on the one hand he says Sophocles was more poet than thinker (cf. the amazing article of N. Vlachos, *Some Aspects of the Religion of Sophocles*) and ignored the whole moral problem (pp. 299, 327), and on the other hand that Sophocles "conceived the matricide as an odious crime," but refrained from saying so out of reverence for the myth (p. 324). However, he seems to feel that the myth did not need criticizing, because Apollo did not order the crime, but only told Orestes how to do it (pp. 302f.). Cf. Sheppard, "Electra: a Defence of Sophocles," *Classical Review*, XLI, no. 1 (1927), 2–9, and the answer of Bowra, pp. 215f. Apollo's authority cannot be read out of Orestes' deed.
16. Kaibel, ed. *Elektra*, pp. 290f., 302, finds in Orestes' speech, "All's well, if Apollo augured well," a subtle indication that Sophocles thought the matricide a crime and that he was verging on an accusation of Apollo, whose responsibility is clearly borne out by *El.* 32ff., 69f., 82f., 1264–1272. Following Erfurdt, *Adnotationes Integrae in*

Sophoclis Tragoedias, p. 403 *ad loc.,* Kaibel maintained that after line 1427 there was a lacuna of three lines which contained the much desired reference to the Furies. It is clear treason, however, first to posit a lacuna, and then to fill it with whatever fits a private theory; besides, the matter of Orestes' guilt, if such is the point of the play, is much too important to entrust to three lines of lyric, while the whole rest of the work shows him in an opposite light. See Steiger, p. 590, and Bowra, pp. 257ff. for refutation. The lacuna may actually exist, but it is by no means certain; cf. Jebb, *Electra,* App. to 1398.

17. Pohlenz, pp. 340–342, thinks Clytaemnestra thoroughly deserves her fate, and cites *El.* 977ff. for the spirit in which the murder should be received. Herein he is no doubt correct, but goes too far when he says that the play is an anti-Aeschylean reversion to an older form of the myth which to "the old Sophocles remained the essence of Tragedy."

18. Cf. Weinstock, pp. 33–35, who calls Electra the incarnation of Divine Justice, and finds the play "an example . . . of that divine command which alone can be the basis of a lasting society." Yet like Pohlenz, Weinstock feels that Sophocles "piously accepts the whole saga as a sacred word," without inquiring after the rightness of the deed. These theories do not fit each other, let alone the play. For the whole idea that the deaths of Clytaemnestra and Aegisthus constitute the main point, that the gods punish sin, and the world is hard, compare Bowra, p. 228.

19. Cf. Bowra, p. 260, who notes the absence of conflict over the murder.

20. Those who hold this view, besides T. v. Wilamowitz, are: U. v. Wilamowitz, *Hermes* (1883), pp. 233f. (*Electra* as simple "heroic action," with all moral problems overlooked); Steiger, p. 584 (Sophocles piously related the sacred story without trying to apply any standards, but simply following Homer); Beloch, *Gesch. Gr.* II², 1, 221, speaks of the play's "jesuitical morality." Reinhardt does not commit himself openly about the moral point.

21. T. v. Wilamowitz, pp. 174, 211f., 215–220; cf. p. 183, on the character of Electra.

22. Pohlenz, pp. 342f., makes a curious attempt to correct Wilamowitz' "pure art" view by saying that not the whole play but the recognition scene only was written for purely artistic effect. It does not seem to improve matters much. His further statement that these recognition scenes are Sophocles' own discovery seem to jar slightly with his other statement (p. 338) that the recognition scene is due to the direct influence of Euripides. See Reinhardt's answer, p. 278, n. 2.

23. *Odyssey* I, 40.

24. *Pyth.* XI, 34–37.

25. Proclus, *Chrest.,* Νόστοι, *Homeri Opera,* Oxford, V, 109, line 3.

26. Diehl, *Anth. Lyr. Gr.* II, vi, 12–15.

27. Cf. Bowra, pp. 214ff.

28. *Eum.* 94–116.

29. *El.* 1415f.

30. *El.* 1426f. The reference is designedly made to Clytaemnestra's criminal treatment of her daughter, in order to prevent sympathy from rising for her.

31. *El.* 1445ff. Note the rude repetition of σέ, and compare *Ajax* 1226, 1228, 1234; *Ant.* 441, 444, 446, 508, 510, 531, 534, 573; regular tyrannical speech.

32. *El.* 1458–1463; cf. *Ajax* 1253f.; *Ant.* 477f.

33. *El.* 1487ff.

34. χωροῖς ἂν εἴσω σὺν τάχει, *El.* 1491.

35. Cf. T. v. Wilamowitz, p. 218.

36. See Schadewaldt, p. 65 and n.

37. στυγερή, *Od.* III, 309f. See Steiger's comment, pp. 564f.

38. Bowra, p. 212, is surely wrong in saying that there is no really ancient evidence that Orestes killed Clytaemnestra, and that Homer shut his eyes to the question of whether he did or not. The ancient Mycenaean seal stone found near Thisbe, and published by Sir Arthur Evans in *Journal of Hellenic Studies*, XLV (1925), 38, fig. 38, is thought to represent the vengeance of Orestes, and the interpretation seems most probable. On this gem, Orestes has already slain Aegisthus and is definitely attacking the fleeing Clytaemnestra. See Evans' remarks on how well the figures bear out the Homeric attitude toward the story. Cf. also *Pyth.* XI, 36.

39. See Bowra, pp. 231ff., for a general summary of her evil characteristics.

40. αἰκία, *El.* 515.

41. *El.* 516–518.

42. *El.* 612–615, 626f.; 1196.

43. *El.* 417ff.; 780ff. On the former passage see Bowra, p. 225; Herodotus I, 107–108; Robert, *Bild und Lied*, pp. 170f.

44. *El.* 244ff.

45. *El.* 378ff.

46. *El.* 766ff., 770f. Bruhn (*ad loc.*) seems practically alone in calling this hypocrisy. Kaibel has a very good explanation (ed. *ad loc.*, 764) and Jebb (Introduction, p. xxxv), T. v. Wilamowitz (p. 181, n. 1), and Schadewaldt (p. 66), all agree that her grief, what there is of it, is genuine. Why should it not be, now that her fear is relieved? Electra's infinitely greater loss accounts for her taunts at 788ff., 804ff.

47. *El.* 244ff., 229ff.

48. *El.* 236f.

49. See Chapter V on *Antigone*, and notes 34–36.

50. El. 150ff.; cf. 1076f.

51. *El.* 100–120, 145ff., 185ff.

52. *El.* 131f., 222.

53. *El.* 254f.

54. *El.* 352–356.

55. *El.* 338–340.

56. *El.* 332–334.

57. *El.* 400.

58. *El.* 356.

59. *El.* 221, 256, 308f., 619f. Cf. Bowra, p. 240.

60. σωφρονεῖν, *El.* 307.

61. *El.* 257–260, 349f.

62. *El.* 321, 1026.

63. Eur. *El.* 61ff., 175–189, 1004. Soph. *El.* 239ff., 309. Cf. also the chorus' remonstrances with her choice, 217–220; 233–235. She will carry her choice to the utmost consequence, 399. The chorus finally gives full approval, 1082–1089. Note the εἴλου.

64. Weinstock, p. 34.

65. *El.* 947ff.

66. *El.* 977–985.

67. Cf. Weinstock, p. 37. He feels that the narrative is the main block on which Electra's heroism is built. I feel rather it merely changes the course of her heroism.

68. *El.* 1019f. The parallels between this stichomythy and the prologue of *Antigone* are obvious.

69. *El.* 1032. It will be noticed that in this play the function of the chorus is slightly different from that of earlier ones. They are fundamentally in agreement with Electra, and though they do remonstrate with her in the parodos, yet when she conceives her great daring plan, it is not they, but only Chrysothemis, who accuses her of folly. The chorus sings a song to speed her on (1058ff.). The reason seems two-fold: (1) Sophocles perhaps felt that the audience would need constant reminders

of the justice of Electra's position, and so made the chorus and even Chrysothemis acknowledge it (338f.); (2) there was a tendency to try to draw the chorus into the action more and more in the later drama. It is equally apparent in *Philoctetes* and *Oedipus at Colonus.*

70. *El.* 117–120.
71. Reinhardt, p. 166, recognizes this fact, but fails to explain Orestes' full function.
72. W. B. Yeats, *Sailing to Byzantium.*
73. T. v. Wilamowitz, p. 166.
74. *El.* 179, 331f., 1464f.
75. *El.* 1253–1255.
76. Contrast the judgment on Aegisthus, 1484f., who is involved in evil, and for whom it can be no gain to put off death. Time is fruitless to the man who cannot live nobly.
77. *El.* 1273ff.
78. *Ajax* 646f.; *Oed. Rex* 1213; *Oed. Col.* 437ff.
79. Electra had said she could not endure unless Orestes came, 117ff.; now it is Orestes' arrival which is the unhoped for, 1262f. Yet both of these unhoped-for things, her own strength and Orestes' coming, are equal to the same thing — moral salvation.
80. *El.* 1264, 1270, 1306 (τῷ παρόντι δαίμονι).

IX. The Paradox of Will: *Philoctetes*

1. See Reinhardt, *Sophokles*, p. 148.
2. *Phil.* 954–960; 1146–1161.
3. *Phil.* 199, 285, 306, 598, 715, 795, 1041, 1114, 1446. Cf. on *Electra*, notes 74–78.
4. *Phil.* 8–11.
5. See below, and n. 17.
6. *Phil.* 610–619.
7. Thus Pohlenz, pp. 344–356, who further states, p. 352, that Sophocles had a special reverence for Heracles, and dedicated a chapel to him. Sophocles seems to have performed numerous acts of public piety, like a good citizen. But how is his special reverence for Heracles compatible with the rough treatment of him in the *Trachiniae?*
8. Cf. Bowra, p. 263, who asserts that clarity is only achieved finally through the intervention of the gods.
9. *Phil.* 1373.
10. Solon, I, 67f. (Diehl).
11. Weinstock, pp. 88f., actually asserts that the chief person of the play is Neoptolemus. This despite the title.
12. Cf. Pohlenz, pp. 345, 355.
13. *Phil.* 108–111.
14. *Phil.* 96–99.
15. σοφία and καλοκἀγαθία, *Phil.* 119. Note the specific contrast of 1246.
16. τὰ συμφέροντα, *Phil.* 131.
17. δριμύς, ἀκριβής, πολιτικός, Dio Chrys., *Or.* 52, 15.
18. Weinstock, pp. 91f., makes him a tool in the hands of the gods, but he seems to be totally outside whatever divine force operates in the play. In fact, that is exactly why he fails, while Neoptolemus, in a sense, succeeds. In any case, there is never any real divine teleology in Sophocles.
19. *Phil.* 1243, 1250, 1257.

20. Cf. *Phil.* 1251, for instance; the opposition of τὸ καλὸν or τὸ δίκαιον and τὸ συμφέρον is familiar as the starting point of Greek conceptual ethics.

21. *Phil.* 874, 1310f.; J. A. Moore, p. 68, takes the character of Neoptolemus as illustrative of Sophocles' belief that arete was φύσει not νόμῳ.

22. *Phil.* 389f., 405ff.

23. The choral strophe which follows this speech at 343 has aroused some curiosity. Granted the chorus as a rule is swept away by the action, still it goes pretty far here. Why suddenly swear to Neoptolemus' fiction, and why, above all, invoke the Magna Mater? Of many explanations, the most plausible seems to be Zielinski's ("De Sophoclis fabula ignota"), though it rests on much hypothesis. Zielinski thinks the passage is a reference to a very early lost play, the *Neoptolemus*, in which this scene actually took place, and the chorus did invoke the Dea Magna, since they were really in Phrygia at the judgment of the arms. His argument is greatly reinforced by comparisons of the fragments of Accius' *Neoptolemus*, Soph. *Phil.* 357, 562, and *Fr. Tr. Adesp.* 363. He furthermore sees evidence for thinking this lost play the second part of a trilogy, produced in 474/3, just after Cimon had conquered Scyros and brought back the bones of Theseus. The other two parts were the *Scyrii* and the *Polyxena*. See also Zielinski, *Tragodoumena*, pp. 41ff., 110ff. In spite of the slight nature of the evidence, the reconstruction seems extremely likely and quite worthy of its author's brilliance and insight.

24. *Phil.* 426ff., 446ff. Cf. 1035.

25. *Phil.* 436–440.

26. *Phil.* 453–460.

27. *Il.* IX, 356–363; 414–416.

28. *Phil.* 77f.

29. *Phil.* 1055–1062.

30. *Phil.* 833ff., 850–864. Those who believe that Sophoclean choruses contain the true morals of the plays seldom mention this passage.

31. Cf. Reinhardt, pp. 192f., 202; Reinhardt is surely a little perverse to say that Neoptolemus deserves no credit for these lines. Cf. Bowra, p. 281.

32. *Phil.* 839–842.

33. Bowra, pp. 265ff., says it must be fulfilled because otherwise trouble will ensue; but to say merely this seems empty and a trifle superstitious.

34. See the *Gorgias* especially for the general exposition of moral goodness as the only really expedient course.

35. *Phil.* 671–673.

36. *Phil.* 195ff. Cf. also the chorus at 676ff., with its long speculation on the innocent suffering (esp. 686) and the extraordinary endurance of Philoctetes (esp. 689f.).

37. *Phil.* 533–538; cf. 794–795, 894.

38. *Phil.* 1046.

39. *Phil.* 1063f.

40. *Phil.* 1066–1078.

41. *Phil.* 1186f., αἰαῖ δαίμων δαίμων.

42. *Phil.* 1197–1201.

43. ἔτ' οὐδέν εἰμι *Phil.* 1217. Cf. 946 and 1030.

44. *Phil.* 1316–1320 (cf. 1387), 1329–1332, 1344–1347, 1373–1375.

45. *Phil.* 1348–1352.

46. *Phil.* 1352ff. The τῷ προσήγορος surely means, "complying, or agreeing in what respect" — in other words, "What have I in common with the Greek host that I should yield?"

47. *Phil.* 1358–1360; *Soph. Trag.*, pp. 292ff. Bowra feels that Philoctetes is terribly wrong, almost impious, to refuse Neoptolemus' full revelation of the situation. But

Bowra is forgetting the free-will problem. In fact, he is trying to get around the oracle!

48. *Phil.* 1392.

49. *Phil.* 1399–1402. I cannot agree that Philoctetes was gradually purified of obstinacy, and was on the point of yielding. See C. Post, *HSCP* (1912), p. 104, and Moore's answer, p. 58. Philoctetes never even came near yielding, and loss of his obstinacy would not have been a purification, but a moral fall.

50. See H. Kuhn, "The True Tragedy," *HSCP*, 52 (1941), p. 13, on the divine nature of the idea of τὸ μεταγνῶναι, and some interesting remarks on this passage, and the final scene.

51. *Phil.* 1405–1407.

52. *Phil.* 1418–1422.

53. Cf. Jaeger, *Paideia* I², 9, "Areté *is* mortal man," etc. Cf. *ibid.*, p. 13, on Aristotle's poem to the "immortal arete" of Hermias, and the element of moral fortitude therein. Furthermore, see Plato, *Symp.* 208c, and Norden who refers to this passage, *Kunstprosa*, pp. 110f., noting the verse (hexameter) rhythms of this passage, which represents not merely sophistic oratorical techniques, but the older heroic morale as well. For a late occurrence of the idea, doubtless suggested by Sophocles' own concern with it, see *Anth. Pal.* VII, 21.

54. *Phil.* 1420, 1425, 1429.

55. *Phil.* 1437ff.

56. εὐσέβεια *Phil.* 1440ff.; this "piety" is, of course, the respect for inner worth (τὸ καλόν) which both already possess and share.

57. Cf. Perrotta, p. 468.

58. T. v. Wilamowitz, pp. 311f.; cf. *ibid.*, p. 316 (U. v. Wilamowitz, who says the *deus ex machina* is inartistic!).

59. ἡδονὴν μετὰ ὕψους καὶ σεμνότητος, Dio Chrys. *Or.* 52, 15.

60. Cf. Bowra, pp. 301f. He concludes, rather characteristically, that the moral of the play is that man must reverence the gods, p. 304.

61. Weinstock, p. 93.

62. *Phil.* 1452–1468 (Francklin).

X. Apocalypse: *Oedipus at Colonus*

1. Cf. Carl Robert, *Oidipus*, for a complete and searching history of the myth.

2. *Homeri Opera*, V, 112ff.

3. *Il.* XXIII, 679; *Od.* XI, 271–280.

4. Paus. I, 28, 7.

5. Eur. *Phoen.* 1703–1707. Cf. I. Muller, *Handbuch d. Kl. Altertumswissenschaft*, VII, I, 1, p. 340.

6. Diod. Sic. XIII, 72; Cf. Bowra, p. 308.

7. Paus. I, 30, 4. The relation of the *Oedipus at Colonus* to the hero cult has been studied with interesting, if not conclusive results by G. Méautis, *L'Oedipe à Colone et le culte des Héros* (Neuchâtel, 1940).

8. *Oed. Col.* 421ff., 765–771.

9. *Oed. Col.* 14–18.

10. *Oed. Col.* 75–76.

11. *Oed. Col.* 562–568.

12. *Oed. Col.* 576ff.

13. *Oed. Col.* 602–605.

14. *Oed. Col.* 607–623.

15. *Oed. Col.* 637, reading ἔμπολιν with Musgrave and Jebb. Cf. *Oed. Col.* 1156 for the implications of the word. Cf. *Ant.* 370.

16. *Oed. Col.* 668ff.

17. Euripides sometimes inverted the process, in his more cynical moods, even as he carried it to extremes in his chauvinistic ones. But in either case it arose from the same consciousness of cultural and ideational standards.

18. *Oed. Col.* 3–8.

19. *Oed. Rex* 1082–1083.

20. *Oed. Rex* 1213.

21. Cf. *Oed. Col.* 7, 22, 437f., 580; in Creon's case, it has failed to teach wisdom, 930f. See also on the *Electra*, and notes 74–78.

22. *Oed. Col.* 804f., 852f.

23. *Oed. Col.* 1454f.

24. *Ajax* 678–682. Cf. *Oed. Col.* 614f. In the *Ajax* passage, such caution and reserve about friendships is an utter reversal of the Homeric standard. For Oedipus, however, the man of γνώμη, these changes are in the order of things, and consistent with wisdom. So also the concept of τὸ μαθεῖν appears (lines 117f.) in a constructive and good light, impossible to the hero of the strictly aristocratic tradition of φυά.

25. *Oed. Col.* 392–395. Cf. *Philoctetes* 1030. Is it conceivable that Sophocles counted the lines of this play as we do in our editions, and purposely placed this essential paradox at line 393? The technique was not unknown to Dante. See note 38 of this chapter.

26. *Oed. Col.* 403.

27. *Oed. Col.* 385f. See U. v. Wilamowitz, in T. v. Wilamowitz, p. 334, and Pohlenz, *Erläut.*, p. 364, for interpretation of σωθῆναι as "homecoming." This idea is well answered by Reinhardt, p. 214, n. 1.

28. Cf. E. Rohde, pp. 535ff. Perrotta, who agrees that Oedipus is unchanged, apparently for this reason makes light of the apotheosis and claims that a hero is not really a demigod (*Sofocle*, pp. 560f.). Once more, the interpretation of the play had suffered from an unhistorical intrusion of basically Christian values in the case of Perrotta, and perhaps of basically Orphic ones in the case of Rohde, who feels that Oedipus lacks purification.

29. See, for instance, *Oed. Col.* 760ff., 960ff. (against Creon); 1383ff. (against Polyneices); 593 (to Theseus).

30. *Oed. Col.* 39–46.

31. *Oed. Col.* 17–18.

32. Pausanias, I, 28, 6, notes the specific absence of horrendous attributes in the Athenian cult of the Eumenides, in contrast with the picture given by Aeschylus. This whole austere but terrorless conception of the Erinyes appears to have been a typically Athenian one.

33. For this aspect of ancient psychology, see Thomas Mann, "Freud and the Future," *Essays of Three Decades* (New York, 1947), esp. pp. 420–426. See also the Joseph series in general.

34. Simonides, 4, 7–12 (Diehl).

35. *Oed. Col.* 228f.

36. *Oed. Col.* 252ff.

37. Besides the passages already quoted, see *Oed. Col.* 142, 266ff., 258–291, 521–548, and 960ff.

38. The importance of the triad in Sophocles, and especially of the third member of the triad, has been studied with illuminating results in an essay by St. John Thackeray, "Sophocles and the Perfect Number," *Proceedings of the British Academy*, 16 (1930), pp. 15–44.

39. *Oed. Col.* 263–272.

40. *Oed. Col.* 966–968.

41. *Oed. Col.* 539f. Solon I, 63–64 (Diehl); cf. *Il.* III, 64–66; cf. Soph. *fg.* 964 (Pearson) and Hesiod *Erga* 82–88. These are the clearest examples of the idea in Sophocles, but "gift" frequently has sinister overtones, especially in the *Trach.* 494ff., 555f., 758, and *Ajax* 662, 665, 817, and most of all 1029–1037, where the gift of an enemy is described in the light of a device of the gods. This comes close to being the "gift of the gods," which is inescapable, and has nothing to do with moral deserts, as Oedipus' distinction, lines 539f., shows.

42. *Oed. Col.* 345–352.

43. *Oed. Col.* 337ff., 1365–1368.

44. *Oed. Col.* 76. Δαίμονος is perhaps correctly "luck," but it is luck with a divine element, in contrast to τύχη.

45. *Oed. Col.* 292ff.

46. *Oed. Col.* 631f.

47. *Oed. Col.* 569, 1042f.

48. *Oed. Col.* 562–568.

49. *Oed. Col.* 74. The blind man's insight recalls, of course, Teiresias, and the whole knowledge problem of the former play.

50. Cf. Dopheide, *De Sophoclis arte dramatica*, p. 77, who says the Polyneices episode is no part of the plot, but a little tragedy in itself. The suggestion of C. Robert, *Oidipus* I, 474ff., only seems more historical than this. Robert thinks that Polyneices represents Sophocles' own son Iophon, who is thought to have tried to seize his heritage before his father's death by having him pronounced *non compos mentis*. Even if Iophon's suit actually took place, which is doubtful, it is very unlike Sophocles to dramatize a humiliating family dispute in a tragedy, and thrust himself to the fore. In any case, it explains nothing about the play.

51. Cf. U. v. Wilamowitz in Tycho v. Wilamowitz, p. 371 (answer to Robert), and pp. 317f., and 367, where it is skillfully shown that the Polyneices scene is firmly connected with the original saga. Wilamowitz exhibits his customary acumen in unearthing sources, but he too has failed to integrate Polyneices artistically with the play.

52. Cf. Allègre, *Sophocle*, pp. 299–305; Bowra, pp. 329ff.; Pohlenz, pp. 364f.; and Reinhardt, p. 227 for such views.

53. *Oed. Col.* 431–444; 765–771; 776–780.

54. The writer of the ancient *Argumentum*, however, feels it is inadequately motivated: ὅ τε ἐπὶ πᾶσι μετ' ᾠδῆς ἀδολέσχου φυγαδενόμενος Οἰδίπους προσέρραπται διὰ κενῆς.

55. *Oed. Col.* 418–420; 448f.

56. *Oed. Col.* 406–408.

57. *Oed. Col.* 399f.; 600–602.

58. *Oed. Col.* 412–415.

59. *Oed. Col.* 636–641; 643.

60. *Oed. Col.* 834ff.

61. *Oed. Col.* 851.

62. Herod. III, 80. Creon's attack on Antigone suggests his character in the *Antigone*.

63. *Oed. Col.* 733f., 758f.; esp. 737f.

64. *Oed. Col.* 944–949.

65. *Rhet.* I, 8 (1366a).

66. *Oed. Col.* 913–923.

67. *Oed. Col.* 960–1002. This passage, the fullest defense which Oedipus gives, should long ago have silenced the argument that he was responsible for his misfortunes through his bad temper. The simple truth of Oedipus' remarks at 991–996 seems inescapable.

68. *Oed. Col.* 1003–1009.

69. *Oed. Col.* 887–890; 897–903.

70. Thuc. II, 37. See Chapter IV above. Reinhardt, p. 223, goes so far as to suggest that Pericles himself is behind the figure of Theseus. But Pericles had been dead now for twenty years, and the shape in Sophocles' mind was more ideal and generally historical than specific.

71. For instance, *Oed. Col.* 703ff., 1533f.

72. See the Oxyrhynchus Historian, Grenfell and Hunt, *Ox. Pap.*, no. 842, col. xiii, 28ff.

73. Xen. *Hell.* II, 2, 19.

74. Thuc. II, 41, 1.

75. *Oed. Col.* 1264.

76. Perrotta, p. 606, feels he is quite as much a hero as Eteocles in the *Septem*, and is modeled on him.

77. *Oed. Col.* 1269f.

78. *Oed. Col.* 1418f.

79. Cf. *Oed. Col.* 1280 with 1344f.

80. Cf. Perrotta, p. 610, who thinks Sophocles disapproved of the curse and that the thunder which follows it is a correction of his attitude. Actually, Oedipus himself tells us the sign is a summons from Zeus. Perrotta feels that Oedipus is exalted in spite of his character, and with as little reason as he was destroyed in the former play. Cf. Reinhardt, p. 230.

81. Cf. Allègre, pp. 299ff., and Bowra, pp. 329ff. Also, apparently, Turolla, *La poesia di Sofocle*, p. 197 (I have this reference second-hand). Patin, *Sophocle*, p. 243, thinks Sophocles did not know what to think of it!

82. Pohlenz, *Gr. Trag.*, p. 365, and *Erläut.*, p. 102, urges the laws governing τροφή and θρεπτήρια. He suggests comparison of *Oed. Col.* 352, 446, 1265, 1362–1365. Cf. Bowra, pp. 327ff. for a similar view and more evidence, and Weinstock, p. 197.

83. Cf. *Oed. Col.* 1429f., 1402–1404; 1432ff.

84. Cf. *Oed. Col.* 374ff.

85. *Thebaid*, fgs. 2 and 3; cf. Bowra, p. 325.

86. *Oed. Col.* 371ff.

87. *Oed. Col.* 1433. Note the characteristic "double motivation."

88. See Thomas Mann, *Joseph and His Brothers*, trans. by H. T. Lowe-Porter (New York, 1945), pp. 141f.

89. *Oed. Col.* 1391. Oedipus does mention having cursed both his sons before, lines 1375f., but the context indicates no more than that he had stated before what he states now, and that both times it was true. Curses take the form of a wish, as oracles of a command, but both essentially only indicate what must be true, when it is viewed without the element of time. Oedipus is so near the state of a god that he can speak as from outside of time.

90. *Oed. Col.* 1540 (τοὐκ θεοῦ παρόν); cf. 1520f. and 1542ff.

91. Cf. Pohlenz, p. 363, and Bowra, pp. 314ff.

92. *Oed. Col.* 1565ff.

93. ἀκερδῆ χάριν, *Oed. Col.* 1484.

94. *Oed. Col.* 1489.

95. *Oed. Col.* 394–395.

96. *Oed. Col.* 1536ff.; 607ff.; 560ff.

97. "An das Göttliche glauben/ Die allein, die es selber sind," F. Hölderlin, "Menschen beifall" (trans. F. Prokosch).

98. *Oed. Col.* 1640f.

99. *El.* 836ff.

100. *Scholia in Soph. Trag. Vetera*, ed. P. N. Papageorgius (Leipzig, 1888), p. 139.

101. Cf. *Od.* XI, 482ff., and Aesch. *Choeph.* 354ff., which Liddell and Scott cite in support of the scholiast's first suggestion.

102. The phrase πάμψυχος ἀνάσσει cannot mean any of the things the scholiast suggests. The difficulty of the usual interpretation lies in the analogy between πάμψυχος and other words like Παναχαιοί and πανδήμιος, where the first part of the compound modifies the second while retaining its root meaning. Sophocles, in *Ant.* 1140ff., uses such a word: — ὡς βιαίας ἔχεται πάνδαμος πόλις ἐπὶ νόσου, "since the city with all its people is caught by a mighty disease." It will be seen at once, however, that this construction, comprehensible enough as it is, is not analogous to πάμψυχος ἀνάσσει, where the adjective in agreement with the subject is made by the scholiast to equal πασῶν ψυχῶν, object of the verb. It seems more likely that πάμψυχος is formed on the analogy of πάμμορος (*Oed. Col.* 161) or παγκάκιστος, and all the other words in which the παν- is merely intensive. This interpretation would give a concessive ring to the phrase, "although all-shade [i.e., nothing but a shade] he rules." Cf. the meaning of περ (intensive) passing into περ (concessive). In exactly the same spirit, involving eternal continuation of a human characteristic, and quite analogous to the whole idea of "immortal arete" in its timeless aspect, is Homer's line about Niobe, *Il.* XXIV, 617: ἔνθα λίθος περ ἐοῦσα θεῶν ἐκ κήδεα πέσσει. Cf. the excellent and brief summary of such ideas in early Greece by M. P. Nilsson, *A History of Greek Religion*, pp. 100–104.

103. τὸ θεῖον. I am indebted to Werner Jaeger's *Theology of the Early Greek Philosophers* for this conception of the research of the Ionians, which seems to me absolutely correct and inevitable. See the following chapter and notes.

104. The quotation is taken from Middlemore's translation of Burckhardt's *Civilization of the Renaissance*.

XI. Sophocles and the Fifth Century

1. Thuc. II, 38, 2.

2. *Ant.* 836–838.

3. Jaeger, *Theology*, pp. 172–174. Cf. his distinction in the Orphic cult between παθεῖν and μαθεῖν, *ibid.*, p. 88.

4. For the view of Ionian philosophy herein adopted, the reader is earnestly referred to Jaeger's *Theology*, which takes its place beside the same author's *Aristotle* as one of the most enlightened, if not the most enlightened, book ever written about Greek philosophy.

5. Xenoph. *fg.* 10 (Diehl); cf. Jaeger, *Theology*, pp. 47–50.

6. Diels, *Vorsokr.* II⁵88B25; cf. Jaeger's exposition of the fragment, *Theology*, chapter x.

7. Cf. Jaeger, pp. 174ff. and chapter x *passim*, esp. note 10, for a brilliant and clear exposition of how Sophistic thinking arose from and transformed the theological speculations of the early philosophers.

8. Cf. Dodds, "Euripides the Irrationalist," *CR*, 43, pp. 94–104.

9. Eur. *Hipp.* 1146.

10. *Ibid.* 1420–1422.

11. See Jaeger, p. 164, for this interpretation of the *Nous* of Anaxagoras. Cf. Diogenes Ap., Diels, *Vorsokr.* II⁵64B4 and 5.

12. Jaeger, pp. 165; 167–171. Diels, *Vorsokr.* II⁵64B3. I have here followed Professor Jaeger implicitly in his attribution of the teleological ideas expressed by Xenophon in *Memorabilia* I and IV to Diogenes.

13. *Ajax* 646f., 669–676. Perrotta (see above, Chapter IV, note 51), thinks this speech reflects the doctrine of Archelaus of Miletus, but it seems to me that Diogenes is perhaps the more likely candidate. Cf. Bowra, p. 42.

14. *Ajax* 678–682; cf. Jebb, ed. *Ajax, ad loc.*, where other examples of this maxim are quoted, and traced back to Bias of Priene; also Plut. *Per.* 39, where Pericles boasts he has never treated an enemy as incurable.

15. Plato, *Crito* 49d. The real battle over the matter of faith, of course, is in the *Gorgias.*

16. I have admittedly treated Socrates from the purely Platonic sources, which I believe, at least up to and including the *Gorgias*, represent him largely as he was. Plato's picture shows a man such as only the fifth century could produce, a man whose whole personality transcended the ideas he dealt with. He is not to be identified with his ideas, but with his moral being: and this, the moral being of Socrates, was one piece of fifth-century tradition which Plato seems to have been content to keep. The fourth century, with its moral and social diffusion, had lost the perspective of action and could produce Plato but not Socrates. Plato's early political aims and their debacle (see the VIIth Letter) seem to represent the last stirrings of the fifth century in him. There was no longer any channel for them, and they died, or perhaps better, passed into the somewhat idealized but basically faithful memoir of the moral heroism of Socrates, which, without example, Plato alone could never have made up.

17. For Socrates as hero, see the beginning of his "serious" defense, in the *Apology* 28 (chapter xvi), with its paradigmatic reference to "demigods who died in Troy."

18. Cf. Jaeger, p. 173: "The Greeks always thought of the word *God* as predicative."

19. Eur. *Her.* 342.

20. *Oed. Col.* 1225.

21. *Il.* XI, 761.

22. Simonides, 5 (Diehl); in Simonides this idea exists side by side with its contrary — that gods and men are widely divided (cf. *fgs.* 6–12) and in general the division rather than the union received the greater emphasis. Yet the idea in *fg.* 37 of the Arete that dwells on high among the nymphs and is achievable by sweat and vigor has about it the implication of divine achievement by man. Cf. *fgs.* 10 and 184.

23. *Ibid.* 118, on those dead at Plataea.

24. *Ibid.* 121. Cf. *Il.* V, 448, for association of verb κυδαίνω with restoration to life.

25. Aesch. *Epigram* 2 (Diehl).

26. *Scolia Anonyma*, 11 (Diehl).

27. *Od.* XI, 487ff.

28. Tyrt. 9, 31; Heraclitus B24, 25, Diels *Vorsokr.*5 Cf., incidentally, B62.

29. Plut. *Per.* 8, quotes Stesimbrotus as his source for this speech; it is interesting to compare therewith Gorgias' *Epitaphios*, Sauppe, *Or. Att.* II, 130, where the immortal element is πόθος. Nevertheless, Gorgias plays deliberately on the paradox of death and immortality. Cf. also, of course, the passage in the *Funeral Oration*, Thuc. II, 43.

30. Thuc. II, 65, 9.

31. Thuc. II, 41, 4.

XII. Metaphysic of Humanism

1. See above, Chapter V, and nn. 35f.

2. *Eth. Nic.* 1145a20–25.

3. *Il.* XXIV, 258.

4. *Eth. Nic.* 1151b7–22.

5. *Ibid.* 1148a22–b5.

6. Cf. *Il.* XXIV, 617; and above, Chapter X, n. 102.

7. Arist. *fg.* 5 (Diehl).

8. Plut. *Dem.* 20. Entirely in keeping with Sophocles' use of oracles, as well as with the "enlightened" fifth-century view, is the interpretation given by Thuc. II, 18. Cf. Diod. Sic. XV, 52, 4, where the episode, however, concerns the fourth century, not the fifth.

9. *Oed. Col.* 403.

10. Cf. Reinhardt, p. 70, who notes how the protagonist, when destroyed, regularly calls upon the roots of his life, not on external fate.

11. The theory is very widespread, but see especially, Pohlenz, p. 235 *et passim.* Cf. Bowra, p. 380.

12. Pohlenz, pp. 212f.

13. See *Ajax* 125f., 301, 394, 646f. (on the fading products of time); *Ant.* 1170; *Oed. Rex* 1186f., 1273f.; *El.* 1159, 1166; *Phil.* 946f., 1030; *Oed. Col.* 109f., 393, 567f.; *fgs.* 13, 331, 945 (Pearson).

14. *Il.* VI, 146ff.; Mimnermus 2 (Diehl); Pindar, *Pyth.* VIII, 95; Aesch. *fg.* 5, l. 9, in Fritsch's *Neue Fragmente*, where I think the correct reading must be βροτός.

15. *Phil.* 1030.

16. *Oed. Col.* 393.

17. Bowra, p. 201, cites Parmenides, *fgs.* 1 and 6, Heraclitus, *fgs.* 78 and 79, and Alcmaeon of Croton, *fg.* 1, as forerunners of this whole kind of distinction between real and unreal. Certainly for them, too, the commonplace had taken on a special significance. Peculiarly interesting is Parmenides' heroic conception of himself as the prophet of the Real.

18. It is perhaps Sophocles' full admission of this fact at the outset that leads to the conclusion that he was a pessimist; cf. Perrotta, *passim*, and J. Opstelten, *Sophokles en het Pessimismus.* (The latter book is known to me only through the review by W. C. Greene, *AJP*, LXVII [October 1946], which in itself is a judicious brief discussion of the whole optimism-pessimism question.) The opposite view, that he was an optimist, appears in Pohlenz, and is equally defensible. Neither view is very valuable, since ultimately these tags are meaningless to an intellect such as Sophocles'.

19. See Greene, *Moira*, for a comprehensive study of this concept.

20. *Oed. Col.* 607ff.

21. *Oed. Col.* 1663–1665.

A SELECTED BIBLIOGRAPHY

Abbott, Evelyn. "The Theology and Ethics of Sophocles," *Hellenica*, London, 1880, pp. 33–66.

Allègre, F. *Sophocle, Etude sur les ressorts dramatiques de son théâtre, et la composition de ses tragédies.* Lyon, Paris, 1905.

Barstow, Marjorie. "Oedipus Rex: A Typical Greek Tragedy," *Classical Weekly*, October 5, 1912.

Beazley, J. D. *Attic Black Figure.* London, 1928.

Böckh, August. *Des Sophokles Antigone.* Berlin, 1843.

Bowra, C. M. *Sophoclean Tragedy.* Oxford, 1944.

Bruhn, Ewald. "Lucubrationum Euripidearum Capita Selecta," *Jahrbücher für Classische Philologie*, XV (Suppl.), 1886, 225–324.

Butcher, S. H. *Aristotle's Theory of Poetry and Fine Art.* 3rd ed., London, New York, 1902.

Bywater, Ingram. *Aristotle on the Art of Poetry.* Oxford, 1909.

Campbell, Lewis. "Le point culminant dans la tragédie grecque," *Mélanges Weil*, Paris, 1898, pp. 17ff.

Cooper, Lane. *The Greek Genius and Its Influence.* New Haven, 1917.

Croiset, Maurice. *Oedipe-Roi de Sophocle, Etude et Analyse.* Paris, 1931.

Denniston, J. D. *Electra.* Oxford, 1939.

Dieterich, Albrecht. "Schlafscenen auf der attischen Bühne," *Rheinisches Museum*, 46 (1891), 25–46.

Dodds, E. R. "Euripides the Irrationalist," *Classical Review*, 43 (1929), 97–104.

Dopheide, Wilhelm. *De Sophoclis arte dramatica.* Westfalen Universität Diss. Münster, 1910.

Earle, M. L. "Studies in Sophocles's Trachinians," *TAPA*, 33 (1902), 5–29.

Earp, F. R. *The Style of Sophocles.* Cambridge, 1944.

Farnell, L. R. *The Higher Aspects of Greek Religion.* London, 1912.

Ferguson, W. S. "The Attic Orgeones," *Harvard Theological Review*, vol. 37, no. 2, pp. 61ff.

Finley, J. H., Jr. "Euripides and Thucydides," *HSCP*, 49 (1938), 23–68.

———— "The Origins of Thucydides' Style," *HSCP*, 50 (1939), 35–84.

———— *Thucydides.* Cambridge, Mass., 1942.

Fritsch, Carl-Ernst. *Neue Fragmente des Aischylos und Sophokles.* Hansische Universität Diss. Hamburg, 1936.

Greene, William C. *Moira: Fate, Good, and Evil in Greek Thought.* Cambridge, Mass., 1944.

———— "The Murderers of Laius," *TAPA*, 60 (1929), 75–86.

Gruppe, Otto F. *Ariadne: Die tragische Kunst der Griechen.* Berlin, 1834.

Hagelueken, Hugo. *Quo tempore Sophoclis Oedipus Rex acta sit.* Rostock Diss. Rostock, 1873.

Harsh, Philip W. " 'Αμαρτία Again," *TAPA*, 76 (1946), 47–58.

Hegel, G. W. F. *The Philosophy of Fine Art*. Translated by F. P. B. Osmaston. London, 1920.

Jacob, A. L. W. *Sophocleae Quaestiones*. Warsaw, 1821.

Jaeger, Werner. *Paideia*. English translation by Gilbert Highet. Oxford, I (2nd ed., 1945), II (1943), III (1944).

———*The Theology of the Early Greek Philosophers*. Oxford, 1947.

Jebb, Sir Richard C. "The Age of Pericles," *Essays and Addresses*. Cambridge, 1907.

———*Sophocles: The Plays and Fragments*. Cambridge, 1885–1902.

Kaibel, Georg. *Sophokles Elektra*. Leipzig, 1896.

Kitto, H. D. F. "Sophocles, Statistics and the Trachiniae," *AJP*, April 1939, pp. 178–193.

Kleeman, August. "Grundgedanke und Tendenz des Sophokleischen Dramas, 'König Oedipus,' " *Wiener Studien*, 44 (1924–25), 33–48.

Kraus, F. *Utrum Sophoclis an Euripidis Electra aetate prior sit quaeritur*. Erlangen Universität Diss. Passau, 1890.

Lessing, G. E. *Leben des Sophokles*. Berlin, 1790.

Linde, P. *Sophokles' Elektra in Verhältnis zu den des Euripides*. Königshütte, O.-S., 1910.

Lübker, Friedrich. *Die Sophokleische Theologie und Ethik*. Kiel, 1851–55.

Macurdy, Grace H. *The Chronology of the Extant Plays of Euripides*. Columbia Diss. New York, 1905.

Méautis, Georges. *L'Oedipe à Colone et le Culte des Héros*. Neuchatel, 1940.

Moore, J. A. *Sophocles and Arete*. Cambridge, Mass., 1938.

Murray, Gilbert. *Five Stages of Greek Religion*. New York, 1925.

Nilsson, M. P. *A History of Greek Religion*. Trans. by F. J. Fielden. Oxford, 1925.

Nock, Arthur D. "The Cult of the Heroes," *Harvard Theological Review*, vol. 37, no. 2, pp. 61ff.

———"Religious Attitudes of the Greeks," *Proceedings of the American Philosophical Society*, 85 (1942), 472–482.

O'Connor, Margaret B. *Religion in the Plays of Sophocles*. Chicago Diss. Chicago, 1923.

Page, Denys L. *Actors' Interpolations in Greek Tragedy*. Oxford, 1934.

Papageorgius, P. N. *Scholia in Sophoclis Tragoedias Vetera*. Leipzig, 1888.

Pearson, A. C. *The Fragments of Sophocles*. Cambridge, 1917.

———*Sophoclis Fabulae*. Oxford, 1924.

Perrotta, Gennaro. *Sofocle*. Messina, 1935.

Petersen, Eugen. *Die attische Tragödie als Bild und Bühnenkunst*. Bonn, 1915.

Pohlenz, Max. *Die griechische Tragödie*. Leipzig and Berlin, 1930.

Reinhardt, Karl. *Sophokles*. Frankfurt am Main, 1933.

Robert, Carl. *Bild und Lied*. Berlin, 1881.

——— *Oidipus: Geschichte eines poetischen Stoffs im griechischen Altertum.* Berlin, 1915.

Rohde, Erwin. *Psyche: Seelencult und Unsterblichkeitsglaube der Griechen.* Freiburg and Leipzig, 1894.

Schadewaldt, Wolfgang. "Sophokles, Aias und Antigone," *Neue Wege zur Antike*, VIII, 61–109.

Schlegel, A. W. *Lectures on Dramatic Art and Literature.* Translated by J. Black. 2nd ed., New York, 1892.

Schmid, W. "Probleme aus der sophokleischen Antigone," *Philologus*, 62 (1903), 1–34.

Sheppard, J. T. "Electra: A Defence of Sophocles," *Classical Review*, vol. 41, no. 1 (1927), pp. 2–9.

——— *The Oedipus Tyrannus of Sophocles.* Cambridge, 1920.

Siess, H. "Chronologische Untersuchungen zu den Tragödien des Sophokles," *Wiener Studien*, 36 (1914–15), 244–294; 37 (1915), 27–62.

Steiger, Hugo. "Warum schrieb Euripides seine Elektra?" *Philologus*, 56 (1897), 561–600.

Sudhaus, Siegfried. *König Oedipus' Schuld.* Kiel, 1912.

Templin, P. W. *De Fabulae Sophocleae Oedipus Coloneus quae inscribitur tempore.* Westfälische Wilhelms-Universität Diss. Münster, 1930.

Thackeray, H. St. John. "Sophocles and the Perfect Number," *Proceedings of the British Academy*, 16 (1930), 15–44.

Vlachos, N. "Some Aspects of the Religion of Sophocles," *Reformed Church Review*, vol. 10, no. 2 (April 1906).

Weinstock, Heinrich. *Sophokles.* Leipzig, Berlin, 1931.

Welcker, F. G. "Über den Aias des Sophokles," *Rheinisches Museum*, 1829, pp. 43–92, 229–271.

Wilamowitz-Moellendorff, Tycho von. *Die dramatische Technik des Sophokles.* Berlin, 1917.

Wilamowitz-Moellendorff, Ulrich von. *Analecta Euripidea.* Berlin, 1875.

——— "Die Beiden Elektren," *Hermes*, 18 (1883), 214–263.

——— *Einleitung in die griechische Tragödie.* Berlin, 1910.

——— "Excurse zum Oedipus des Sophokles," *Hermes*, 34 (1899), 55–80.

——— *Der Glaube der Hellenen.* Berlin, 1931–32.

——— *Griechische Tragödien übersetzt.* Berlin, 1899–1929.

——— *Herakles.* 2nd ed., Berlin, 1895.

——— "Oedipus auf Kolonos," in T. v. Wilamowitz, *Dramatische Technik* (q.v.).

Wilson, Edmund. *The Wound and the Bow.* Boston, 1941. Title essay, pp. 272–295.

Zielinski, Tadeusz. "De Sophoclis fabula ignota," *Eos*, 27 (1924), 59–73.

——— "Excurse zu den Trachinierinnen," *Philologus*, 55 (1896), 491–633.

INDEX

INDEX